SYNGE CENTENARY PAPERS

J. M. SYNGE

CENTENARY PAPERS

1971

Edited by Maurice Harmon

THE DOLMEN PRESS

Printed and published at the Dolmen Press Limited
8 Herbert Place, Dublin 2 in the
Republic of Ireland

1972

Distributed outside Ireland
by Oxford University Press

CONTENTS

FOREWORD. Maurice Harmon. *page* vii

PREFACE. Roger McHugh. ix

I SYNGE AND THE IDEA OF A NATIONAL LITERATURE. Seán Ó Tuama. 1

II SYNGE'S USE OF IRISH FOLKLORE. Seán Ó Súilleabháin. 18

III THE LANGUAGE OF SYNGE. Alan J. Bliss. 35

IV SYNGE AND THE ACTOR — A CONSIDERATION OF STYLE. Hugh Hunt. 63

V EIGHT NIGHTS IN THE ABBEY. Hilary Berrow. 75

VI DEIRDRE OF THE SORROWS: *LITERATURE FIRST . . . DRAMA AFTERWARDS*. Ann Saddlemyer. 88

VII THE PROSE OF JOHN MILLINGTON SYNGE. T. R. Henn. 108

VIII SYNGE'S POETIC USE OF LANGUAGE. Seamus Deane. 127

IX THE POETRY OF SYNGE AND YEATS. Jon Stallworthy. 145

X SYNGE AND MODERNISM. Thomas Kilroy. 167

XI J. M. SYNGE — A CENTENARY APPRAISAL. David H. Greene. 180

CONTRIBUTORS 197

INDEX 199

FOREWORD

The J. M. Synge Centenary Commemoration which took place in Dublin from April 27 to May 1, 1971 was sponsored jointly by Trinity College, Dublin, and University College, Dublin, under the patronage of His Excellency Eamon de Valera, President of Ireland. Its activities were planned by a distinguished committee under the chairmanship of the Chief Justice Cearbhall O Dálaigh.

Some of the essays included in this book were read to the eminent scholars, dramatists and producers, who had assembled in Dublin to honour the occasion. Among those present were members of the Synge family from all over the world. The other essays were specially commissioned.

I should like to thank the contributors for their generous response to my request for papers and for making my task so agreeable and rewarding by the high quality of their work. They have, I think, deepened our understanding of the man and his work and have extended our knowledge of the contexts from which it comes. Finally, I wish to thank the committee for the honour of being editor of this centenary volume.

Maurice Harmon
University College, Dublin

PREFACE

ROGER McHUGH

It might be said of Dr MacLiammóir, who was to deliver this Address, that 'there's not his like for eloquence or talk at all', as Pegeen said of the Playboy. We all regret the absence of that many-sided artist, and no one regrets it more than I do. However, I am consoled by the fact that I am addressing an audience which, as far as it is possible in human affairs, has already achieved that somewhat difficult state which Yeats so much desired, Unity of Being; or at any rate, unity of purpose; the fitting commemoration of a great writer, a century after his birth.

'That praise or censure is certainly the most sincere,' wrote Dryden, 'which *unbribed* posterity shall give us.' The writer of any age might fittingly utter the words of that comic eighteenth-century character, Boyle Roche, 'What has posterity ever done for us ?' Like most Irish bulls this is a pregnant bull, for it is a jest which is an earnest in the womb of time; but given sufficient time, posterity may make amends, and it inevitably does so with a great writer when his centenary comes round. The whirligig of time brings in its justices (including Chief Justices) as well as its revenges.

What is one to say of John Millington Synge at the beginning of a commemoration week, during which his work will be discussed by scholars and writers, his manuscripts exhibited, his plaque unveiled, his plays performed and the man himself impersonated?

I think that one must risk platitudes and talk about two chief matters of this commemoration. The first is Synge's stature as a poetic dramatist, a stature achieved in the seven last years of his 38 years of life. It was an extraordinary achievement comparable to that of Keats, manifest in six plays, and undertaken under the same shadow of disease and death.

Ibsen, a dramatist whom Synge disliked, probably because he had read or had seen his work only in joyless and pallid translation, was one of the great poetic minds of the century into which Synge was born and, in an address to the Norwegian students in 1874, spoke of the task of the dramatic poet :

> What does it mean to be a poet? . . . to be a poet means essentially to see, but mark well, to see in such a way that whatever is seen is perceived by the audience just as the poet saw it. But only what has been lived through can be seen in that way and accepted in that way . . . no poet lives through anything in isolation. What he lives through, all of his countrymen live through with him. If that were not so, what would bridge the gap between the producing and the receiving minds?

Potentially, before he shared the life of the people as fully as he did on Aran, Synge was a writer. He had the trained eye of the naturalist, which this College helped to train. He had the trained ear of the musician, which our Academy of Music helped to train. He knew a little Irish—enough to win a prize here but in those days (as I think it is recognised) that was not very much. And then, in his travels in Europe, in his study of Racine and Molière, of Petrarch or of Villon, he had some experience of the highest literary standards.

But the catalyst which matured his genius as a writer was the shock of discovery of the life of Aran, of the people of Wicklow (whom he already knew but not so fully), and of the people of West Kerry.

He told Yeats that literature is born out of the shock of new material. He was awakened by Hyde's little play *Casadh an tSugáin* to the possibilities of the peasant play. Lady Gregory's *Cuchulain of Muirthemne* reinforced his realisation of the literary possibilities of Irish-English, which, he wrote, unites an Elizabethan vocabulary with plaintive Gaelic constructions. And from his own experience of hearing an old man reciting verse in Gaelic which, though he did not fully understand it, brought tears to his eyes, he discovered that a writer's personal rhythm and cadence could arrest the hearer and compel his feelings.

This is to speak mainly of technical experiences in his formation as a dramatist. But they are also important to his psychological development as an artist.

There was, however, a deeper thing that underlay his art, as it underlies that of all great artists: a contemplative cast of mind which made him try to seize the individuality of the thing contemplated. This is reflected in his notebooks: 'The profound is always inimitable . . . Things have always a character and characters always a mood. These moods are perpetually new, as the sunsets. Profound insight finds the inner and essential mood of the things it treats of and hence gives us art that is absolutely distinct and inimitable.'

Yeats's description, 'that meditative man John Synge' is well chosen. Synge had a habit of quietly watching, of soaking-in a thing, a scene, a person, of catching its mood and essence. That is why there is no standard Synge style in his plays, although each has a recognisably individual quality. The austere style of *Riders to the Sea* is very different from the exuberant style of the *Playboy*. His other plays move between these two extremes. *Deirdre of the Sorrows* was being toned down in style when he died. And to mention death is to recall another factor that deepened his work, especially in his last years. Synge, like Webster, was 'much impressed by death' but this consciousness, while it shared something of Webster's realisation of the cruelty of life, operated also in the direction of 'astringent joy and hardness,' in the thought, reflected all through his plays, that no man can be living forever, that it is no small thing to be rid of grey hairs and of the loosening of the teeth, that even 'the great catastrophies of life give substance and power to the tragedy and humour which are the two poles of art.'

Ibsen gave one marvellous description of poetry—'Doom-session upon the soul'—and in Synge that sense of doom heightens the enjoyment of life and is reflected in the savour of his speech. He was no theorist; he believed, in fact, that 'all theorising is bad for the artist because it makes him live in the intelligence instead of the half sub-conscious faculties by which all real creation is performed"; yet we learn more about the nature of art from his few prefaces and notes than from all of *A Vision*.

Synge literally gave us great riches in a little room. The exigencies of the Abbey Theatre, for example, made his *Playboy* rather different from what he had planned. The audience is not shown, as Synge had originally intended, the fight with his father which starts Christy on his travels, does not know from the beginning that Old Mahon is coming hot from Hades, thirsting for revenge. Frank O'Connor thought that this would have made it a better play but that is highly debatable.

The dramatic sense of Synge is observable in the last-known draft of *The Playboy*, which Professor Frenz has brought to this Conference from the Lilly Library of Indiana University, a generous gesture. He has brought, too, a Xerox copy for the National Library and, if you read the ending of that draft, you will see that in it Synge makes Pegeen Mike rush out after the Playboy to make sure she hasn't lost him. In the play as we have it in its acting version, she throws her shawl over her head and wails that she *has* lost him. It is much better so. Synge, who worked close to his company (as Molière and Shakespeare did), must have realised this in rehearsal. Art loves chance and chance art, Aristotle said truly, and the seizing of the happy chance of speech, of event, of cadence and character runs all through the art of Synge.

But to labour his greatness is unnecessary. And when his work is being played in our theatres one cannot easily resist the temptation to quote lavishly from his plays. Indeed so quotable is Synge that much of what passes for Synge criticism consists of joining together lengthy extracts from what he wrote, the scholar supplying mainly conjunctive phrases.

So I turn instead to my second general point, the fact that Synge is being commemorated in his own country. All of us know now what he meant when he told Maud Gonne, as the current Abbey Theatre programme reminds us, that his plays were his way of doing something for Ireland. What many of us sense is what Synge in fact intended, his capturing of the individuality of a nation: 'The individuality of mood is often trivial, perverse, fleeting (he wrote) but the national mood is broad, serious, provisionally permanent.' He argued that a writer needs a national mood as well as an intellectual temper and that place, period and personal distinction, inspired by this mood, give great art.

It was chiefly the people of Aran and of Cois Fhairrge from whom he caught it, a people who were and perhaps still are its last repository. 'These people,' wrote John Butler Yeats, 'believe everything to be carried on by a miracle, and the civilized man, who does not know that behind all science and reason and all moral systems there is something transcending all knowledge and which is a continued miracle of love and beauty, is not only incapable of culture, he is incapable of deserving it.'

And what of that people now? There are two questions which will interest most of you. Have these people shut their lips on poetry? And what are the prospects of their continuing individuality, which can leaven the individuality of the nation?

I believe that both of these questions can be answered by something I am going to read for you. These words were spoken last week by an old man of Cois Fhairrge. He was talking of the threatened withdrawal of the dole from countrymen like himself who in fact did not want doles but work; and when work was not provided for such as he, felt that this blow was the last:

> Má ghabhann an fear tuaithe scíos, an fhaid a bheas gob ar an bhfiach dubh ní thiocfaidh sé aníos. An bhlian seo chugainn beid muid i dteach na mbocht nó san uaigh a cheannaigh airgead Judas. Tá an spiorad briste ionainn agus nuair a bhriseann an spiorad, leann a bhFian ní thabharfadh sé an spiorad ar ais.

I translate: 'If the countryman gets worn out, as long as there's a beak on the raven he'll not come up again. The coming year we'll be in the poorhouse or in the grave that the money of Judas bought. The spirit is broken in us and when the spirit is broken, the ale of the Fianna itself will not bring the spirit back.'

Yes, poetry still lives in the people of the West but the individual leaven of their existence is in danger of extinction. I do not ask you to leave ten per cent of pity under your commemorative plate. All I ask is that we realise the score and perhaps try to help to pay it.

J. M. SYNGE

16 April 1871
24 March 1909

I: SYNGE AND THE IDEA OF A NATIONAL LITERATURE

SEÁN Ó TUAMA

The problem of how to create an individual Irish literature in the English language began increasingly to exercise the minds of writers in Ireland in the second half of the nineteenth century. Yeats, following Ferguson and others, seems to have thought in his early years that such a literature could be achieved mainly by transposing the matter of Ireland into English. In a letter published in *United Ireland* in 1892 he said: 'Can we not build up . . . a national literature which shall be none the less Irish in spirit from being English in language ? Can we not keep the continuity of the nation's life . . . by retelling in English which shall have an indefinable Irish quality of rhythm and style, all that is best of the ancient literature . . . until there has been made a golden bridge between the old and the new ?' One wonders, however, if Yeats felt, even at that stage, that this was the complete answer.

In the last analysis, the continuing individuality of any national literature is primarily going to depend, not on the past artistic achievements of the nation, but on its present and enduring special pattern of life; on the nation's culture rather than on its Culture. Yeats, however, found himself unable to make any extensive contact with the more traditional Irish community mind. Even the Hiberno-English he so often lauded, he was quite unable to master. His advice to Synge then to go and live on the Aran Islands could be seen in the light of his own failure to respond adequately to a way of life not his own. One might even say that Synge, another member of the Anglo-Irish nation, was carrying out, on behalf of Yeats, a major step in the programme for building up a national Irish literature in the English language; a step, incidentally, which entailed using, not an 'indefinable Irish quality' of English, but an English so palpably, and so definably Irish, that one still feels somewhat disconcerted, even shocked, by it.

Synge, by his very nature, saw drama as emanating from the observable realities of known life, rather than, as Yeats saw it, from the life of myth. 'I do not believe,' he wrote to Stephen MacKenna, 'in the possibility of a purely fantastic unmodern ideal breezy springdayish Cuchulainoid National Theatre. We had the "Shadowy Waters" on the stage last week, and it was the most *distressing* failure the mind can imagine—a half-empty room with growling men and tittering females.'[1] The living Aran Irish-speaking community then was much more likely to be a source of drama for a person such as Synge than all the myth and literature of past centuries. Indeed so successfully did Synge allow his feelings to interact with those of this most traditional of Irish-speaking communities that it was he, and not Yeats, who shaped the future of the Abbey Theatre. So it was that our national theatre, in the process of being saved from becoming 'Cuchulainoid,' tended to become 'peasantoid' instead.

I am unaware that any detailed scholarly analysis has been made of the ascendancy culture to which Synge and other Anglo-Irish writers belong. On the surface, certainly, it would appear to have been the very antithesis of the peasant culture he came to identify with. It was traditionally middle-class urban or landed gentry; inheriting post-reformation ethics, enjoying formal educational and institutional butresses, but not very deeply rooted outside its Dublin base. On the other hand the Aran world was rural, Catholic and tentacularly rooted, inheriting an oral learning and the widespread medieval type of Irish community life. It might seem rather improbable that a person of Synge's background could have made a successful emotional transition from the one world to the other.

This, however, is to speak of the two cultures—one rural-based, one Dublin-based—as if they had co-existed in Ireland, without change throughout some three centuries. The truth is that a complicated two-way assimilative process had been at work from quite early on. Swift, in the eighteenth century for instance, not alone spoke on behalf of the people of Ireland, but even learned some Irish. Later on in the nineteenth century, just as the mass of Irish people, under increasing pressure from the English political and economic machine, tended to become Anglicised, ironically enough there was a gradual withdrawal of the Anglo-Irish nation from its dependency on the English mother-culture, and an effort to identify with the older Irish culture. In the final decades of the nineteenth century there is real evidence for the mingling, in varying degrees, of the Irish and Anglo-Irish traditions. This tendency to merge the two traditions is more profoundly institutionalised, perhaps, in the Abbey Theatre, than in any other of the cultural or nationalistic societies which were founded at that time.

As a result of this assimilative process, it is more than possible that the Irish-speaking world Synge encountered in the Aran Islands, and elsewhere, was not as foreign to him as it might appear on the surface. Because, of course, the Aran-island community should not be thought of as being, in most essential ways, a special community in late nineteenth-century Ireland. Irish may have been its language, it may have had its local and regional customs and emphases, but fundamentally it shared the same value-system with the West Cork district where Synge's mother had been born, and with the Wicklow district where Synge's father had been born, where many of Synge's numerous childhood nurses must have come from, and where he himself had spent a good deal of his boyhood. One must postulate then that, long before Synge went to Aran, part, at least, of his psychological make-up responded to that special network of feelings and thinking which is characteristically Irish. Synge, in learning Irish and observing life in the islands was not only enhancing his previous intuitive knowledge of the traditional mind, he was building himself up immensely in the process as a responding and feeling person. Otherwise one cannot adequately explain how, as has been so justly remarked, a very minor poet became practically overnight a dramatist of major significance : in my opinion the one dramatist of enduring quality to come out of the Abbey Theatre.

Synge might, of course, have found Aran community life particularly appealing even on a purely personal plane, had he never been pre-conditioned culturally to understand it. Because of his own morbid obsession with death, the spectacle of human beings living fully, almost ritualistically, on the brink of death made a deep impression on him, as did the fact also that this simple, almost primeval people, articulated their life in a highly refined and poetic manner. However, this personal empathy with some features of the island way of life cannot in any real measure help us to understand why it is that Synge, in his very restricted *opus,* has captured more fully than any other Irish writer who has written in English, the deeper resonances of the traditional Irish mind : some of its basic attitudes to life and death, to religion and to heroism, to man-woman and mother-son relationships, to poetry, entertainment, work and a host of other values. Synge, then, is not to be reckoned as a dramatist who merely observed and reported with sympathy on a quasi-medieval way of life full of poetry, quaint customs and folkloric odds and ends. Rather is he the Anglo-Irish writer *par excellence* who responded to the basic values underlying that life; and managed to recreate it unerringly in artistic form in two classic pieces, *Riders to the Sea* and *Playboy of the Western World.*

The culture which provided the basic material for the plays of Synge may in one sense be called a 'peasant' culture; but the term 'peasant,' in the Irish context, needs more careful interpretation than usual. Obviously country people in Aran and elsewhere inherited what is usually thought of as a 'peasant' culture with all its restrictions and advantages. But they were also the inheritors of the remnants of a 'high Culture,' an aristocratic tradition which lasted strongly in Ireland for practically two thousand years, down into the seventeenth century. The Irish aristocratic structure, as distinct from most other similar structures in Western Europe, was rural and highly decentralised. The entire country, even in late medieval times, was a mosaic of some one hundred and fifty small kingdoms, each containing, on average, quite a small population. Aristocrats and peasants lived in close proximity to one another, and must have shared to a great extent the same world-view, the same primary attitudes to life in general.

One of these primary attitudes, firmly established throughout the whole historic Irish community, is the high status accorded to poetry, music, and story-telling. Quite clearly a large factor in preserving and disseminating this attitude was that in all the rural kingdoms special arrangements obtained for the provision of these arts. Each chieftain permanently employed professional poets and musicians and, doubtless, encouraged other professional and semi-professional artists to entertain himself and his people. Consequently, great numbers of people throughout rural Ireland were brought into constant contact with various levels of poetry, music and storytelling, unlike people in rural communities in countries such as England and France where the arts were mostly confined to the urban centralised centres of government. This more than anything else explains the esteem for poetry and music, the flair for fine talk and for story-telling, which still exists even in our rather characterless modern Ireland.

Synge, who has said that 'in a good play every speech should be as fully flavoured as a nut or apple,' accepted quite naturally this basic community attitude. What is more significant still is that all his own work contains, in a quite uncontrived manner, many of the most typical and well-recognised traits of the two thousand-year-old native Irish literary tradition. One could argue, for instance, that the type of dramatic sequences or juxtaposition he employs, or his lyric changes of mood from situation to situation, owe more to the modes of Irish story-telling and the native dramatic monologue than to any established Anglo-Irish or foreign theatrical tradition. It is quite certain, however, that the concrete, sharp and dramatic quality of the best Irish verse is everywhere present in his work. Even the simplest speeches in *Riders to the Sea* have these characteristics:

> Cathleen: . . . 'Give me a knife Nora; the string's perished with salt water, and there's a black knot on it you wouldn't loosen in a week . . . . Ah Nora, isn't it a bitter thing to think of him floating that way to the far north, and no one to keen him but the black hags that do be flying on the sea?'[2]

One is inevitably reminded here of a score of poems in Irish where the same detailed and intense intimacy makes itself felt:

> A widow and a virgin
> I am left still so young,
> And go say to my people
> That my treasure was drowned;
> Had I been in the boat then
> And my two hands on the sheet
> Take my word, Mrs. O'Reilly,
> I'd have cured all your grief.
>
> The eels have your eyes
> And the crabs have your mouth
> Your two shining bright hands
> Under sway of the salmon;
> I'd give five pounds to anyone

Who would lighten my sorrow,
A sad solitary woman
Poor bright Nelly Sheridan.
(Trans. O Riada and Lucy)

Una Ellis-Fermor has rightly remarked on the strange affinity between Synge's nature-passages and the nature-poetry of Irish monks from the ninth or tenth centuries. It is equally true that the Old Irish delicate and impressionistic reactions to natural phenomena—'natural magic' was Matthew Arnold's description of this quality—must have remained a rooted characteristic of the Irish community mind. Several such passages in Synge are echoed again and again in Irish folksong, or in books such as *Allagar na hInise,* by Tomás O Criomhthain, the fisherman from the Blasket Islands. Compare these two passages for instance.

> 'There's the sound of one of them twittering yellow birds do be coming in the spring-time from beyond the sea, and there'll be a fine warmth now in the sun, and a sweetness in the air, the way it'll be a grand thing to be sitting here quiet and easy, smelling the things growing up, and budding from the earth.'[3]

> 'It's in the white strand field I'm working. It's a sweet day . . . the sea calm, curaghs coming and going, a single person in one of them—Seán Léan, as stately in it as the Prince of Wales in his ornate coracle; the fish showing their heads above water, the birds with their music, human beings on dry land, dressed only in shirts, earthing potatoes; a crowd coming from the two sides of the hill carrying handfuls of bracken, another gang running eastwards across the hillside after school at mid-day; smoke coming from every house just now—dinner is on, no doubt.'[4]

Not alone are such undoubted characteristic Irish literary traits to be found in abundance in Synge, but his two major works seem to mirror, respectively, the two main streams of the whole Irish literary tradition. While Irish verse tends mostly to be concrete, and intense in quality, Irish prose, from its very beginnings, inclines towards fantasy, burlesque or phantasmagoria. This prose tradition remains mainly, down through the centuries, a comic or satiric tradition finally manifesting itself indirectly, and in another language, in the works, say, of Stephens, Myles na gCopaleen and the early Beckett. Synge's *Playboy* stems quite clearly from this prose tradition, while his 'poetic' play *Riders to the Sea* remains firmly within the main mode of the much more ascetic verse tradition, 'pared to the bone.'

Just as Synge's plays seem to be unusually in accord with the main Irish literary tradition, so also do they contain basic insights not alone into the *psyche* of Aran life, but by extension into the *psyche* of Irish life generally. I will mention a few of what seem to me to be major points of creative contact.

The attitude of the old woman, Maurya, in *Riders to the Sea,* worn out by the attrition of the sea, finally and quietly accepting death—so long as the requisite rituals are at hand to assuage its bitterness—is all of a piece with anything similar I know of in Irish life or literature. Synge poses no theories here about her death or about tragedy in general; while religious consolations are used more as ritual than reality. In so far as one can deduce a general statement from the play about death, it seems to say quite simply : 'having lived fully, using whatever props or illusions that are necessary, death can be borne with some dignity.' As Maurya has used to the full her six sons as props for her living, so also has Deirdre used to the full her ideal love for Naisi, and can finally 'put away sorrow like a shoe that is worn out and muddy,' finding that 'in the grave we're safe surely.' These words of Deirdre echo lines from the famous last speeches of Maurya; and Maurya's last speeches, in turn, echo in their tone and in their intensely subdued feeling a passage from Tomás O Criomhthain's biography, *An tOileánach,* where in a short passage at the end of a chapter he describes incidents in his personal family life which many other writers would have made the main subject-matter of their memoirs:

> Ten children were born to us, but ill-luck dogged them, God help us. The first child of mine christened was seven or eight years of age when he fell down the cliff and was killed. From that time on as quickly as a child came, another went. Two of them died of the measles, and every disease that came swept some one from me. Donal was drowned trying to rescue the lady on the White Strand. I had another fine boy, growing up and helping. Shortly he was taken from me too. The sorrow of all these things affected their poor mother and she was

> taken from me. I was never blinded until then .... One boy only is with me now at home. Another boy in America. That is the end my children came to. God be with them—all of them who are dead—and with the poor woman whose spirit broke because of them.[5]

Compare this with :

> I've had a husband, and a husband's father, and six sons in this house . . . and some of them were found and some of them were not found, but they're gone now the lot of them .... There was Sheamus and his father, and his own father again, were lost in a dark night .... There was Patch after was drowned out of a curagh that turned over .... They're all together this time, and the end is come. May the Almighty God have mercy on Bartley's soul, and on Michael's soul . . . and may He have mercy on my soul, Nora, and on the soul of every one is left living in the world .... Michael has a clean burial in the far north, by the grace of the Almighty God. Bartley will have a fine coffin out of the white boards, and a deep grave surely .... What more can we want than that? No man at all can be living for ever, and we must be satisfied.[6]

This intense, near-fatalistic acceptance by the old of the brutal fact of death—once the props had gone—did not mean at all that life before death was futile. Life itself need not in any way be futile, because it could always be transformed into poetry, fantasy, burlesque, anything one willed. If myth, illusion or ritual helped one to master life so much the better. Use it, Synge seems to say, in his comic interpretation of the Irish mind, but do not depend on it. The Playboy grew in stature because he enjoyed the illusion that he had killed 'his da.' This illusion was punctured, but in the meantime he had mastered life (including his overbearing father) and could live life in future more independently. Similarly Nora, in the *Shadow of the Glen,* briefly enjoyed the illusion that her crusty old husband had died. This illusion was again crudely shattered, but she seemed in the meantime to have mustered up the courage—though dramatically speaking, this is not at all rendered sufficiently credible— to risk a new and fuller life with a man of the roads.

On the other hand, in *The Well of the Saints,* the two old blind beggars, have been living adequately, sometimes uproariously, with the illusion that if their sight were restored all should be well. Unfortunately for them their wish is granted, their illusion shattered; and because of their not being sufficiently equipped to deal with the raw reality of life, they choose rather pathetically to return to their former blind state. The comic vision cedes rather shakily here to the tragic vision, making the overall mood and effect of the play somewhat uncertain.

Synge uses anecdotes and folk stories as the basis for these plays, but he re-shapes his material in such a fashion that he leaves us in no doubt as to his own emotional involvement with this particular way of viewing life. Mastering life after all was of the most immediate importance to himself personally, given that this world was for him the only reality and afterlife a matter of lying in Mount Jerome graveyard 'with worms eternally.'

Some critics, notably Daniel Corkery, have argued that Synge fails to come to grips with the religious element in the Irish consciousness. It is, of course, true that what we have been used to think of as the traditional Catholic Ireland gets very little showing in his plays. One must say here, however, that, firstly, our concept of a traditional Catholic Ireland is to a large extent a nineteenth century urban concept; and, secondly, that Synge's plays make no realistic attempt to reflect any section of life, in its particularity, as lived in the Aran islands, or anywhere else. Neither, of course, do Shakespeare's plays represent, in any detail, life in Elizabethan England. Synge possibly stays closer to lived life than does Shakespeare, but he still uses only the very basic elements.

Synge, no doubt, could have quite legitimately omitted the Catholic part of the Irish consciousness if he found it did not accord with his own temperament, or with his own particular artistic needs, thereby losing out somewhat on his claim to be a faithful interpreter of the traditional mind. One doubts, however, if this is the way to look at it. It seems to me that Synge, intuitively and by observation, felt that the pre-Christian substratum of the Irish mind was still the more potent factor in the conduct of daily life. His description of a funeral in Aran makes this quite clear:

> After Mass this morning an old woman was buried. She lived in the cottage next mine, and more than once before noon I

heard a faint echo of the keen. I did not go to the wake for fear my presence might jar upon the mourners, but all last evening I could hear the strokes of a hammer in the yard, where, in the middle of a little crowd of idlers, the next of kin laboured slowly at the coffin. To-day, before the hour for the funeral, poteen was served to a number of men who stood about upon the road, and a portion was brought to me in my room. Then the coffin was carried, sewn loosely in sailcloth, and held near the ground by three cross-poles lashed upon the top. As we moved down to the low eastern portion of the island, nearly all the men, and all the oldest women, wearing petticoats over their heads, came out and joined in the procession.

While the grave was being opened the women sat down among the flat tombstones, bordered with a pale fringe of early bracken, and began the wild keen, or crying for the dead. Each old woman, as she took her turn in the leading recitative, seemed possessed for the moment with a profound ecstacy of grief, swaying to and fro, and bending her forehead to the stone before her, while she called out to the dead with a perpetually recurring chant of sobs.

All round the graveyard other wrinkled women, looking out from under the deep red petticoats that cloaked them, rocked themselves with the same rhythm, and intoned the inarticulate chant that is sustained by all as an accompaniment.

The morning had been beautifully fine, but as they lowered the coffin into the grave, thunder rumbled overhead and hailstones hissed among the bracken.

In Inishmaan one is forced to believe in a sympathy between man and nature, and at this moment when the thunder sounded a death peal of extraordinary grandeur above the voices of the women, I could see the faces near me stiff and drawn with emotion.

When the coffin was in the grave, and the thunder had rolled away across the hills of Clare, the keen broke out again more passionately than before.

This grief of the keen is no personal complaint for the death of one woman over eighty years, but seems to contain the whole passionate rage that lurks somewhere in every native of the island. In this cry of pain the inner consciousness of

> the people seems to lay itself bare for an instant, and to reveal the mood of beings who feel their isolation in the face of a universe that wars on them with winds and seas. They are usually silent, but in the presence of death all outward show of indifference or patience is forgotten, and they shriek with pitiable despair before the horror of the fate to which they are all doomed.
>
> Before they covered the coffin an old man kneeled down by the grave and repeated a simple prayer for the dead.
>
> There was an irony in these words of atonement and Catholic belief spoken by voices that were still hoarse with the cries of pagan desperation.
>
> A little beyond the grave I saw a line of old women who had recited in the keen sitting in the shadow of a wall beside the roofless shell of the church. They were still sobbing and shaken with grief, yet they were beginning to talk again of the daily trifles that veil from them the terror of the world.
>
> When we had all come out of the graveyard, and two men had re-built the hole in the wall through which the coffin had been carried in, we walked back to the village, talking of anything and joking of anything as if merely coming from the boat-slip, or the pier.[7]

Synge's viewpoint here, and elsewhere, that Christian dogmas and rituals have been quite often a mechanical super-imposition on pagan attitudes of mind, I find quite convincing; so much so that I consider him to have been much more discerning than Anglo-Irish writers in general in plumbing the Irish religious consciousness.

A culture, anthropologists tell us, is a community's design for living, handed down from generation to generation, refurbished, perhaps, from time to time, but always retaining a certain structural permanency. The community's language as a part of this design reflects and transmits a particular and evolving network of feeling, thinking and behaving. Theoretically, no other language can in any satisfactory way express that culture, or reproduce elements of it in that new extension or metamorphosis of life (i.e. life as understood within that culture) which we call art.

Essentially then the main stylistic problem facing Synge as a dramatist, who was expressing the elements of one culture in terms of a language not expressly of that culture, was quite similar to that facing a writer translating literature from one language to another. 'To translate well,' Roger Caillois writes, 'is to "invent" the text (vocabulary, syntax, and style) that the translated author would have written if his native language had been that of the translator, and not his own.'[8]

Synge, of course, did have the advantage here that a good deal of the translation he required had been done for him by the country people of Ireland in their nineteenth century change-over from Irish to English. But even at that Synge clearly had to 'invent': he took up the incipient Hiberno-English dialect, elaborated on it, and shaped from it a fully-fashioned diction, which I would say, had never been spoken at this consistency by any community of people. He is, perhaps, the only widely-known writer to build up an authentic and individual style based on the translation of one language into another.

It must be stressed, however, that the Hiberno-English on which Synge built is in many ways a very restricted dialect. It may have managed to express adequately some or even all of the most basic attitudes and feelings of a community which had historically been Irish-speaking, but it was utterly defective as an instrument which would serve the same wide range of linguistic functions as the Irish language did serve within such a community—functions associated with a whole spectrum of formal, semi-formal and informal speech (i.e. orations, sermons, story-telling, various conversational tonalities, etc.). Synge's dialect, then, while it contains some rather exotic elements, has little tonal subtlety, and cannot be used effectively to reflect situations in any kind of realistic manner: it is very formalised 'peasant' diction, much more distanced from life and live situations than, one feels, has generally been realised. Moreover, this dialect is an isolated 'language in itself,' having no conventional sociolinguistic relationship with a standard, or higher-class language, much as, say, a Yorkshire dialect would have with standard English.

Some consequences arise from these linguistic factors which are crucial both in the production and criticism of Synge's work. One of the most obvious of these is that Synge's style maintains credibility only in certain limited circumstances. In *Deirdre of the Sorrows,* for instance, despite its many very magnificent passages, the language is completely inadequate tonally to create a milieu in which kings and princes can operate. Here is Conchubar, the High-king, speaking in turn to Deirdre's nurse and to Deirdre herself:

> Conchubar . . . She's coming now, and let you walk in and keep Fergus till I speak with her a while.
> Lavarcham . . . If I'm after vexing you itself, it'd be best you weren't taking her hasty or scolding her at all.
> Conchubar . . . I've no call to. I'm well pleased she's light and airy. . . . The gods save you Deirdre. . . .
> Deirdre . . . The gods save you. . . . I have no wish to be a queen.
> Conchubar . . . You'd wish to be dressing in your duns and grey, and you herding your geese or driving your calves to their shed . . . like the common lot scattered in the glens?[9]

The style here has become rustic fancy dress, it has not evolved in any way out of the various kinds of emotional and linguistic relationships existing between different strata of people. The High-king cannot be distinguished stylistically from the 'common lot scattered in glen,' and thereby loses dramatic credibility. One doubts very much, even had Synge lived long enough to rewrite it, could he have made *Deirdre of the Sorrows* a true theatrical event.

On the other hand, the consequence for even the classic pieces such as *The Playboy of the Western World* and *Riders to the Sea* is that the style works only if the plays, in production, are sufficiently distanced from the life from which they have emanated. *The Playboy,* because of its being so patently in the realms of fantasy or phantasmagoria, is generally accorded an adequate treatment, from this point of view, in professional productions; *Riders to the Sea* never, or almost never, in my experience. The basic situation of this play is so familiar to people acquainted with the west coast of Ireland, that the tendency has been to produce it in a much more naturalistic manner than its formalised mono-toned style allows. Given this style one can see *Riders to the Sea* successfully produced only as a sort of ritual, where actors gesticulate most sparingly, where actions such as removing a cake from the fire become virtually sacramental acts, where the movements of girls crying together are stylised, yet natural, as in a Greek funeral *stele.* More particularly, the dialogue throughout needs to be spoken, simply, though ritualistically, and be seen as a part of a build-up for the last great litanies of Maurya, which should finally overwhelm us as surely as the sea has overwhelmed her.

Produced or interpreted at this sort of lyric-ritualistic level it can be shown, I think, that *Riders to the Sea* is functional in every line, full of the most intense dramatic action, one of the greatest works ever written in Ireland.

A host of considerations such as I have mentioned flow from Synge's highly successful attempt to recreate West of Ireland life in terms of Hiberno-English—an attempt which we have been looking at as an essential part of a programme to build up a national literature in the English language.

In this regard it must be remembered that Yeats and Joyce, as well as Synge, were also intensely concerned with the 'west,' and all its implications. In their case, however, it became less and less an identifiable place, and more and more a territory or a tension of the mind. Yeats, on the evidence of his writings, spent his life working out in poetry and drama his tortured and ambivalent relationship with 'Connaught,' his synonym for the older native Culture (or culture). But the poet who declared in his younger days 'Connaught for me is Ireland' was increasingly to renounce this concept until finally he felt he had nothing left to lean on but 'the foul rag-and-bone shop of the heart.'

Joyce, unlike the other two, being of native Catholic stock, and sensing, perhaps, more acutely the future cultural pattern of the country, had his own cunning answer to the east-west dilemma:

> He even ran away with hunself and became a farsoonerite, saying he would far sooner muddle through the hash of lentils in Europe than meddle with Irrland's split little pea. *(Finnegans Wake).*[10]

He did not run away, however, without having worked out his cultural problem also in terms of literature. *Ulysses* bears ample and complicated testimony of this; but *The Dead* is Joyce's most straightforward account of his situation. In this story Gabriel, the Dublin Palesman, having discovered an emotional chasm between himself and his Galway-born wife, seems to have resolved to 'journey westward.' Joyce himself, however, chose to go east . . . .

He must have felt finally that trying to assimilate 'Connaught' as Synge did, and as, after his own fashion, Yeats tried to do for a time, was at best a make-shift literary ploy. Absolutely revealing, however, in its depiction of his splitmindedness, is his account in *Portrait of the Artist* of an Irish-speaking old man a friend of his had encountered in the west of Ireland. Joyce declares with feverish clarity: 'I fear him . . . . It is with him I must struggle all through the night till day come, till he or I lie dead, gripping him by his sinewy throat till . . . . Till what? Till he yield to me? No, I mean no harm.'

For Joyce and Yeats, the conflict arising from the problem of whether to identify or not to identify with facets of Irish culture was clearly one of the most dynamic and productive factors in their whole work. For Synge, a much more monolithic character, the effort to identify never assumed the proportions of a problem : he merely went through the process simply, rigorously and successfully.

In either case the question of whether or not to identify could never have arisen had there not been a recognisable Irish culture, or pattern of life. Synge discerned this pattern of life, at its most elemental, on the west coast; and, as an artist, sensed that Hiberno-English was the only language which could successfully express it. Hiberno-English, however, has shown itself to be a very ephemeral dialect. It is quickly receding both as a spoken and a written tongue; so, of course, are many of the features of the more traditional Irish life. Synge's solution, then, is not finally a viable one.

Mention was made earlier in this essay of the rather ironic fact that, while the Anglo-Irish nation tended to identify increasingly with the native traditions right down through the nineteenth century, the older culture, at the same time, was being swiftly eroded by the English language and its traditions. Despite the establishment of an Irish state in the twentieth century, this assimilative process has continued inexorably. Indeed, it is more than probable that since the time of Synge the individuality of the whole of Irish life has diminished severely; and that this diminution has occurred not alone on the surface of life, but in that fundamental network of values and attitudes which is surely the basis on which the permanency of a culture depends.

In the early thirties, Daniel Corkery, in his book *Synge and*

Anglo-Irish literature, summed up the state of Irish culture thus: 'Everywhere in the mentality of Irish people are flux and uncertainty. Our national consciousness may be described, in a native phrase, as a quaking sod. It gives no footing. It is not English, nor Irish, nor Anglo-Irish . . . .' Numerous contemporary commentators—much less involved with traditional nationalism than Corkery—have been taking the view that our consciousness is, in fact, rapidly becoming less and less Irish or Anglo-Irish, and more and more provincial British. A foreign scholar, Dr. M. W. Heslinga, in his book *The Irish Border as a Cultural Divide,* finds that the whole country, North and South, shares by and large (except in the matter of religion) the one British culture. One feels, or at least hopes, that here the case has been overstated.

Corkery, in that controversial first chapter of his book on Synge—a book which, incidentally, still contains some of the best critical analysis of the plays—doubts if an eroded culture such as ours could, in the long term, produce an individual literature in English. The tone of this particular chapter is very much of its time, sharply polemical and rather condemnatory of Anglo-Irish writers in general. This is unfortunate: one cannot readily or generally condemn writers for being caught up willy-nilly in a complicated assimilative process. Corkery's main thesis, however, seems to me to have even more force today than at the time he stated it.

In this regard, the rôle attributed to a language by anthropologists in general, and by linguistic anthropologists in particular, in the formulation and transmission of a culture, has special relevance: 'The fact of the matter,' says Edward Sapir, 'is that the "real world" is to a large extent unconsciously built up on the language habits of the group. No two languages are ever sufficiently similar to be considered as representing the same social reality. The worlds in which different societies live are distinct worlds, not merely the same world with diffierent labels attached. The understanding of a single poem, for instance, involves not merely an understanding of the single words in their average significance, but a full comprehension of the whole life of the community as it is mirrored in the words, or as it is suggested by their overtones. Even comparatively simple acts of perception are very much more at the mercy of the social patterns called words than we might suppose.'[10]

In the circumstances, then, that Hiberno-English has clearly lost ground, and that standard English is increasingly bringing with it, and imposing on us a 'world,' a 'design for living,' a 'value-system' at variance with our own, one cannot hope in the long term for a national literature in English, i.e. a literature which shall have an individual Irish way of seeing and expressing reality : a literature as specifically Irish *in its attitudes to life* as Synge's plays. Given what could be the present irreversible position, where the Irish 'experience' is so often an echo of the English 'experience,' all one could visualise evolving finally in Ireland would be a British regional literature, containing, perhaps, a large residual element of 'Irishness'—remnants of Irish attitudes, customs and manners—but, in essence, growing gradually out of an overall British (or Anglo-American) way of viewing life. Whether one should call such a literature Irish (or even Anglo-Irish) is merely a matter of acceptable nomenclature, and almost irrelevant. Whether one calls Languedoc cooking French, or Scottish sculpture British, is equally irrelevant.

Synge is possibly the only major writer of the Anglo-Irish nation to have achieved satisfactory identification with the historic Irish ethos. But the uniqueness, indeed the near-grotesqueness of his achievement, highlights the immense complexity of the task of any Irish writers of English in the future who feel they should have something to say which would recognizably grow out of the Irish way of encompassing reality.

NOTES

1 See *Irish Renaissance,* ed. Robin Skelton and David R. Clark, (Dublin, 1965), p. 67.
2 *Collected Works* III, pp. 15-17.
3 'The Well of the Saints', *Collected Works,* III, p. 131.
4 *Allagar na hInise* (Dublin 1928), p. 66; trans.
5 *An tOileánach* (Dublin 1929), p. 163; trans.
6 'Riders to the Sea', *Collected Works,* III, pp. 21-27.
7 *Collected Works,* II, pp. 74-5.
8 *Times Literary Supplement,* 25 September, 1970.
9 *Collected Works,* IV, pp. 189-191.
10 *Finnegans Wake* (London 1939), p. 171.
11 See *The Status of Linguistics as a Science,* p. 162, in Selected Writings of Edward Sapir, ed. David G. Mandelbaum. (University of California Press, 1963).

II: SYNGE'S USE OF IRISH FOLKLORE

SEÁN Ó SÚILLEABHÁIN

The very acute eye and the sensitiveness to Nature with which Synge was endowed have left us, in his writings, vignettes of places and people, which are at once colourful and vivid. He had also an ear alert for local dialects and lore, which he later used to good effect in his prose and plays. He preferred, in his wanderings in parts of Ireland, to mix and converse with the ordinary people rather than with the upper classes; thus farmers, shepherds, fishermen, tramps and tinkers form the majority of the people whom he met.

In Wicklow he had no difficulty in understanding the local speech which, like his own, was English. He was an unflagging note-taker, always jotting down words, phrases, snatches of songs and other items of lore, which served as material for his written works. Although handicapped at first by his lack of knowledge of the local dialects of Irish in Kerry and the West of Ireland, he succeeded in time, by study and the aid of tutors, in learning the language sufficiently well to understand what was being said or told in the form of a story.

His prose writings concerning Wicklow, Aran, Connemara, Mayo and Kerry are very rich in documentation about social and economic conditions, and are useful sources for historians, ethnologists and sociologists. The present article does not afford scope, however, for the discussion of these aspects of his writings. It must confine itself to their purely folklore content: folktales, legends, anecdotes, motifs, songs, folk beliefs and their associated customs. Social customs such as patterns, dancing, the playing of music and cards, storytelling and horse-racing will have to be excluded.

FOLK LITERATURE

The items of folk literature noted or used by Synge may be divided as follows:

A. *International Tale-Types*[1]

1. Types 882 *(The Wager on the Wife's Chastity)* and 890 *(A Pound of Flesh)* in combination.[2] The first element concerns a wager made by a merchant with a sea-captain about the chastity of the former's wife; the second tells of the defeat of a money-lender's attempt to extort a pound of flesh from the merchant in lieu of money he has borrowed. Shakespeare's use of the former in *Cymbeline* and of the latter in *The Merchant of Venice* will be remembered. Synge's version reverses the normal rôles in the Irish and international type, in which it is the merchant who usually pretends to have succeeded in seducing the captain's wife. Eighty-two versions of the first Type and thirty-six of the second have been recorded in Ireland.

2. *cf.* Type 1350 is the index number to be assigned to the tale recorded by Synge in Inishmaan and used by him as the theme of *The Shadow of the Glen.*[3] By this is meant that it is an ecotype (by-form) of Type 1350 *(The Loving Wife),* in which, when the husband feigns death, the credulous wife is ready to take as husband the man who brings her the news—this main Type is not found as an oral tale in Ireland. While Motif H466 *(Feigned death to test wife's faithfulness)*[4] is relevant for all the many Irish versions of the ecotype, these have no connection with Type 1510 *(The Matron of Ephesus),* which is a different tale. Synge pointed this out also. As in Synge's Aran version, the tale is often told in the first person, but he has not given the more usual Irish form in which the narrator tells of some other frightening experiences which he has had either before or after his visit to the house in which the husband is feigning death. Synge's version also differs from the normal Irish ones in which the main episode always ends with the wife and her lover being beaten by the enraged husband and the narrator fleeing from the scene. This ecotype was very popular in Ireland.

3. Two other Types, 1640 *(The Brave Tailor)* and 300 *(The Dragon-Slayer)* are combined in a version noted by Synge in Inishmaan. This is a rare fusion in Irish storytelling, however. The small hero (not necessarily a tailor) boasts of his prowess in killing a large number (of flies) at a blow and later goes on to slay three giants and to rescue a princess from a sea-monster. Synge gives a fairly full summary of this usually very long tale, which was the

most popular of all with Irish storytellers (six hundred and fifty-two versions of *The Dragon-Slayer* have been recorded in Ireland, as against three hundred and eight of *The Brave Tailor).*

4. In Aran again, Synge heard a version of Type 567 *(The Magic Bird-Heart.)* He summarises a rather poor form of the tale which has been recorded one hundred and thirty-six times in Ireland. It centres about a bird which lays golden eggs and will enable the person who eats its heart and liver to become king of Ireland; as might be expected, several persons contend for possession of the bird.

5. In *Deirdre of the Sorrows,* Synge gets Naisi to say to Fergus : '. . . and I see we're as happy as the leaves on the young trees and we'll be so ever and always though we'd live the age of the eagle and the salmon and the crow of Britain.'[5] The reference here is to Type 1927 *(The Cold May Night),* which I suggested to Stith Thompson for inclusion in his register of folktale types. The tale describes the search for information about the coldest night which has ever occurred, involving visits to an old otter, and aged eagle (hawk or crow) and finally to the oldest of all, a salmon at Assaroe in Co. Donegal. Forty-three versions of this unusual tale have been recorded in Ireland. Type 244[xx] *(The Crow and the Titmouse),* not recorded in Ireland, in which the great age of the titmouse and the cold which she has endured occurs, has motifs which echo our own main Type.

6. In the Glenbeigh district Synge noted two versions of Type 1305 *(The Miser and his Gold)*[6] and one of Type 1305C *(Miser Would Drink Molten Gold);*[7] the latter describes how an old woman who melts down her golden sovereigns to swallow them before she dies and thus deprive her relatives of their benefit is foiled by the substitution of melted butter.

7. In a public house near Swinford, Co. Mayo, Synge met an old man who was said to have killed three wild ducks 'with one skelp of a little gun he had.'[8] Although Synge does not give the complete tale, what he does tell is recognisable as an ecotype of Type 1894 *(The Man Shoots a Ramrod Full of Ducks).* This tale savours of the fantastic exploits of Baron Münchausen and of other 'tall stories' which are so popular in North America, and are also found in Europe.

B. *Other Tale-Types*

1. Synge heard in Aran a story about a famous horse-rider,

Charlie Lambert, who, by riding to victory the horse of an Irish gentleman against an English opponent, saved its owner from losing his property. This tale-type is well-known in Ireland and has been recorded in different areas; the hero is sometimes either an Irish soldier who is 'on the run' after the Rebellion of 1798, or else an outlaw; both are pardoned on the strength of their prowess as riders.[9]

2. A somewhat similar tale, noted by Synge in Aran, describes how a fairy man rides to victory the nag of a farmer who has been kind to him and thus enables him to become a rich man.[10]

3. 'And now, here's to your good health, and may you live till they make you a coffin out of a gooseberry bush, or till you die in childbed.' This drinking toast to Synge brings to mind the humorous story so common in Ireland about a trickster, condemned to the gallows, who was offered his own choice of tree from which to be hanged; he chose a gooseberry bush, saying that he would wait until it grew, if it proved too small!

4. The basic theme of *The Well of the Saints* (the blind, having been cured, wish to be blind once more) occurs in the folk story of a blind man who, having been cured, similarly asks to be made blind again in order that he may not commit sin.

5. The legend of Mary, who scattered the seeds of a medicinal plant all over the world to benefit mankind,[12] is reminiscent of many similar legends concerning the origins of particular beneficial herbs and plants.

6. The story told to Synge in Inisheer, purporting to explain the stammering in speech and inefficiency in performance of the Inishmaan people,[13] belongs to the genre of tales about *Fools* (Motif J1700 - Motif J1729), on a parallel with the Men of Gotham tale-types found in many countries.

7. In his book about Aran,[14] Synge devoted merely ten lines to the local story on which he later based *The Playboy of the Western World*. According to what Synge was told, the young man 'killed his father with the blow of a spade when he was in passion.' Professor Tomás O Máille of Galway carried out research into the basic tale and later criticised Synge for veering, for artistic reasons, from the actual facts, which I summarise as follows from his account[15]: a young man named O Máille (named 'The Playboy' by Synge) was born about 1838 either in Iorras Mór or near Calath in Connemara; his father drank heavily, and young

O Máille went to sea at an early age; he sent home money with which his father bought some extra land; when his wife died, the father re-married and refused to give the land to his son when he returned home and married; in the course of a quarrel in the potato-field, the father was injured (not killed) by the son; both wives advised him to flee and, after hiding here and there in Connemara, he reached Aran *via* Garumna and was sheltered there by a kinswoman who was married to a man named O Hiarnáin; the local people of Inishmore took pity on the fugitive who was downcast on account of what had happened between himself and his father and provided him with gifts and entertainment to cheer him up; when the search for him became intensified, two Conneely men rowed O Máille to Inishmaan, where he was taken in by an old man; the house was surrounded one night by the police, who, in error, allowed O Máille to escape in the belief that he was the old man; he hid in a cave near the shore until some time later a boat, which was taking potatoes from Aran to Tralee, took him on board; he finally reached Cork and later arrived in America; a few years later, as a sea-captain, he brought his ship into Galway, making himself known only to a few trusted friends. Professor O Máille, as already stated, found fault with Synge for having misinterpreted the kindness of the Inishmore people to the young man and for having misused this part of the story in the play.

C. *Heroic Tale-Types and Motifs*

The older Ulster Cycle of tales is represented in Synge's writings by his unfinished play, *Deirdre of the Sorrows.* He does not mention having heard the basic story told orally anywhere in his travels, although its currency is shown by the fact that some fifty versions of it have been recorded in Ireland. It may have originally been a literary creation, more suited to the banqueting hall and court than to the fireside. Synge's treatment of it points to a manuscript or printed source rather than to an oral version. Had he lived to finish the play, he might, had he heard the folk-version, have worked in the usual folk-ending (Type 970 : *The Twining Branches),* which tells how two trees planted on the lovers' graves became entwined.

The sole mention of Cú Chulainn, the Ulster hero, in Synge's writings is a reference to 'Cúchulainn's house,'[16] a large cairn of stones on a mountain near Aunascaul in Kerry.

The only tale of the later Fianna Cycle which Synge has given, at some length, tells of the visit of Oisín to Tír na n-Og; he had heard it near Glenbeigh.[17] He also gives some minor scraps of lore about Diarmaid O Duibhne and Gráinne, but these are associated with local places and not developed by Synge. Both the Oisín tale and the story of the pursuit of Diarmaid and Gráinne were very popular with Irish storytellers.

Apart from such motifs as occur in the tales already mentioned, the following may be noted: T52.3 *(Bride purchased for her weight in gold),* which Synge records twice; Deirdre's wish for a man whose hair, skin and lips are of a certain colour—a motif which occurs in other tales also; and the rhetorical close to a tale told by Mourteen—we do not know what tale it was; these passages (rhetorics, runs, *côraithe catha* or *cultacha gaisce,* or even 'nonsense endings,' as Synge styles them) were a common feature of Gaelic, Slav and Scandinavian folktales. Synge noted from an old man in Inishmaan a single riddle, which is of common currency.

D. *Folk Poetry*

Synge occasionally gives verses of songs, either in the original or in his own translation from Irish, most of which are well-known.

1. 'The White Horse' ('an extraordinary English doggerel,' as Synge styled it[18]) gives extravagant praise to a horse, which is said to have served as a mount for many famous people, from Adam to Daniel O'Connell. This type of song was popular in Ireland, in both Irish and English, under such titles as 'The Old Grey Mare,' 'The Paidireen Mare,' *'Ceann an Chapaill'* and others.[19]

2. 'Phelim and the Eagle' is a translation, made by Synge, of another song he heard in Aran.[20] Its usual Irish name is *An tIolra*[*ch*] Mór (The Great Eagle); it was composed by a Connemara poet, Féidhlim Mac Dhubhghaill. It is based on the secret killing of a cock by a woman as a treat for a visitor and the supposed subsequent search by her husband for the eagle which she had blamed.

3. Another search-song, this time for a horse, supposed to have

been taken by the fairies, is entitled 'Rucard Mor' by Synge in his own translation.[21] The owner of the horse, Riocard Mór de Búrc, a fish jolter, visits in turn many fairy centres, but is told at last that the horse has been killed to provide a hunting-cap from her skin for somebody named Conall Cat[h].

4. Synge gives some scraps of a ballad about the Russo-Japanese War, sung as a duet at Puck Fair by a man and a woman.[22]

5. Among other broken verses quoted by Synge,[23] occurs the couplet used by a roulette man at Rossbeigh races :

> Come play me a game of timmun and tup,
> The more you put down the more you take up.

I heard a roulette man at a pattern in South Kerry using this same exhortation fifty years ago, using 'toodlembuck' instead of 'timmun and tup.'

6. Synge gives an Aran version[24] of the reason why 'the poet MacSweeny' composed a song which Synge styles 'The Big Wedding;' he does not, however, give a translation of the song itself, which, he says, was known in both Irish and English. The poet was Mícheál Mhac Suibhne, who was born near Cong in Co. Mayo about 1760 and died sometime around 1820. His published poems give a different reason for the composition of the song, *Bainis Pheigí Ní Eádhra* (Peggy O'Hara's Wedding), a very popular song in Connemara. It consists of eleven verses which give a fanciful description of the magnificent wedding of Peigí.

7. In his Aran book, Synge gives his own translation of some verses of another song concerning the whiskey available from the tavern of a Mr. Sloper near Galway.[25]

8. Synge tells us that, on the Blaskets, he heard sung 'a long English doggerel' about a poor Maynooth student, who was falsely accused of seduction by a woman but was finally acquitted 'when a man rode up on a horse and said it was himself was the lover of the lady and the father of her child.'[26] Synge does not give the words of the ballad, however, and I have not been able to trace it. The basic theme of the maligned student is to be found in some Irish folktales.[27]

FOLK CUSTOM AND BELIEF

Synge was attracted to the exotic wherever he went, and his

notes about it, as well as his reaction to it, make very interesting reading, which, however, contains nothing very new for those who know how Irish country people traditionally feel and conduct themselves.

In his own poem, *To the Oaks of Glencree,* he refers to his own death :

'There'll come a season when you'll stretch
Black boards to cover me :
Then in Mount Jerome I'll lie, poor wretch,
With worms eternally.'

The theme of death occurs frequently in his works, and may have held a kind of fascination for him personally and as a writer.

In *The Shadow of the Glen,*[28] the reason given by Nora for the delay in laying-out the body of her (supposed) dead husband—that only his sister should do it—is certainly a dramatic device of the playwright, and not based on traditional custom.

During his stay in Aran especially, Synge observed wakes and funerals of both young and old and has well described the atmosphere on such sad occasions, while not entering to any great depth into the manifold customs and beliefs which come into play at such times of human crisis. Still, by combing through his works, we can discover the following : the provision of boards from the mainland for the coffins of persons, still alive, on treeless Aran;[29] the provision of whiskey, pipes and tobacco at wakes and funerals;[30] burial scenes on Aran;[31] a funeral near Swinford in Mayo;[32] the wake and funeral of drowned men[33] (Synge, in *Riders to the Sea,* has the drowned body of Bartley carried into the house to be waked;[34] this is contrary to the normal Irish custom of waking in an outhouse the body of a person who has died out of doors); the keening of the dead at wakes and funerals[35] (do 'the black hags that do be flying on the sea,'[36] which are mentioned as the only keeners of the drowned Michael, represent relatives who have died abroad and return in the guise of sea-birds?—a common Irish folk belief); and finally, the mention of 'the way murdered men do bleed and drip,'[37] which may refer to the belief that the corpse of a murdered person will bleed in the presence of, or when touched by, the murderer.

Belief in the return of the dead to this world on particular occasions and for certain reasons was very strong in Ireland and elsewhere, and it does not surprise us to find Synge noting and using it. In *Riders to the Sea,*[38] old Maurya speaks of 'the day Bride Dara seen the dead man with the child in his arms.' Again, in Aran, we are told how a woman 'saw all the people that were dead a while back on this island and the south island, and they all talking with each other;'[39] also how two dead men (his grandfathers) had helped a man to lead his horse through a fair on the road, 'with the people buying and selling and they not living people at all.'[40] A very common facet of folk belief concerning the supposed return of the dead is that they occasionally come back to take some living person with them into the kingdom of the dead. This is vividly illustrated in *Riders to the Sea,* where the already drowned Michael is seen riding the grey pony in the company of Bartley (who is to be drowned) on the red mare.[41] This belief is the base of most stories about a person who meets a ghost late at night and dies at home shortly afterwards—the ghost had come to take him away.

Synge noted a few omens of death in Aran. Of a man who had been drowned, we are told that 'before he went out on the sea that day his dog came up and sat beside him on the rocks, and began crying;'[42] also 'we don't like a cock or hen to break anything in a house, for we know then someone will be going away'[43] (through death, perhaps, although this is not expressly stated).

Lore about death and the kingdom of the dead leads us on to associated beliefs of another kind. Synge's comment that the people of Inishmaan 'make no distinction between the natural and the supernatural'[44] is, to my mind, an overstatement. Had he said that the natural and the supernatural were equally real to them (though still distinguished), he would have summed up the belief traditionally held by people everywhere in the existence of some kind of world outside of our material one, peopled by beings of various kinds, friendly or malignant, who could and did involve themselves in worldly affairs. Among the malignant beings, we may place the Devil as an active agent in certain happenings which were otherwise inexplicable; the Playboy even refers to the Devil's 'four fathers,'[45] whoever they might have been.

'The Joeys will be out walking if you sit delaying like that,'[46] Pegeen Mike remarks to Shawn Keogh in an endeavour to get him to leave. She was referring to the common belief in the existence of the fairies, as inhabitants of the other world already mentioned.

Synge's book about Aran shows the strength of fairy-belief among the islanders. The fairies could take away people into their own world[47]—a world which, in folk belief, is often confused and mixed up with the world of the dead. Such abducted humans, who might have been supposed to have died in the normal way, could occasionally return to this world, and Synge gives the extraordinary story about a woman who bore children after her return from fairyland.[48] The fairies could take off animals and crops also: 'the old man told me,' Synge says, 'that the fairies have a tenth of all the produce of the country and make stores of it in the rocks.'[49] Again, like humans, they played music[50] and ball-games [51] and rode across the hills.[52] Their origin, as given to Synge by an old Aran man,[53] is in accord with the normal Irish tradition that they are some of the rebellious angels who fell with Lucifer from Heaven. Such are the items of fairy lore mentioned by Synge, a few gleanings from the rich harvest which still awaits scholarly study, so far as Ireland is concerned.

Several other facets of belief in the supernatural are also illustrated in Synge's works. 'My intercourse with these people,' he remarks of Aran, 'has made me realise that miracles must abound wherever the new conception of law is not understood. On these islands alone miracles enough happen every year to equip a divine emissary. Rye is turned into oats, storms are raised to keep evictors from the shore, cows that are isolated on lonely rocks bring forth calves, and other things of the same kind are common,'[54] It may be well to enumerate here those 'other things' of which he writes: a voice issues from a hole into which a rabbit has been hunted, begging for mercy: 'Ah, Phaddrick, don't hurt me with the hook!';[55] strange music distracts a man who is about to take aim at a rabbit, the rabbit vanishes and, when the man looks over a wall, he sees 'a rabbit sitting up by the wall with a sort of flute in its mouth, and it playing on it with its two fingers;[56] a man who is out late at night hears a noise 'as if there was a man trying to catch a horse on the rocks,' and then 'as if twenty horses, and then as if a hundred or a thousand, were galloping after him;'[57] the same man told Synge that he had been coming home before dawn and had heard a flute playing at a hole under a cliff;[58] old Pat Dirane tells Synge that one night he had heard a voice crying out in Irish, '*A mháthair, tá mé marbh*' ('O mother, I'm killed'), 'and in the morning there was blood on the wall of his house, and a child in a house not far off was dead;'[59] similarly, 'There was a woman went to bed at the lower village a while ago, and her child along with her. For a time they did not sleep, and then something came to the window, and they heard a voice and this is what it said—"It is time to sleep from this out." In the morning the child was dead, and indeed it is many get their death that way on this island;'[60] a man is asked by a woman to take her into his cart at night and, when he refuses to do so and looks back, he sees only a pig;[61] and finally, a warning of the approach of the peelers in search of poteen is given by a strange fisherman.[62]

The underwater world and its inhabitants are also noted by Synge. In Lough Nahanagan in Wicklow 'the spirit came down out of the clouds and rifted the water asunder' and later killed a dog that was swimming in the lake.[63] In Glenbeigh district, Synge heard the well-known story of the man who married the mermaid, after stealing her *cochall* (underwater cloak); she finally recovered her 'covering' and returned to the sea; 'I'm told from that day there isn't one of the Shees can go out in a boat on that bay and not be drowned.'[64] Under that same bay lies 'Tir-na-nOg' which Oisín visited,[65] and when a local man looked down into the water from his boat one morning he saw 'people walking about, and side-cars driving in the squares.'[66] Synge also heard stories about strange ships which appeared and vanished when approached by human beings.[67]

Holy wells, festivals and the saints associated with them are mentioned a few times by Synge. The water from a holy well near the ruined church of the 'Ceathair Aluinn' (*recte* 'An Ceathrar Alainn') in Aran is said to be famous for its power to cure blindness and epilepsy.[68] Bonfires on the eve of the Feast of St. John were noted by Synge in both Aran[69] and Erris.[70] The practice of killing a sheep on the night of the Feast of St. Martin (10 November) is also mentioned by him.[71] And we find the Saint, in *The Well of the Saints,* saying that he will go to Glendalough to sleep in the bed of holy Kevin (his grave.)[72]

There are several references in Synge's works to insanity[73] and to the effect which a change of moon may have on human beings.[74] The Irish term *'le gealaigh'* ('with the moon') for 'insane' and the Latin root of the word 'lunacy' seem to be associated with this belief. References to 'the old screeching madwoman running round in the glen'[75] and to 'the madmen of Keel, eating muck and green weeds on the faces of the cliffs,'[76] have a probable connection with Gleann na nGealt (The Glen of the Mad People) between Camp and Aunascaul in Kerry; tradition says that in olden times insane persons went to this glen in the hope of being cured by eating the watercress which grew in the healing spring there[77]—this may be the 'weeds' referred to above. Still in the field of folk medicine, Synge tells of an old bonesetter, 'said to have done remarkable cures,' whom he met in Aran.[78]

In Synge's writings, we find many references to persons who were said to be possessed of special powers or capabilities. The Saint in *The Well of the Saints* restored their sight to Martin Doul and his wife, Mary[79]. Then there was the witch who raised a storm in Aran to prevent the bailiffs from landing and carrying out an eviction.[80] 'Among the country people of the East of Ireland,' says Synge, 'the tramps and tinkers who wander round from the West have a curious reputation for witchery and unnatural powers.'[81] Again, the Saint in the aforementioned play advises his listeners 'to be saying a prayer for your own sakes against false prophets and heathens, and the words of women and smiths.'[82] In *The Tinker's Wedding*, Mary accuses Sarah that she 'quenched the flaming candles on the throne of God the time your shadow fell within the pillars of the chapel door.'[83] A French priest, who had visited Aran, is hinted at as having changed the rye crop into oats and brought poor crops.[84] Finally, in the list of such persons, comes the man who brings ill-luck to any curagh in which he is a passenger.[85]

Things to which special powers are attributed are also mentioned a few times by Synge: holy water, so often used as a magical element in Irish folk practice;[86] and the use of a sharp needle to afford protection against harm from the fairies.[87]

His references to the use of speech in swearing, blessing and cursing are also to be noted here. In *The Well of the Saints*, Martin Doul speaks of the noises he hears 'till you'd take your dying oath on sun and moon a thing was breathing on the stones.'[88] Again, in *Deirdre of the Sorrows*, Ainnle says: 'By the sun and moon and the whole earth, I wed Deirdre to Naisi.'[89] Later, in the same play, Lavarcham says: 'It's a hard thing surely, but let you take my word and swear Naisi by the earth, and the sun over it, and the four quarters of the moon he'll not go back to Emain for good faith, or bad faith . . .'[90] As regards the use of speech in blessings, reference is to be made to the fact that the departing Bartley wishes the blessings of God on his mother as he sets out, while she refrains from returning it,[91] and so, possibly, contributes to his death. In Aran, Synge noted that as men crossed the threshold of the house where he was staying they usually murmured 'The blessing of God on this place,' or some similar words.[92] So too, in Aran, the phrase 'God bless it' should be added when a child is being praised (probably to prevent harm from evil eye or malicious tongue).[93] Maledictions are often referred to by Synge. In *The Shadow of the Glen,* Nora says of her supposedly dead husband : 'he put a black curse on me this morning if I'd touch his body the time he'd die sudden, or let anyone touch it except his sister only.[94] In *The Playboy of the Western World,* Christy Mahon says: '... and not a one of them to this day would say their seven curses on him.'[95] In *The Well of the Saints,* Martin Doul says to Molly: 'Won't you raise your voice, Molly, and lay hell's long curse on his tongue.'[96] And finally, writing of the people of Wicklow, Synge tells of an old man from Glenmalure, who had not been sent financial help by his wealthy children in California, and quotes him as saying 'may the devil ride with them to hell!'[97]

A few final items illustrative of folk belief and practice in Synge's works may be listed : the symbolic action of old Maurya in placing the empty cup mouth downwards on the table to signify that the end had come;[98] the dream of the Sligo woman about a healing well in Aran which proved true;[99] and the ill-luck which follows the breaking of certain tabus (fishing on the eve of a holy day,[100] or wearing the shirt of a dead man[101]). Bogeys to frighten children are mentioned twice by Synge.[102]

For the purposes of this necessarily short article, I have analysed Synge's works from the view-point of their folklore content,[103] and have synthesised what I have found into various relevant categories. It has been a worthwhile task. Synge has emerged as a reliable collector of traditional lore in the course of his visits to parts of Wicklow, Kerry, Galway and Mayo. The tales, motifs, verse, folk beliefs and customs, which he has noted or used in his plays, are all verifiable as belonging to genuine oral tradition. For this, as well as for other reasons, he deserves commendation.

NOTES

CW: *The Collected Works of J. M. Synge*. General Editor: Robin Skelton. (Oxford University Press 1962-8)

1 Antti Aarne and Stith Thompson, *The Types of the Folktale* (Helsinki, 1961). For a discussion of international folktale types, see Stith Thompson, *The Folktale* (New York, 1946). For Irish versions, see Séan Ó Súilleabháin and Reidar Th. Christiansen, *The Types of the Irish Folktale* (Helsinki, 1963).

2 CW II, pp. 61-64. Synge published this tale, with comment, in *New Ireland Review* (Dublin, November, 1898), p. 153.

3 For a comment on Synge's sources for the play, see P. S. O'Hegarty, *The Irish Book Lover* (Dublin, 1918), IX, pp. 126-127; also Reader, *The Irish Book Lover* (Dublin, 1921), XIII, pp. 37-38.

4 For Motifs, see Stith Thompson, *Motif-Index of Folk Literature* (Copenhagen, 1966), 6 vols.

5 CW IV, p. 229. For an English translation of a Galway version of this tale, see Sean O'Sullivan, *Folktales of Ireland* (London, 1966), pp. 15-18; see also Eleanor Hull, 'The Hawk of Achill, or the Legend of the Oldest of the Animals', in *Folk-Lore* (London, 1932), XLIII, pp. 376-409.

6 CW II, pp. 261-262.

7 *idem*, pp. 262-263.

8 *idem*, p. 332.

9 *idem*, pp. 166-167. See Irish Folklore Commission's MS. Vols. 24, pp. 385-389, and 534, pp. 439-455. Also *Our Boys* (Dublin, October, 1915), p. 52.

10 CW II, p. 167. See Irish Folklore Commission's MS. Vol. 244, pp. 261-264; also *An Stoc* (Gaillimh, Eanáir/Feabhra, 1931), p. 10.

11 CW II, p. 183.

12 *idem*, p. 244.

13 *idem*, pp. 178-179.

14 *idem*, p. 95.

15 Tomás O Máille, *An Ghaoth Aniar* (Baile Atha Cliath, 1920), pp. 93-98. See also Irish Folklore Commission's MS. Vol. 79, p. 437, for an Inishmaan version, recorded by Gordon Quinn, 1931.

16 CW II, p. 268. See *Journal of the County Louth Archaeological Society* (Dundalk, 1914), III, p. 193, for legend and photograph.

17 CW II, p. 270.

18 *idem*, pp. 167-171.

19 See Michael F. Cox, *Notes on the History of the Irish Horse* (1897), pp. 106-111; *Journal of the Royal Society of Antiquaries of Ireland* (Dublin, 1909), XXXIX, p. 206; Colm O Lochlainn, *Irish Street Ballads* (Dublin, 1939), pp. 70-71; *An Macaomh* (Baile Atha Cliath, Bealtaine, 1913), p. 47, contributed by the editor, Patrick Pearse; ed. James N. Healy, *The Mercier Book of Old Irish Street Ballads* (Cork, 1969), III, pp. 137-138; for a version in the Irish language, see Irish Folklore Commission's MS. Vol. 52, pp. 114-119.

20 cw II, pp. 175-178. See Domhnall O Fotharta, *Siamsa an Gheimhridh* (Baile Atha Cliath, 1892), pp. 108-110, 115-116; *An Stoc* (Gaillimh, Eanáir/Feabhra, 1931), p. 3; Irish Folklore Commission's MS. Vols. 109, pp. 24-28, 229, pp. 45-48, 237, pp. 4-5, and 1281, pp. 61-64.
21 cw II, pp. 172-175. For some verses of the original Irish song (said to have been composed by Seán Bacach O Guairim about 1860), see *Irisleabhar Muighe Nuadhad* (Baile Atha Cliath, 1916), pp. 74-76; also Irish Folklore Commission's MS. Vols. 74, pp. 280-281, 79, pp. 314-315, 1130, pp. 258-262; and Oireachtas MSS., National Library, Dublin, No. 251.
22 cw II, p. 267.
23 *idem,* p. 272.
24 *idem,* p. 183. For the other story and the Irish song, see ed. Tomás O Máille, *Mícheál Mhac Suibhne agus Filidh an tSléibhe* (Baile Atha Cliath, 1934), pp. 3, 23-28.
25 cw II, pp. 183-184. See O Máille, *Micheál Mhac Suibhne,* pp. 10-11, 111.
26 cw II, pp. 256-257.
27 Seán O Súilleabháin, *Scéalta Cráibhtheacha* (Baile Atha Cliath, 1952), Nos. 26, 34 and 44.
28 cw III, 35.
29 cw II, p. 158; *idem,* III, p. 25.
30 cw II, p. 171; *idem,* III, Appendix A, p. 249; *idem,* IV, pp. 77, 151, and Appendix B, pp. 321, 323; *idem,* III, pp. 36-37; Seán O Súilleabháin, *Irish Wake Amusements* (Cork, 1967), pp. 16-25.
31 cw II, pp. 74-76, 160-162, 171.
32 *idem,* p. 329.
33 *idem,* pp. 158, 160-162.
34 *idem,* III, p. 23.
35 cw II, pp. 74-76, 160-162. For 'The Keening of the Dead', see Seán O Súilleabháin, *Irish Wake Amusements,* pp. 130-145.
36 cw III, p. 17.
37 cw IV, p. 97.
38 cw III, p. 19.
39 cw II, p. 157.
40 *idem,* p. 182.
41 cw III, pp. 19, 23.
42 cw II, p. 164.
43 *idem,* pp. 164-165.
44 *idem,* p. 128.
45 cw IV, p. 81.
46 cw III, Appendix B, p. 311.
47 cw II, pp. 54, 80, 165.
48 *idem,* p. 159; for a translation of a Connemara version of this story, see Sean O'Sullivan, *Folktales of Ireland* (Chicago and London, 1966), pp. 176-179.
49 cw II, p. 82.
50 *idem,* p. 165.
51 *idem,* p. 80.

52 *idem*, p. 216.
53 *idem*, p. 56.
54 *idem*, p. 128.
55 *idem*, p. 154.
56 *idem*, p. 154.
57 *idem*, p. 180.
58 *idem*, p. 180.
59 *idem*, p. 80.
60 *idem*, p. 160.
61 *idem*, p. 182.
62 *idem*, p. 157.
63 *idem*, pp. 189-190.
64 *idem*, p. 271. For another Kerry version of this story, see ed. Seán O Súilleabháin, *Diarmuid na Bolgaighe agus a Chomhursain* (Baile Atha Cliath, 1937), p. 2; for Scottish versions, see David Thomson, *The People of the Sea* (London, 1954), pp. 157-163, 211-212.
65 cw II, pp. 270-271.
66 *idem*, p. 271.
67 *idem*, pp. 165, 181-182.
68 *idem*, pp. 56-57; cw III. p. 79. For the four 'beautiful persons' (Saints Fursey, Brendan of Birr, Conall and Berchain), see the *Journal of the Royal Society of Antiquaries of Ireland* (Dublin), XVII (1885-1886), p. 491.
69 cw II, p. 102.
70 *idem*, p. 327.
71 cw III, Appendix A, p. 244. See Seán O Súilleabháin, 'The Feast of Saint Martin in Ireland', in *Studies in Folklore* (Bloomington, Indiana, 1957), pp. 252-261.
72 cw III, p. 101. References to sleeping in 'saints' beds' as a cure for sterility in women occur frequently in Irish oral tradition.
73 cw II, pp. 209-210, 217, 219.
74 cw IV, pp. 7, 23, 31.
75 cw III, p. 97.
76 cw IV, p. 169.
77 See Gearóid Mac Eoin, 'Gleann Bolcáin agus Gleann na nGealt', in *Béaloideas* (Baile Atha Cliath, 1962), XXX, 105-120.
78 cw II, p. 95.
79 cw III, Act I.
80 cw II, pp. 88, 128.
81 *idem*, p. 203.
82 cw III, p. 91; see note about 'Saint Patrick's Breastplate', idem. p. 90.
83 cw IV, p. 33.
84 cw II, pp. 127-128.
85 *idem*, p. 117.
86 cw III, p. 25.
87 cw II, p. 80; idem, III, p. 41.
88 cw III, p. 127.
89 cw IV, p. 215.
90 *idem*, p. 217.

91 cw III, p. 11.
92 cw II. p. 59.
93 *idem,* p. 51.
94 cw III, p. 35.
95 cw IV, p. 85.
96 cw III, p. 123.
97 cw II, p. 216.
98 cw III, p. 25.
99 cw II, p. 57.
100 *idem,* p. 137.
101 cw III, p. 15.
102 cw II, p. 111; idem, III, p. 121.
103 In 1932, a German student, Herbert Frenzel of Dresden, presented an inaugural dissertation for Doctorate at Bonn University, entitled 'John Millington Synge's Work as a contribution to Irish Folklore and to the Psychology of Primitive Tribes' (Düren/Rheinland, 1932). Apart from its inverted title, it was not a satisfactory study from the folklore point of view, as it veered rather to the anthropological approach.

III: THE LANGUAGE OF SYNGE

ALAN J. BLISS

I

The English language has been spoken in Ireland for eight hundred years, but its history has been very chequered. During the Middle Ages the Norman and English settlers in Ireland were rapidly assimilated to the native stock, and attempts to stem the tide of Gaelicization were ineffective. Already by 1500, English was hardly spoken outside the garrison towns, and the advent of the Reformation served to hasten the decay of English, since the Irish language came to be the symbol of the old religion; sixteenth-century English visitors to Ireland observed that even those who were able to speak English among themselves would not speak it to them.[2] By 1600, the old English of Ireland was effectively extinct, except in two small areas, the baronies of Forth and Bargy in Co. Wexford and the district of Fingall in north Co. Dublin, where it survived until the early nineteenth century.[3]

Present-day Anglo-Irish has no continuity with the Anglo-Irish of the Middle Ages; the English language was introduced into Ireland for a second time with the Cromwellian settlements of the 1650's.[4] For a century and a half English remained the language of the land-owning class; and, isolated as it was from the main stream of English culture, the English spoken in Ireland stagnated, and preserved features of seventeenth-century English which had long become obsolete in England. From the beginning of the nineteenth century onwards the Irish-speaking population began with increasing momentum to acquire the English language.[5] The relaxation of the Penal Laws facilitated the spread of education which, because English was the 'prestige' language, meant education in English; the rapid increase in population meant that emigration was for many the only alternative to starvation, and the English language was the passport both to Britain and to the United States.

The peculiarities of present-day Anglo-Irish stem from the exceptional political and social conditions of eighteenth- and nineteenth-century Ireland. The only speakers of Standard English in Ireland were the landed classes, who regarded their tenants, and were in turn regarded by them, as aliens different in political and social values, in culture, and in religion;[6] the Irish were taught their English by people of their own race, whose English was itself at several removes from Standard English, and had been learnt in part from books.[7] The Irish are not lacking in mental ability, and there is no reason why they should not have learnt to speak English perfectly, if they had been given the opportunity of doing so; but they were not. Because they learnt from each other, not only were the archaisms of seventeenth-century English preserved and propagated, but the influence of the Irish language on Anglo-Irish speech was cumulative; even in those areas where Irish has long ceased to be spoken, its influence on pronunciation, on vocabulary, and above all on syntax, is paramount.

If Ulster is left out of account, there is much less regional variation in Anglo-Irish than might have been expected. Of course there are differences in pronunciation, and even in vocabulary;[8] but, though it may be easy enough to place a man by his 'accent,' it is very difficult to place a piece of *written* Anglo-Irish into its regional context. Even in Co. Wicklow, where Irish has hardly been spoken for nearly two hundred years, the influence of the Irish language is still strong, because the transmission of the knowledge of English has a continuous history, unaffected by Standard English, reaching back to the time when Irish was still the vernacular of the county. On the other hand, the English of those Western counties where the use of Irish has only recently died out shows many of the peculiarities of 17th-century English, since the Irish-speakers there learned their English from those whose language still preserved these features.

II

The representation in writing of the peculiarities of Anglo-Irish speech goes back to the time of Swift,[9] whose *Irish Eloquence* and *Dialogue in the Hibernian Style*[10] castigate a number of non-Standard words and idioms which are still in common use. In the 1820's Banim and Griffin, and a little later Lover and Lever, made use of Anglo-Irish dialogue for comic purposes; Carleton's purpose was more serious, but he, too, used Anglo-Irish only in dialogue. The first use of Anglo-Irish as a literary medium was made by Douglas Hyde in 1890, when in his *Beside the Fire* he published a series of folk-tales in the original Irish, and accompanied them with a translation into Anglo-Irish.

Hyde's preface to *Beside the Fire* is well worth study,[11] since he devotes several pages[12] to a discussion of the rationale of his method of translation. After criticizing some collectors of folk-tales for presenting them in a fully anglicized form, and Campbell of Islay for translating his Scottish Gaelic sources too literally, he points out[13] that 'it is not very easy to make a good translation from Irish into English, for there are no two Aryan languages more opposed to each other in spirit and idiom.' Whereas many Irish idioms and turns of phrase are reproduced in Anglo-Irish, many others are not; so that, though the use of Anglo-Irish is a help, it is not a complete solution to the problem. 'I have not,' he says,[14] 'always translated the Irish idioms quite literally, though I have used much unidiomatic English, but only of the kind used all over Ireland, the kind the people themselves use . . . Where, as sometimes happens, the English language contains no exact equivalent for an Irish expression, I have rendered the original as well as I could, as one generally does render for linguistic purposes, from one language into another.'

Interesting though this discussion is, it does not tell the whole story. It has not, apparently, previously been noticed that Hyde deliberately introduces into his translations Anglo-Irish expressions which have no counterpart in the Irish original.[15] In the following examples (all taken from the story of 'Paudyeen O'Kelly and the Weasel') the phrases italicized have either been added in the translation, corresponding to nothing in the Irish, or are much less in accordance with English idiom than a literal translation would be :

> He wanted to go to the fair of Cauher-na-mart to sell a sturk of an ass *that he had*.[16]
>
> When he got to the house he found the door open *before him,* and in with him.[17]
>
> But at last, *when he got her gone* [lit. *when she went away*] Paudyeen rose up.[18]
>
> . . . instead of coming home with the money he got for his old ass, *as he thought would be the way with him in the morning* [lit. *as he thought in the morning he would be doing*] . . .[19]
>
> but don't be afraid *before him*.[20]

Hyde (though he did not admit it in his introduction) was therefore intentionally using the Anglo-Irish dialect to reproduce not the letter but the spirit of the Irish folk-tale; that is, he was using it as a literary medium. The effect is sometimes not too far removed from that of the language of Synge, as the following brief passage shows:

> And why did you bring away my gold that I was for five hundred years gathering throughout the hills and hollows of the world.[21]

Here the achievement is wholly Hyde's, for the Irish equivalent of the characteristic phrase 'throughout the hills and hollows of the world'[22] means, more literally, 'among the hills and valleys of the world.'[23]

In the same year, 1890, Hyde began the serial publication of his *Songs of Connacht,* at first in *The Nation,* subsequently in *The Weekly Freeman.*[24] Of this collection the most important chapter is the fourth, containing *The Love Songs of Connacht,* published separately in book form in 1893. In his preface Hyde says[25] that this 'little work . . . was originally all written in Irish, but the exigencies of publication in a weekly newspaper necessitated the translation of it into English;' 'My English prose translation,' he adds, 'only aims at being literal, and has courageously, though no doubt ruggedly, reproduced the Irish idioms of the original.' Posterity has reason to be grateful to the ephemeral press in this case, since it is generally recognized that Synge was much indebted to Hyde's translation of these love songs. '*The Love Songs of Connacht,*' says Boyd,[26] 'were the constant study of the author of *The Playboy,* whose plays testify, more than those of any other writer, to the influence of Hyde's prose.'

In *The Love Songs of Connacht* Hyde translates his own Irish prose commentary much more accurately than he had translated the folk-tales in *Beside the Fire.* The Irish verses which form the major part of the book are sometimes translated into English verse, and these verse translations, though an improvement on most earlier attempts to translate Irish into English verse, are not of outstanding merit in spite of their metrical ingenuity. It is the prose translations which Hyde provides as well as or instead of the verse translations that are of startling excellence; these for the first time revealed the astonishing resources of the Anglo-Irish dialect as a medium for poetic prose. Attempts have been made to trace instances in which Synge may have been directly indebted to Hyde, but none of the resemblances is really very striking;[27] Synge's debt is subtler and less easily formalized than this. Perhaps the following passages will indicate how close the tone of Hyde's translation may come to Synge's characteristic style :

> 'Tis a pity without me to be married, with the bright treasure of my heart, on the brink by the great river or at the nearer ditch by its side. Company of young women, it is they who would raise my heart and I would be a year younger if I were married to my desire.[28]
>
> And O Nelly, Oh, dear God, it is not proper for thee to be forsaking me, and sure it was beside thy white skin I had desired to be coaxing thee, my hand on the Bible and I down on my knees, that I would never part with thee until I should be stretched in the clay.[29]
>
> It is my destruction and spoiling, without my love, and me (to be) in Spain or far away from our kin, in the dwelling of a wood beside shore or wave, and without a person in the world in our vicinity. It is closely I would approach to the flower of the affections, and it is mildly I would kiss her little mouth. I would arrange for her a couch and would repose near her, and I would give a little to coaxing her.[30]

III

Synge's first attempt to write in the Anglo-Irish dialect seems to have been the poem which Skelton entitles 'Ballad of a Pauper,' and which he tentatively dates in 1895.[31] It appears to owe nothing to Hyde, whom Synge may not yet have read. It is unique among Synge's Anglo-Irish writings in that it makes use of the non-Standard spellings traditionally used to denote pronunciations current in Ireland : *Misther, thrade, thruth, thrifle; wid; dacent; niver, jist; evenin, goin', schoolin, etc.* This is a device which Synge never used again;[32] for, as Johnston remarks,[33] 'Synge was writing for a group of players who knew how to pronounce his words, so he does not bother to substitute apostrophes for terminal *g*'s and *d*'s.'[34] This, however, is not the whole of the story, for in two later poems, 'Danny' (1907) and 'The Mergency Man' (1908),[35] the Anglo-Irish is not adorned with non-Standard spellings;[36] and here the knowledge of the players cannot be relevant. It is very probable that Synge had learnt from his dramatic experience that the spirit of the Anglo-Irish dialect can best be reproduced by the accurate rendering of its syntax and idiom.

Synge's literary ambitions were transformed by his meeting with Yeats in 1896.[37] 'Give up Paris,' Yeats said to him,[38] 'Go to the Aran Islands. Live there as if you were one of the people themselves; express a life that has never found expression.' Synge went to the Aran Islands, not once but many times. He had already studied Irish in Dublin and Paris, and in Aran he learned to speak the language well. Between 1903 and 1909 he produced the series of six plays on which his reputation mainly rests. All are written in a type of Anglo-Irish distinguished by a characteristic flavour and rhythm. Synge's use of Anglo-Irish has been attacked—and defended—on two grounds: that, taken as a whole, it is unrealistic and unrepresentative of peasant speech, even though it may be accurate in detail; and that, whether or not it conveys an effect of realism, it contains numerous features totally alien to the Anglo-Irish dialect. These two charges are independent of one another, and need to be considered separately. However, before this can be done there are two general questions which need to be discussed.

IV

In the first place, it is for most purposes a convenience to speak of 'the language of Synge' as if it were homogeneous; but in fact it is not. As Johnston points out,[39]

> The type of dialogue now familiar as Synge's did not spring into existence fully equipped from the first moment of its appearance, but it is something that the dramatist experimented with from play to play, until it reached its final flowering in *The Playboy*. Indeed, the earliest form in which we find it is perilously like some of the parodies of 'the Abbey play' that have appeared in skits from time to time.

This process of development can be studied and analysed in detail. As will appear below,[40] certain 'inaccuracies' in Synge's use of Anglo-Irish appear to be confined to the two earliest plays, *Riders to the Sea* and *The Shadow of the Glen*. More interesting and more significant, perhaps, is the analysis of certain features of syntax and vocabulary as they occur in all six plays. The following table, adapted from Professor Taniguchi's forthcoming *Studies on the Structure of the Dialogue in Synge's Plays,*[41] shows the average number of occurences per sentence of each of a number of selected syntactic features in each of the plays. The syntactic features in questions are the following:[42] (1) emphasis by means of introductory *it's,* etc.; (2) the use of 'progressive' tenses formed with present participle; (3) the form *do be,* etc.; (4) the construction *I am after doing,* etc.; (5) the subordinate clause introduced by *and* and lacking a finite verb; (6) the imperative formed with *let.* The total, of course, shows the average number of occurrences per sentence of all these features taken together.

	Riders to the Sea	The Shadow of the Glen	The Well of the Saints	The Tinker's Wedding	The Playboy	Deirdre of the Sorrows
(1)	0.20	0.58	0.30	0.34	0.22	0.16
(2)	0.84	1.60	1.48	1.18	1.70	0.44
(3)	0.00	0.04	0.20	0.06	0.00	0.00
(4)	0.10	0.06	0.04	0.06	0.04	0.00
(5)	0.22	0.18	0.08	0.10	0.22	0.04
(6)	0.02	0.12	0.06	0.20	0.02	0.06
Total	1.38	2.58	2.16	1.94	2.20	0.70

In the introduction to my 'Synge Glossary'[43] I have given figures for the occurrence of words and phrases which do not occur in more than one of Synge's plays. The following table shows the average occurrence of such 'unique' words in each ten pages of the *Collected Works:*

Riders to the Sea	The Shadow of the Glen	The Well of the Saints	The Tinker's Wedding	The Playboy	Deirdre of the Sorrows
1.7	4.8	5.4	5.2	17.0	5.5

These two tables show that both in syntax and in vocabulary there is something approaching a norm for the plays of Synge (about two syntactic features per sentence, and about five 'unique' words in ten pages). However, only two plays, *The Well of the Saints* and *The Tinker's Wedding,* follow the norm in both respects. *Riders to the Sea* falls a little below the norm in syntax and well below it in vocabulary; *The Shadow of the Glen* rises well above the norm in syntax, but follows it in vocabulary; *The Playboy* follows the norm in syntax but shows more than three times the norm in vocabulary; *Deirdre of the Sorrows* is well below the norm in syntax but follows it in vocabulary. Chronologically there is a progressive change of emphasis from syntax to vocabulary. *The Playboy* in particular relies for its effect very largely on its exotic vocabulary; in *Deirdre of the Sorrows* the relative emphasis as between syntax and vocabulary is much the same as in *The Playboy,* but its effects are considerably more subdued.

In the second place, it is necessary to realise that the dialogue of the plays is not always presented to us in the form of the words supposedly used by the personages concerned. Johnston remarks[44] that 'it is a common misconception to suppose that these people are not supposed to be speaking English at all, and that the plays are presenting us with a translation of what they are actually saying.' Whether or not this belief is really widespread, it is certainly not entirely a misconception. In only two of the six plays,[45] *The Shadow of the Glen* and *The Tinker's Wedding,* is it quite certain that the characters are English-speaking : the first is set in 'the last cottage at the head of a long glen in County Wicklow;'[46] the second is set only in 'a road-side near a village,'[47] but references in the text make it clear that the village is in Co. Wicklow.[48] In *Deirdre of the Sorrows* it is certain that the dialogue does not represent what was actually said, since the action takes place long before the first introduction of English into Ireland, and indeed before the English language had come into existence. *Riders to the Sea* is set on 'an island off the West of Ireland'[49]—presumably one of the Aran Islands, with which Synge was familiar;[50] and even today the common language of Aran is Irish. *The Well of the Saints* is set in 'some lonely mountainous district on the east of Ireland, one or more centuries ago;'[51] even one century before Synge's time, Irish would almost certainly have been spoken in any 'lonely mountainous district' in eastern Ireland. *The Playboy of the Western World* poses a special problem. 'The action takes place near a village, on a wild coast of Mayo;'[52] but Christy Mahon comes from 'a windy corner of high distant hills,'[53] and boasts of 'wide and windy acres of rich Munster land;'[54] we learn, in fact, that he killed his father in Kerry.[55] In Synge's time Irish was still spoken in many parts of both Mayo and Kerry,[56] so it is not certain that the characters in *The Playboy* would have spoken English; yet, if they had been Irish-speaking, Christy's Munster Irish would have been scarcely intelligible to the people of North Connaught, and there is no hint in the play of any such difficulty. Even if the characters were English-speaking it is perhaps curious that no comment is made on Christy's accent, since the Kerry accent is distinctive and very different from that of Mayo; Michael Flaherty should hardly have needed to ask Christy where it was that he 'did the deed.'[57]

V

The complaint has often been made that all Synge's characters speak alike. Not only is there no discrimination between characters in the same play, but the same form of speech is used irrespective of whether the play is set in Wicklow or in Mayo, on the Aran Islands or in bronze-age Ulster. Thus, Bourgeois complains[58] that 'Synge makes Irish peasants who are not Irish-speaking—such as the Wicklow peasants, whose dialect is more akin to Elizabethan English—speak in the Gaelic fashion like the Western peasants. All his characters, despite geographical differences, talk alike.' Similarly Colum remarks[59] that 'all the characters speak to the same rhythm and their speech is made up of words and phrases from different parts of the country with Gaelic idioms, authorized and unauthorized.'[60] These judgments rest on a number of misconceptions. First, it is not strictly true that the language of the plays is wholly uniform; there is a chronological progression from the early to the later plays.[61] Secondly, if the dialogue of the plays is to be considered as a translation from the Irish—and we have seen that in three of the plays (and possibly in a fourth) it must be so considered[62]—the supposed homogeneity of the language is less open to objection; what needs to be examined is its suitability as a medium for the translation of Irish. Thirdly, the Anglo-Irish dialect is in fact much more uniform throughout the country than these critics are willing to allow.[63]

More serious is the charge that Synge's language is unrealistic, in so far as it is unlike the speech of any kind of Irishman. Some judgments of this kind are purely subjective : thus, Lynd says that Synge's style is 'gauded and overwrought, with bagfuls of wild phrases,' and Ervine calls it 'contrived stuff, entirely unrepresentative of peasant speech.'[64] However, objective evidence is to be found in the well-known fact that the actors of the Abbey Theatre found Synge's dialogue peculiarly difficult to learn and perform : if it had been truly representative of Irish speech they, as Irishmen, should have found no difficulty in it. Yeats himself has testified to this fact:

> He made word and phrase dance to a very strange rhythm, which will always, till his plays have created their own tradition, be difficult to actors who have not learned it from his own lips . . . The players were puzzled by the rhythm . . . Perhaps no Irish countryman had ever that exact rhythm in his voice.

Máire Nic Shiubhlaigh is even more explicit:[66]

> At first I found Synge's lines almost impossible to learn and deliver . . . It was neither verse not prose. The speeches had a musical lilt, absolutely different to anything I had heard before. Every passage brought some new difficulty and we would all stumble through the speeches until the tempo in which they were written was finally discovered.

Ironically enough, one of the most devastating indictments of Synge's realism is Quin's attempt to defend it:[67]

> It was of course this quality [of great originality and vividness] that earlier attracted J. M. Synge, and which, in the highly concentrated form in which he used it in *The Playboy of the Western World,* so astonished his hearers that he found it necessary to devote a whole preface to affirming its very existence in the mouths of Irish speakers of English. No one who reads Dr. Henry's book need have any further doubt about Synge's highly-coloured language.

But the book referred to, a scholarly study of an Anglo-Irish dialect,[68] chooses its examples precisely because they are striking, unusual, and therefore worth analysis; to compare Synge's plays to an anthology of out-of-the-way idioms does little to defend their realism.

VI

It is important to remember that Synge never claimed that his language was realistic. In his Preface to *The Playboy*[69] he claimed no more than that nearly every word and phrase he used was genuine Anglo-Irish:

> In writing *The Playboy of the Western World,* as in my other plays, I have used one or two words only, that I have not heard among the country people of Ireland, or spoken in my own nursery before I could read the newspapers. A certain number of the phrases I employ I have heard also from herds and fishermen along the coast from Kerry to Mayo, or from beggar-women and ballad-singers nearer Dublin.[70]

Synge's claim, if it could be justified, would not exempt him from the charge of lack of realism, as Strong has vividly pointed out:[71]

> The language of Synge's plays is *not* the language of the peasants, insomuch that no peasant talks consistently as Synge's characters talk; it *is* the language of the peasants, in that it contains no word or phrase a peasant did not actually use.[72]

It remains to be seen, however, whether Synge's claim that his language is accurate in detail, even if it is unrealistic in general effect, can in fact be justified.

Some of the accusations of inaccuracy that have been made are ill-founded. Bourgeois, for instance, says[73] that 'such voluminous, mouth-filling "jaw-breakers" as "potentate," "retribution," are not to be heard on the lips of the real Irish countryfolk, however great their well-known love of the word for the word's sake may be.' In fact such unnecessary Latinisms are a commonplace in all types of rural Anglo-Irish, and Frank O'Connor has explained why this should be so :[74]

> Because they did not wish to be educated according to what Protestants thought their station in life, the people had to turn for education to the hedge-schools — those nurseries of the secret societies—and the very few Church schools, in both of which Latin was taught.
>
> But there was still a linguistic difficulty. If the people were to survive they had to speak English, and any little knowledge they had was based upon Latin. Accordingly they tended to avoid Anglo-Saxon words, the connotations of which they were not familiar with; were chary of Norman-French words, and as often as possible opted for Latin.

There is equally little foundation for Bourgeois' objection[75] that

'Synge puts in the mouth of his Western peasants (Pegeen in the present instance) such Elizabethan, hence Eastern, archaisms as "bedizened," "inveigle," "pandied;" Christy is called with Shakespearean aptness the "looney" of Mahon's; and Deirdre speaks of having been "spancelled" seven years with Naisi.' Nevertheless, it is a fact that Synge's Anglo-Irish is inaccurate in a number of respects. Since he makes no attempt to indicate pronunciation, it is only in the realms of vocabulary and of syntax that he is open to attack. Even here some caution is necessary. It is always impossible to prove a negative, and the statement that a given word or idiom is 'never' used in Anglo-Irish can be refuted by the demonstration that it was used by a single speaker on a single occasion. If, however, a word or idiom is so exceedingly rare that it strikes even the Irish ear as wholly unfamiliar and unnatural, then for all practical purposes it is 'never' used in Anglo-Irish, and would be out of place in any realistic representation of the dialect.

A substantial number of the words and phrases used by Synge appear to be unique, or at least unique in the meaning required by the context. Some of them appear also in the note-books, and it is difficult not to suspect that in some cases Synge may have misinterpreted the context and therefore misunderstood the meaning[76]. Among the words which appear not to occur outside the works of Synge are *bias* (CW iv 49) meaning uncertain, *dreepiness* (CW iii 109) 'appearance of having a cold in the head,' *hoop* (CW iv 225) 'become crooked,' *louty* (CW iv 153) 'clumsy' *pitchpike* (CW iv 75) 'pitchfork', *scruff* (CW iv 59) 'back (of a hill)', *sloppy* (CW iv 243) 'tear-stained', and *swiggle* (CW iv 109), a portmanteau word combining *swing* and *wriggle.* The word *streeleen* (CW iv 81) is used in the sense 'flow of discourse;' it must be a transliteration of Irish *s(t)raoillín,* but this means 'a garter, a tape, a swathe or band; a string of beads, *etc.,* a connected series, a queue of persons, *etc.,* a train; an untidy or dishevelled person.'[77] The word *honey* is used as a form of address in many English dialects, but it is rare in Ireland, and the combination *Mister honey,* which recurs again and again in *The Playboy,* is incredible. Anglo-Irish *let* is regularly used in the sense 'utter,' as in *let a cry* (CW iii 35), *let a shout* (CW iii 167), *let a grunt or groan* (CW iv 73), *let a roar* (CW iv 123), *let a gasp* (CW iv 243); but its use in *let a cough or a sneeze* (CW iv

85) strains the credulity, and *let a wink* (CW iv 89) is quite unparalleled, and in fact unbelievable. The phrase *on the ridge of the world* (CW iii 97 iv 231), translating Irish *ar dhruim an domhain* 'in existence' is improbable and unconvincing.

Some of Synge's inaccuracies in the realm of syntax have been pointed out by Frank O'Connor.[78] The normal English perfect tense is not used in Anglo-Irish,[79] yet it occurs twice in the following short passage from *Riders to the Sea* (CW iii 25):

> It isn't that I haven't prayed for you, Bartley, to the Almighty God. It isn't that I haven't said prayers in the dark night till you wouldn't know what I'd be saying . . .

The normal Anglo-Irish idiom would be *It isn't that I didn't pray* and *It isn't that I didn't say prayers.* Also in *Riders to the Sea* (CW iii 7) Synge uses the phrase *Shall I open it now,?* though in Anglo-Irish the Standard *shall I?* is invariably replaced by *will I?*[80] O'Connor also calls attention to Synge's fondness for the omission of the relative pronoun, even when it is the subject of the relative clause (as in the phrase *of all are living or have been),* 'a construction,' he says 'that in my experience does not occur at all.' O'Connor is certainly wrong in his suggestion that the construction does not occur at all: Taniguchi [81] cites instances from the works of a number of Irish writers.[82] Nevertheless, the frequency with which Synge omits the relative pronoun is so high that the construction appears to have become an obsession with him; Taniguchi points out[83] that 'Synge sparingly uses the relative pronouns, and in "Deirdre of the Sorrows," for instance, no relatives are used except in a few cases.' On the other hand van Hamel[84] notes that Synge never uses a construction common enough in spoken Anglo-Irish, and much favoured by Yeats, the use of the infinitive to represent the Irish verbal noun in a subordinate clause, as in *It is a pity he not to awaken at this time.*

There are other syntactical inaccuracies in the work of Synge which seem never to have been noticed before. In standard English an indirect question not introduced by some interrogative word is introduced by *if* (or more rarely by *whether*), and the word order is that of a statement, as in *I wonder if he will come.* In Anglo-Irish this use of *if* is unknown, and the indirect question has exactly the same form as a direct question, as in *I wonder will he come.* In his first two plays Synge sometimes uses *if* as in standard English :

We're to find out *if* it's Michael's they are.[85]
Isn't it a queer hard thing to say *if* it's his they are surely.[86]
Lay your hand on him now and tell me *if* it's cold he is.[87]

Yet elsewhere in the same two plays Synge sometimes uses the regular Anglo-Irish formula :

Did you ask him would he stop going this day with the horses to the Galway fair?[88]
. . . . she'll be going down to see would he be floating from the east.[89]

In standard English the contraction *'s* may stand either for *is* or for *has,* and *'d* for *would* or for *had.* In Anglo-Irish, however, the verb 'to have' is never contracted, so that *'s* and *'d* are unambiguously *is* and *would* respectively. From his earliest to his latest works Synge occasionally uses *'s* and *'d* for *has* and *had* :[90]

The young priest says he*'s* known the like of it. 'If it's Michael's they are,' says he, 'you can tell herself he*'s* got a clean burial by the grace of God.[91] *(Riders to the Sea.)*
She*'s* no shame the time she*'s* a drop taken.[92] *(The Tinker's Wedding)*
. . . its the like He's done, many*'s* the day, with big and famous sinners.[93] *(Translation.)*
I*'d* no way be looking down into your heart.[94] *(Translations.)*

It would be easy but unrewarding to multiply instances of inaccuracies in Synge's use of the Anglo-Irish dialect. Enough has been said to show that he was using a language of which he was not a native speaker, and with which he was not fully familiar; that, by dint of effort, he succeeded in improving his command of it, though he never came to write it perfectly. It is more interesting to investigate why he should have taken such pains to acquire this difficult language : it was certainly not, as we have seen, in an attempt at realism, an attempt to commit to writing an exact representation of the speech of the Irish peasant.

VII

The problem of Synge's intentions cannot be adequately discussed without a consideration of the nature of the Anglo-Irish dialect which he took as the basis for the language of his plays. Among the different varieties of English this is perhaps the most flexible and the most expressive. To the richness of the English language in one of its greatest periods it has added the subtlety of Irish syntax, and in some respects it has extended Irish idiom beyond the limits imposed on it in the Irish language. Above all, Anglo-Irish is the variety of English which loses least when it is transferred from the mouth of the speaker to the print on the page. Spoken standard English relies very extensively on stress and intonation for emphasis and the expression of nuances; hence it loses very much when it is reduced to written form. In English drama the actor has an important role to play in supplying the appropriate stress and intonation, so that the reader of an English play is inevitably at a disadvantage. In Anglo-Irish emphasis and nuance are integrated into the structure of the sentence,[95] and are not affected by reduction to writing : the dialogue of Anglo-Irish drama and fiction 'reads' much better than dialogue in standard English.

Emphasis in English is achieved mainly by stress; in Anglo-Irish, as in Irish, it is achieved primarily by word-order. The most important element in the sentence is placed at the beginning, preceded only by an introductory *it's, it was,* etc.; the remainder of the sentence is cast in the form of a relative clause, though the relative pronoun is often omitted.[96] A simple example can be found in the following sentence from Synge's *Translations* :[97]

> It's of the like of that that we old hags do be thinking.

Here the structure of the sentence places on *of the like of that* an emphasis which in English could be obtained only by stress, a stress which cannot be recorded in the written form.

Some of the nuances of meaning in the Anglo-Irish verb can scarcely be achieved in English even by the use of stress and intonation. The Irish verb 'to be' has two forms of the present tense, *tá* and *bíonn,* of which the second is habitual or consuetudinal—'always is, is regularly.' The consuetudinal form is rendered in Anglo-Irish by *does be;* in the sentence cited above *do be thinking* means 'are always thinking.' In Anglo-Irish the consuetudinal form is extended to verbs other than the verb 'to be;' *does have, does go,* etc.[98] The normal English perfect *he has written (the letter)* is not used in Anglo-Irish: instead, there are four different constructions which may be used, each with a different nuance of meaning. In some contexts, particularly with the verb 'to be,' the present tense is often used instead of the perfect: *she's dead these ten years,* instead of the English *she has been dead for ten years.* In many contexts the simple past is used instead of the perfect.[99] Of the other two constructions, *he's after writing the letter* implies that he has just recently written it; *he has the letter written* emphasizes the completion of the act. Needless to say, none of these nuances is affected by the reduction of speech to writing. There are also many other alternative modes of expression in Anglo-Irish which need not be detailed here.

The effect of this great flexibility of idiom is that the use of Anglo-Irish permits a greater variety of rhythm than is possible in standard English. As Price says,[100]

> The effect of these and other related constructions, as used by Synge, is to produce a sequence of assorted cadences unified in a full sure rhythm which gives unobtrusively a basic pattern, as in some kinds of Jacobean blank verse, yet provides for ejaculations of single syllables or phrases and for numerous variations wherever appropriate.

VIII

This, then, is the dialect of which Synge made use. His dialogue is not, and was not intended to be, an accurate repre-sensation of peasant speech: it is rather a 'distillation' or 'selection' from that speech. According to Saul[101] 'it is a language *distilled* out of everyday west-coast Anglo-Irish;' according to Johnston,[102] 'Synge employs it, after having *distilled* it, as it were, from the verbiage of a community in which he was living.' According to Price[103] 'Synge made a *selection* from the idiom of the peasants and created language authentic and credible[104] and more exact, compact and beautiful than the actual utterance of anyone;' according to Henn[105] 'this "peasant speech" is a *selection,* refraction, compression of the language that Synge had known from boyhood, among the people of the Dublin, Wicklow and Galway countrysides.' The nature of this distillation and selection was acutely observed by Bourgeois:[106] 'even when he is not actually translating Gaelic, he seems to exaggerate the coefficient of Hibernicism.' Huscher, too, refers[107] to his 'gesteigerte Gälicismus.' In other words, when Synge was distilling his brew from the language of the peasants, he concentrated those elements which distinguish Anglo-Irish from standard English, and which render it more flexible, more expressive, and more potent in its rhythm.

Synge, like many other writers before him and after him, was creating a special language to suit his special artistic purpose: the change and development in his usage illustrated above[108] shows his gradual groping towards success. What his purpose was can only be conjectured, since he left no statement of his plan. It is probably very significant, however, that late in his life Synge turned his talents towards translation from the verse of Villon, Petrarch, and other French, Italian and German poets. The translation of poetry presents nearly insuperable problems: translation into verse means that the metrical form imposes additions, omissions, and various other inaccuracies; translation into prose involves the loss of the heightened tone characteristic of poetry. It is instructive to compare Synge's two translations of Colin Muset's 'Complaint to his Patron,' one into verse and the other into prose.[109] The verse translation is inaccurate, and it is not even effective as verse; the prose translation is not only more accurate, it better retains the tone of the original. Anglo-Irish prose is indeed capable of profound poetic effects: the two translations from the work of Villon, free though they are, are among the best ever made.[110] These translations surely show that the language Synge had created in his dramas was intended to achieve the heightened tone of poetry without the artificiality of versification.

Such a conclusion is, of course, by no means new. Bourgeois felicitously remarks[111] that 'Synge wrote in a prose that sets him high among the poets.' All those critics who emphasize the significance in Synge's development of Hyde's *Love Songs of Connacht* at the expense of *Beside the Fire* have implicitly realized that Hyde's prose translation of Irish poetry was a major inspiration to him. Boyd remarks[112] that the language of the love-scenes between Christy and Pegeen Mike is 'poetry untrammelled by the mechanism of verse;' 'the Gaelic-English idiom . . . has now become for the author a perfect instrument of poetic speech;' 'to every breath of passion there is a corresponding heightening of the key in which the language is pitched.' Nevertheless, the full potentialities of Synge's language for poetic expression have not been adequately investigated; in particular, the tendency for the rhythm of his dialogue to pass inconspicuously from that of prose to that of poetry has not attracted sufficient attention.

The rhythm of Synge's dialogue has not yet been systematically studied,[113] but a number of writers have commented on various aspects of it. In particular, it has often been noticed that Synge makes use of various characteristic cadences, predominately at the end of speeches, but also at the end of sentences within a speech and even of mere clauses. Huscher,[114] Henry,[115] and O'Connor[116] have all, apparently independently, noted the frequency of the cadence x x x́ x x́, as in *from this mortal day;* Henry[117] lists more than 60 instances of this cadence in *The Playboy* alone, and his list is not exhaustive. The cadence x x x́ x x x́ is also common; Henry[118] lists eight instances in *The Playboy.* More significant, perhaps, is the fact adverted to by Bourgeois,[119] that Synge's prose contains a considerable number of blank-verse lines. It is indeed true that many of the speeches in the plays end either with blank-verse lines or with alexandrines. The following examples, all from *The Playboy*,[120] illustrate first the blank-verse lines and then the alexandrines:

I'll maybe tell them and I'll maybe not. (61)
the way I wasn't fearing you at all. (81)
That God in glory may be thanked for that! (91)
I'm very thankful to you all today. (99)
I'll bet my dowry that he'll lick the world. (101)
if I did wed him and did save you so. (117)
I seen him raving on the sands today. (131)
there's wonders hidden in the heart of man. (135)
with lamentation in the dead of night. (137)
the champion playboy of the western world. (139)
Run to the right, and not a one will see. (145)
Is it the truth the dispensation's come? (153)
to have you stifled on the gallows tree. (165)

as naked as an ash-tree in the moon of May. (83)
you'll wed the widow Casey in a score of days. (101)
and you can give your answer when you have them tried. (115)
I'll make myself contented to be lodging here. (117)

A hideous, fearful villain, and the spit of you. (123)
I'm thinking I'll go walking for to view the race. (139)
or coining funny nicknames for the stars of night. (149)
It's well enough he's lying for the likes of him. (153)
I felt them making whistles of my ribs within. (163)
and I a proven hero in the end of all. (167)
I've lost the only playboy of the western world. (173)

These examples represent only a selection from the total; and the number could be enormously increased by the inclusion of instances which are not coterminous with clauses. It is noteworthy that nearly all the above examples end with the cadence already referred to above, x x x́ x x́; in other words, a favourite cadence is a blank-verse line in which the third stress is subdued, or an alexandrine in which the fourth stress is subdued.

IX

Any summing up must necessarily be hypothetical, and what follows claims to be no more than plausible conjecture, based on the facts collected in this paper. Synge spent his early manhood in the Paris of the 1890s, the home of self-conscious literary experiment. At this time he had shown no interest in the dialect of his native country, apart from his single stage-Irish poem, 'Ballad of a Pauper.'[121] There is no way of telling whether he first read Hyde's *Beside the Fire* and *Love Songs of Connacht* before or after he met Yeats in 1896, but whatever the date the effect of Hyde's work on him was profound : here was a language, deliberately used as a medium of literary expression,[122] closely related to a dialect familiar to him from the days of his childhood. Acquainted as he was with the literary thought of the Europe of his time, Synge could hardly fail to be aware that the potentialities of the Anglo-Irish dialect had not been exhausted by Hyde. It may be that it was his awareness of these potentialities that led him so readily to accept Yeats's advice that he should go to the Aran Island and live there like one of the people :[123] if he did not read Hyde until later, then his knowledge of the speech of the West would have given him a greater insight into Hyde's achievement.

At all events, he set himself to learn the Anglo-Irish dialect. It may be that, as he himself claimed,[124] he had spoken it in the nursery; men grow out of nursery language, and his education at Trinity College and his residence abroad would both have contributed towards the elimination of Hibernicisms from his speech. The evidence shows [125] that he could not use it accurately: some of the mistakes discernible in his earlier plays he was subsequently able to eliminate; others persisted right through into his latest works. Evidence of a different kind[126] shows that, while he was learning the Anglo-Irish dialect, he was also experimenting with its use as a literary medium. In his earliest plays he was experimenting mainly with syntax and idiom; later he turned his attention to the exploitation of the dialect's rich vocabulary. In his last play, *Deirdre of the Sorrows,* he abandoned the exuberance of *The Playboy* in favour of more sombre, muted effects. At the same time he was experimenting with the varieties of rhythm which are facilitated by the versatility of Anglo-Irish.[127]

Synge's first attempts at the dramatic form were in verse, and in the early part of 1902 his time seems to have been fully occupied with poetic drama.[128] The work of the Elizabethan and Jacobean dramatists had earned for poetic drama a secure place in English literature, but it had long fallen into desuetude. Attempts to revive the form, even by such great poets as Browning and Tennyson, had met with little success. However, around the turn of the century the time was ripe for a revival, and even such inferior efforts as those of Stephen Phillips[129] achieved considerable though temporary popularity. It is not surprising that Synge should have made his first dramatic experiments in verse; it is more surprising, perhaps, that he should have abandoned the attempt so soon. It was part of Synge's greatness that he realized, as Stephen Phillips did not, that the future of poetic drama did not lie within the limits of the traditional blank-verse form—that a new poetic medium needed to be forged, one which would combine the vigour and intensity of poetry with the flexibility and naturalism of prose. He found the makings of such a medium in the Anglo-Irish dialect, and he exploited them to the full.

Synge's fateful encounter with Yeats led to results which Yeats did not expect, and which he may never have realized in full. Certainly Synge did not 'express a life that has never found expression;' that he left to the folk-dramatists among his contemporaries and successors. Rather, he invented a medium of expression capable of the highest flights of comedy and tragedy, with which he brought to life upon the stage situations no more realistic than the language he used. It is, in a sense, accidental that Synge's plays are set in Ireland: the Irish setting has, of course, some congruity with the Anglo-Irish basis of the language in which they are written; the natural Irish tendency towards rhetorical forms of expression justifies an extravagance of language which would hardly be acceptable in an English context;[130] and the remoteness of the settings from civilization as we know it lends plausibility to actions which in themselves make no pretence to realism. The 'Playboy riots' were no more and no less sensible than the protests from the Japanese embassy which followed the first production of *The Mikado* in 1885: Synge set his play in Mayo for exactly the same reasons that Gilbert and Sullivan set their opera in Japan.

It is no more reasonable to censure the homogeneity of Synge's language than it would be to complain because the characters in *Julius Cæsar, Macbeth, Hamlet* and *Romeo and Juliet* all speak in the same kind of blank verse; no more reasonable to worry whether Christy Mahon and Pegeen Mike spoke in Irish or in English than to worry whether the nobles in *King John* spoke in English or in Norman French. The language of Synge ought to be subject to the same mode of criticism as Shakespeare's verse: is it or is it not a suitable medium for poetic drama? The consensus of critical opinion is that it is. The tragedy of Synge is that, because his purpose was misunderstood, he has had no imitators. Boyd's comment[131] is as true now as it was fifty years ago:

> The language of his plays, the most tangible of his debts to the peasantry, has awakened no important echoes in the work of those who came after him. They use the speech of the people, but it is realistic speech, not the re-created dialect which Synge elaborated.

Perhaps Synge's talent was unique; but perhaps some Irish dramatist or poet may yet come who will build upon the foundations he laid so well a structure of poetic prose finer than anything that has yet been seen.

NOTES

1 All quotations from the writings of Synge are taken from *J. M. Synge: Collected Works,* General Editor Robin Skelton (Oxford, 1962-8). Reference to the *Collected Works* is made by the abbreviation CW followed by the volume-number in roman numerals and the page-number in arabic numerals. The following abbreviations are used in the notes:
BOURGEOIS: Maurice Bourgeois, *John Millington Synge and the Irish Theatre* (1913)
BOYD: Ernest Boyd, *Ireland's Literary Renaissance* (Dublin, 1968)
HUSCHER: Herbert Huscher, 'Das Anglo-Irische und seine Bedeutung als sprachkünstlerisches Ausdrucksmittel', *Englische Kultur in sprachwissenschaftlicher Deutung, Max Deutschbein zum 60. Geburtstage* (Leipzig, 1936), pp. 40-59.
JOHNSTON: Denis Johnston *John Millington Synge* (1965)
O'CONNOR: Frank O'Connor, *The Backward Look: A Survey of Irish Literature* (1967)
PRICE: Alan Price, *Synge and Anglo-Irish Drama* (1961)
TANIGUCHI: Jiro Taniguchi, *A Grammatical Analysis of Artistic Representation of Irish English* (Tokyo, 1955)

2 'The English Irish and the very Cittizens (excepting those of Dublin where the lord Deputy resides) though they could speake English as well as wee, yet Commenly speake Irish among themselues, and were hardly induced by our familiar Conversation to speake English with vs.' Fynes Moryson in *Shakespeare's Europe,* ed. Charles Hughes (1903), p. 213.

3 The most convenient collection of material is to be found in William Barnes' edition of Jacob Poole's *Glossary . . . of the Old Dialect . . . of Forth and Bargy,* 1867.

4 The Plantation of Ulster came earlier; since the majority of the planters were Scottish, the Ulster dialect is basically different from that of the other three provinces, and is not further considered in these pages.

5 For a lucid account of the spread of English see Maureen Wall, 'The Decline of the Irish Language', *A View of the Irish Language,* ed. Brian O Cuív (Dublin, 1969) pp. 81-90, and Seán de Fréine, *The Great Silence* (Dublin, 1965), pp. 135-49.

6 The attitude of the gentry towards the peasants and their language is well illustrated by Swift's comments in his 'On Barbarous Denominations in Ireland' [*Prose Works of Jonathan Swift,* ed. Herbert Davis, IV (1957) 281]: 'What we call the Irish brogue is no sooner discovered, than it makes the deliverer in the last degree ridiculous and despised; and, from such a mouth, an Englishman expects nothing but bulls, blunders, and follies. . . . I have heard many gentlemen among us talk much of the great convenience to those who live in the country, that they should speak Irish. It may possibly be so; but I think they should be such who never intend to visit England, upon pain of being ridiculous; for I do not

remember to have heard of any one man that spoke Irish, who had not the accent upon his tongue easily discernible to any English ear.'

7 P. J. Dowling, *The Hedge-Schools of Ireland* (Cork, 1968).

8 Variations in vocabulary are almost entirely limited to Irish loan-words in Anglo-Irish, and reflect limited distributions in Irish.

9 Irish characters appeared in English plays from about 1600, but it is impossible to be certain that their speech is authentic. See J. O. Bartley, *Teague, Shenkin and Sawney* (Cork, 1954).

10 *Prose Works of Jonathan Swift,* ed. Herbert Davis, IV (1957) 277-9. Unfortunately the print does not reproduce the manuscripts accurately. The two pieces are not independent of each other, but represent different arrangements of the same material.

11 The importance of *Beside the Fire* and its preface is pointed out only by BOYD pp. 70-74 and O'CONNOR p. 169.

12 Pp. xlvii-xliv.

13 P. xlvii.

14 Pp. xlviii-xliv.

15 Hyde's alterations of the story are not merely linguistic. The following passage occurs in the translation on pp. 73-5 (the italics are mine). 'He sat down on a stool that was beside the wall, and began falling asleep, when he saw a big weasel coming to the fire with *something yellow in its mouth,* which it dropped on the hearth-stone, and then it went away. She soon came back again with *the same thing* in her mouth, *and he saw that it was a guinea she had.* She dropped it on the hearth-stone, and went away again.' A more literal translation of the Irish version on pp. 72-4 would run as follows. 'He sat down on a stool beside the wall, and it was not long before he began falling asleep, when he saw a big weasel coming to the fire, and she dropped *a guinea* on the hearth-stone, and went away. It was not long before she came back with *another guinea,* and dropped it on the hearth-stone, and went away.' Here Hyde has increased the dramatic quality of the narrative.

16 In Irish, *Bhí dúil aige le dul go h-aonach Cháthair-na-mart le storc asail do dhíol.* Cf. p. 77, 'He came out and set a dog he had after the weasel'; in Irish, *Tháinig sé amach agus chuir sé madadh a bhí aige andhiaigh na h-easóige.* (Here, and in other quotations, Hyde's Irish type is replaced by italic type, but his rather eccentric orthography is retained.)

17 P. 73. In Irish, *Nuair chuaidh sé chum an tíghe, bhí an doras fosgailte, agus asteach leis.*

18 P. 75. In Irish, *Acht faoi dheireadh nuair d'imthigh sí d'éirigh Páidín.* Cf. p. 79, 'I shall be dead a month from this day, and when you get me dead put a coal under this little hut and burn it'; in Irish, *Béidh mise marbh mí ó'n lá so, agus nuair gheobhas tu marbh mé cuir splanc faoi an mbothán agus dóigh é.*

19 P. 75. In Irish, . . . *ann áit é bheith tígheacht a bhaile leis an*

airgiod a fuair sé air a shean-asal, mar shaoil sé air maidin go mbeidheadh sé ag deanamh.

20 P. 79. In Irish, *acht ná bíodh aon fhaitchios ort.* Cf. p. 83, 'Don't be afraid of me at all'; in Irish, *Ná bíodh aon fhaitchíos ort rómham-sa.*

21 P. 77.

22 In the light of the discussion of the rhythm of Synge's language on pp. 52-3 it is perhaps worth noting that not only does this translation from a blank-verse line, but the more literal translation given below also does so.

23 In Irish, *ameasg cnoc agus gleann an domhain.*

24 As Mícheál O hAodha points out in his Introduction to the 1969 reprint of *Love Songs of Connacht,* some of the songs were first published in American periodicals. One appeared in *The Boston Pilot* as early as September 1889.

25 P. 5.

26 BOYD, p. 79.

27 See BOURGEOIS, p. 227 footnote. Some of Bourgeois' comparisons have been repeated without acknowledgement by Mícheál O hAodha in his Introduction to the 1969 reprint of *Love Songs of Connacht,* pp. vii-viii.

28 P. 25.

29 P. 109.

30 P. 120.

31 CW I 8-9.

32 Except in the case of one word. As Corkery points out [*Synge and Anglo-Irish Literature* (1966) p. 100], 'there was one word . . . which Synge often wrote phonetically—"divil".' It is possible that Synge was here influenced by a desire to make it clear that, for the Irish peasant, the use of *divil* is not profanity.

33 JOHNSTON, p. 9.

34 A similar comment appears in HUSCHER, p. 51: 'Soweit es sich um das Drama handelt, lag die Vernachlässigung der Aussprachewiedergabe gewiss auch daran, dass diese Schauspieler selbst Iren waren und keiner besonderen Andeutung heimischer Sprechweise bedurften.'

35 CW I 56-7,8.

36 In 'Danny' the spelling *dyin'* is used for the sake of the rhyme with *nine.* In 'The Mergency Man', though there are no eccentric spellings, some Anglo-Irish punctuations are assured by the rhymes: *Coomasaharn* rhymes with *star in, net* with *bit.*

37 D. H. Greene and E. M. Stephens, *J. M. Synge 1871-1909* (New York, 1959), p. 61.

38 'Mr Synge and his Plays' [Preface to the first edition of *The Well of the Saints*], CW III 63.

39 JOHNSTON, pp. 11-12.

40 Pp. 47-8.

41 I am much indebted to Professor Taniguchi for allowing me to make use of his work.

42 Some of these syntactic features are discussed more fully on pp. 49-50.

43 *Sunshine and the Moon's Delight: J. M. Synge 1871-1971. ed. S.* B. Bushrui (Beirut, 1971), pp. 299-318.

44 JOHNSTON p. 9.

45 In Synge's unfinished play *When the Moon has Set* it is also certain that the characters are English-speaking.

46 CW III 31.

47 CW IV 5.

48 See, for instance, the references to Tibradden (south Co. Dublin) and Rathvanna (CW IV 9); to Wicklow, Wexford and Dublin (CW IV 35); and to 'Wicklow, Wexford, and the County Meath' (CW IV 11, etc.)

49 CW III 3.

50 The frequent references to Connemara (CW III 7 etc.), some ten miles north of the Aran Islands, and to Galway fair (CW III 5), make this identification almost certain. In the original production considerable pains were taken to reproduce the costume of the Aran Islands: see CW III Introduction xviii-xix.

51 CW III 69.

52 CW IV 55.

53 CW IV 75.

54 CW IV 79.

55 CW IV 171.

56 Convenient maps of the survival of Irish in 1851 and 1891 are to be found in Brian O Cúiv, *Irish Dialects and Irish-speaking Districts* (Dublin, 1967), and in *A View of the Irish Language,* ed. Brian O Cuív (Dublin, 1969). As late as 1891 Irish was still spoken by more than half the population over large parts of Mayo and Kerry.

57 Christy shows an unexpected familiarity with the geography of north-west Mayo when he speaks of 'spearing salmons in the Owen or the Carrowmore' (CW IV 149); the Owenmore River runs westward through Bangor Erris and flows into the sea near Gweesalia; Lough Carrowmore lies a few miles north west of Bangor Erris.

58 BOURGEOIS pp. 226-7. Bourgeois' remark (p. 226 footnote) that 'geographically speaking, *Deirdre of the Sorrows* ought to be written in Ulster dialect' is extraordinarily inept.

59 Cited in PRICE p. 44.

60 Douglas Hyde wrote in a letter to Huscher that the language of Synge represented a type of English, almost obsolete. which had once existed in newly anglicized districts of the West. HUSCHER p. 52: 'Douglas Hyde bemerkt dass es sich dabei um eine wirkliche seit Jahrzehnten fast geschwundete Sprechweise damals neuanglisierte Gebiete des Westens handle.'

61 See pp. 41-2.

62 See p. 42
63 See p. 36.
64 Cited in PRICE p. 42.
65 'Mr Synge and his Plays' [Preface to the first edition of *The Well of the Saints*], CW III 64.
66 Máire Nic Shiubhlaigh and Edward Kenny, *The Splendid Years* (Dublin, 1955), pp. 42-3.
67 E. G. Quin, 'Irish and English', *Hermathena* xciii (1959) 26-37. The quotation is on p. 36.
68 P. L. Henry, *An Anglo-Irish Dialect of North Roscommon* (Dublin, 1957).
69 CW IV 53.
70 Cf. also Yeats, op.cit. p. 68: 'For though the people of the play [*The Well of the Saints*] use no phrase they could not use in daily life, we know that we are seeking to express what no eye has ever seen.'
71 L. A. G. Strong, *John Millington Synge* (1941) pp. 81-2.
72 Cf. also JOHNSTON 33: 'It is probably true that he had heard all the words he uses, though probably not in the same order. Synge undoubtedly glorifies the language.'
73 BOURGEOIS, p. 228.
74 O'CONNOR, p. 139
75 BOURGEOIS, 226 footnote.
76 Synge could not always be trusted to explain his own use of words accurately. In a letter to Meyerfeld he explains *griseldy* (CW III 131) as 'grisly'; yet both the context and the comparison of the formation with *spavindy* (CW IV 127) 'spavined' and *wizendy* (CW III 99) 'wizened' show that the meaning is 'grizzled'.
77 P.S. Dineen, *Irish-English Dictionary* (Dublin, 1927) s.v.
78 O'CONNOR, p. 188. It must be emphasized that most of the syntactic inaccuracies discussed occur only or mainly in Synge's earliest plays, *Riders to the Sea* and *The Shadow of the Glen.*
79 For the various means by which this can be expressed in Anglo-Irish see p. 50.
80 Cf. TANIGUCHI ¶43.2-A. Elsewhere in this play Synge follows the regular usage: *What way will I live?* (CW III 11), *Will I be in it as soon as himself?* (CW III 13).
81 TANIGUCHI ¶25.3.
82 After introductory *It's* the ommission of the relative is very common; see TANIGUCHI ¶62.4-A-1. The origin of the usage is far from clear. The omission of the subject relative is common in the northern dialects of Middle English. On the other hand, an Irish origin for the usage is by no means impossible. In the present and future tenses there is in some dialects a special relative form, and in any case the initial consonant of the verb is aspirated by the relative particle *a*; but two of the commonest verbs, *tá* 'is' and *deir* 'says', escape this aspiration for historical reasons, and neither of them has a special relative form in the present tense. It is perhaps

significant that, as Taniguchi points out [loc. cit.], the omission of the relative is most common with the verbs 'to be' and 'to have' (the later being expressed in Irish by an idiom involving the verb 'to be'). In the past tense the initial consonant of the verb is aspirated in any case, and the particle *do* which precedes it is regularly weakened to *a*, so that the relative form is not distinctive.

83 Loc. cit.

84 A. G. van Hamel, 'On Anglo-Irish Syntax', *Englische Studien* xlv (1912) 272-92. The comment in question is on p. 279.

85 CW iii 5.

86 CW iii 15.

87 CW iii 35.

88 CW iii 5.

89 CW iii 7.

90 Some apparent instances of *'s* for *has* may be misleading: in *he's gone,* for instance, the full Anglo-Irish phrase is *he is gone.*

91 CW III 5. Compare the usage later in the play (CW III 27): *Michael has a clean burial in the far north.*

92 CW IV 19.

93 CW I 79.

94 CW I 84.

95 Hence spoken Anglo-Irish tends to sound monotonous to the English ear; there is intonation, indeed, but it is not *significant* intonation in the English sense.

96 See note 82.

97 CW I 80.

98 The use of *do* in Anglo-Irish as a 'consuetudinal auxiliary' seems to represent a specialization of (meaningless) auxiliary *do* current in seventeenth-century English. The origin of this specialization and the manner of its extension to verbs other than the verb 'to be' are interesting problems which I hope to discuss elsewhere.

99 See p. 47.

100 PRICE, p. 46.

101 G. B. Saul, *The Age of Yeats* (New York, 1964) 378.

102 JOHNSTON, p. 10.

103 PRICE, p. 77.

104 In the light of the inaccuracies listed on pp. 47-48, Price's use of 'authentic and credible' can hardly be justified.

105 *The Plays and Poems of J. M. Synge,* ed. T. R. Henn (1963) 11.

106 BOURGEOIS, p. 228.

107 HUSCHER, p. 52.

108 Pp. 41-2.

109 CW I 82-3.

110 D. B. Wyndham Lewis in his *François Villon: A Documented Survey* (1928) prints Synge's 'brief prose-paraphrase of the Ballade to Our Lady' because 'the speech of Catholic Kerry [sic] chimes naturally with the strong and simple passion of this noble poem.' (p. xvii) Elsewhere he refers to 'J. M. Synge's free and lovely prose-

paraphrase' of the Old Woman's Lament. (p.246)

111 BOURGEOIS, p. 230.

112 BOYD, p. 327.

113 See, however, P. L. Henry's study of the rhythm of *The Playboy* in *Philologica Pragensia* viii (1965), pp. 198-204. A more extended treatment of all the plays will appear in Professor Taniguchi's forthcoming study.

114 HUSCHER, p. 46

115 Loc. cit., p. 203.

116 O'CONNOR, p. 189.

117 Ibid. The references are unfortunately not to CW, which was not then available, but to T. R. Henn's *The Plays and Poems of J. M. Synge* (1963).

118 Loc. cit. pp. 203-4.

119 BOURGEOIS 230. According to Bourgeois there are 80 blank-verse lines in *The Playboy* and ten in *Deirdre;* unfortunately there is no indication whether or not these figures refer to blank-verse lines in cadence. Bourgeois is reprehended in PRICE p. 3 for descending 'to such dubious minutiæ as the estimation of the number of blank-verse lines in *The Playboy* and *Deirdre.*'

120 The numbers in brackets refer to the pages of CW IV.

121 P. 39.

122 P. 38

123 P.40.

124 P. 45.

125 Pp. 46-8.

126 Pp. 41-2.

127 Pp. 52-3.

128 CW I Introduction xii-xiii; see also CW I 69, 74, 76. The verse plays are written partly in rhymed and partly in blank-verse lines. Some of the blank-verse lines are very like those which appear in cadence in the 'prose' plays: compare *The long-sailed ships sail from the east and south* (CW I 73) with the blank-verse lines cited from *The Playboy* on p. 00.

129 Phillips' first play *Herod* (1900) was followed during the next fifteen years by a sequence of equally mediocre verse plays.

130 The rhetorical question, so rare in spoken standard English, is very common in Anglo-Irish. One of the two most frequent types, the negative question, is much used by Synge: *Isn't it a hard and cruel man won't hear a word from an old woman?* (CW III 11); *isn't it many another man may have a shirt of it as well as Michael himself?* JCW III 15); *Isn't it a great wonder you're letting him lie there?* (CW IV 33); *Wasn't I the last one heard his living voice in the world?* (CW IV 39); *Wasn't I digging spuds in the field?* (CW IV 75); *Amn't I after saying it is himself has me destroyed?* (CW IV 121).

131 BOYD, p. 334.

IV: SYNGE AND THE ACTOR – A CONSIDERATION OF STYLE

HUGH HUNT

Is there such a thing as a style of acting Synge's plays and is that style fixed irrevocably for all time? Style is a manner of expression. We talk of the style of a painter, of a football player, of an orator, of a writer. Synge as a dramatist had a very definite manner of expression. 'Poetic and dramatic expression in him are one and simultaneous, as they appear to have been with Shakespeare and with Webster.'[1] A Synge sentence is immediately recognisable; it is 'as fully flavoured as an apple or a nut;' its cadence and rhythm, its fusion of imagery and native speech are so shaped and orchestrated that the actors who are the instruments through which this verbal music is played have little room to manoeuvre. If an actor cuts an adjective or alters a word from a Synge sentence we are aware of a loss of balance. Should, therefore, an actor who has not only to interpret Synge's literary style, but the styles of many other dramatists, have a style of his own? Surely this is to negate the purpose of interpretation.

An actor's art is expressed through speech, gesture, movement and the whole range of his physical and spiritual being. Actors who posses a very marked style must necessarily be limited in versatility. We think of such actors as mannered actors, often they become the popular 'stars' of the theatre and cinema. Henry Irving, Sarah Bernhardt and Charlie Chaplin were actors of this kind. When I look back at the pre-War Abbey—the Abbey in which I worked between 1935 and 1938—I can name two of the most loved players of that company—Barry Fitzgerald and Maureen Delaney—who possessed a mannered style. They were always marvellously themselves—immediately recognisable whenever they appeared on the stage.

I find it hard to read the words of Michael James or Widow Quin without conjuring up the vocal inflexions and physical characteristics of these two players. I can also name another actor, perhaps the greatest of all Abbey actors—F. J. McCormick

—whose whole personality, including his manner of speech, seemed to change with every part he played.

The question of an acting style is linked with the question of interpretation. Interpretation is concerned, not only with the rhythms and cadences of the dramatist's literary style, but also with the interpretation of the character the dramatist has created. The dramatist's character as expressed in the text is, however, not a living being; his character lives in the imagination of the reader. Whatever reality Christy Mahon may assume in our imaginations, the living character only exists when there is injected into it the living 'self' of the actor, or as Stanislavsky puts it, when the character assumes the 'life of the human spirit.' It is this that provides a character, not only with a body, but with a soul. There are as many Hamlets as there are actors.

The measure of the actor's art—the degree to which he can make a character live on the stage—depends, first, on the quality of the actor's 'self' which we loosely call his personality. Secondly, it depends on his ability to marry his 'self', or some part of his 'self', consciously or subconsciously with the imaginary character of the play's text. But there is a third demand made upon the art of the actor, and this is his interpretation of the style of the text.

Every dramatist has his particular style. Synge's style is more emphatic and more individual than that of most Irish dramatists. Are we then to assume that, whilst the actor must interpret Synge's characters through the medium of the 'self', he must express that character's speech in a rigid framework ? And is that framework unalterable through all time ?

My answer to the first question is a qualified yes, and to the second an unqualified no. This is the paradox of acting.

If we are to accept that one measure of an actor's art is his ability to marry his 'self' with the imaginary character of the text, then it follows that the actor's self-expression must be injected into the text. An analogy is to be found in the interpretation of a musical composition. There must be harmony in the orchestral interpretation of a score, but we do not expect the conductor and soloist of a Chopin piano concerto to interpret the music in a rigid style. The rhythms and cadences as well as the tempo must be the personal expression of the musicians. Can we then deny to the director and actors of Synge's plays their personal expression of the dramatist's score ? Yet this is an argument frequently used by the traditional theatre critics. Basically it amounts to the statement that there is only one way of speaking Synge's lines. A similar argument was until recently used by the traditional critics of the acting style of the Comédie Française. Here the rigid teaching of inflections and rhythms in the plays of Corneille, Molière and Racine was so governed by tradition that the French national theatre was becoming a museum. What was left of the actor's art was imitation. The measure of his art was judged by the degree to which the actor excelled in speaking the lines according to the rules of tradition.

When I was a student in Paris I once heard a much-loved actor deliver the famous speech in *Le Cid:* 'Percé jusques au fond du coeur . . . .' so beautifully and with such perfect conformity to traditional style that he was not only greeted with cries of 'encore,' but he did so twice ! However poetic such a performance may be, however radiant the personality of the performer, the result is imitation, not acting.

The paradox that lies at the heart of acting throughout history is the conflict between imitation and reality. Theatre is not real. It is, as Aristotle says of tragedy, an imitation of life, but the actor's art is to give life to an imitation through the medium of his own reality. 'Suit the action to the word, the word to the action : with this special observance, that you o'erstep not the modesty of nature; for anything so overdone is from the purpose of playing; whose end, both at the first and now, was and is, to hold as 'twere, the mirror up to nature . . . .'

Shakespeare through the character of Hamlet was expressing the plea for reality in his own time, as opposed to the traditional oratorial style of

> . . . . players that I have seen play, and heard others praise, and that highly, not to speak it profanely, that neither having the accent of Christians nor the gait of Christian, pagan, nor man, have so strutted and bellowed, that I have thought some of nature's journeymen had made men, and not made them well, they imitated humanity so abominably.

Hamlet's advice to the players to reject imitation and hold 'the mirror up to nature' was to be repeated by Garrick, Antoine and Stanislavsky. Each in his own way, and in his own day, sought to re-create reality in a theatre grown stale by tradition—a theatre which no longer reflected the Zeitgeist—the life-style of contemporary society.

Theatre is not a museum of antiquity, and herein lies the danger of all traditional theatres. Theatre is a living art created before a living audience. The art of the actor is to communicate the play to the audience of his own day, to involve them deeply in the action. This is not to deny Brecht's alienation, for how can the theatre help to change or improve the nature of society, unless the audience cares passionately about the action and argument presented on the stage?

To communicate the play to a living audience the actor must communicate it in terms that a living audience cares deeply about. Whilst we admit that the dramatist has his particular style, we must also admit that each age has its particular style. What may have been accepted as reality in the age of Shakespeare is no longer accepted as reality today. It would clearly have been alien to the whole ethos of the eighteenth century if Garrick had attempted to imitate the style of Burbage. It would be equally alien to our own age if the Royal Shakespeare Company were to imitate the style of Garrick.

This applies not only to the setting, costumes, lighting and choreography of Shakespeare's plays, but also to the character interpretation which includes the speech of the actor. It follows, therefore, that there is such a thing as a style of acting, but that the actor's style must change from age to age in order that he may communicate with his audience. 'On the stage,' said Synge in his Preface to *The Playboy,* 'one must have reality and one must have joy.' If the Abbey actors today tried to imitate the style of the Fay brothers in presenting Synge's plays we would, I suspect, find the result lacking in reality, if not slightly ludicrous. The problem of the actor is how far he can temper Synge's style to communicate the play's reality to the reality of the audience of his own day.

When the Irish National Theatre Society first astonished English audiences in the early days of this century it is clear that the actors possessed a definite style. This style was largely created by the teaching of the Fay brothers. The Fays' style was evolved by experiment, using the raw material of untrained actors with no traditional stylistic mannerisms. It could be negatively classified as an attack on the traditional acting styles of the nineteenth century—styles that were already felt to be out of date by an influential section of the audience, and had been under constant attack from such critics as Archer, Shaw, Henry James and C. E. Montague.

The Abbey style was born in 1902 when the amalgamation of the Irish Literary Theatre with the acting company formed by Frank and Willie Fay took place. The style that the Fay brothers developed over the ensuing years was an amalgam of the styles of the dramatists and the actors. The dominating dramatists of the Irish National Theatre Society—as the new company was called—were Yeats and Lady Gregory, whose styles became so closely related that, in the folk plays in which they collaborated (*The Pot, of Broth* and *Kathleen Ni Houlihan*), Yeats was unable to say precisely how much each had contributed to the writing. A year and a half after the new company was formed Synge's first play, *The Shadow of the Glen,* was added to the repertoire, and from 1903 onwards Synge's plays exerted an increasing influence in the development of the Abbey style so far as verbal expression was concerned. But an acting style embraces other elements of the actor's art besides the spoken word.

Gabriel Fallon argues in *The Abbey and the Actor*[2] that what is known of the Abbey Theatre tradition rests on two schools of acting—the style of Antoine and the style of Coquelin. Certainly the work of both Frenchmen was studied and admired by Frank and Willie Fay. Antoine, the father of naturalism, placed his emphasis not only on real props and furniture, but on natural behaviour and on natural speech. Coquelin insisted on the tradition of beautiful speech, the tradition of the Comédie Française, in which for every phrase of an Alexandrine line there was only one determinable inflection, 'la seule inflexion juste.' Fallon suggests that, had the Fays not left the Theatre, 'it is not unlikely that Frank would have staked all on Coquelin as the greater of the two actors and by doing so have preserved the tradition of beautiful speech for which the company which he himself trained were famous.' But what is beautiful speech to one generation has no reality to the next. To *preserve* tradition is to kill the art of the theatre; to *develop* it in terms of the living audience is to create a living art.

But actors lacking music
Do most excite my spleen
They think it is more human

To shuffle, grunt and groan
Not knowing what unearthly stuff
Rounds a mighty scene.

Yeats was right; but the music must be played in terms of the reality of the age.

In the second volume of his autobiography[3] Frank O'Connor gives an entertaining and coloured account of Yeats's fury at my production of his play, *Deirdre,* with Jean Forbes-Robertson in 1937. What this actress brought to the part was to substitute passion for poetic recitation. Passion was something that the Abbey style at this time singularly lacked. A new production of *The Playboy,* in which Cyril Cusack made his first appearance as Christy Mahon, was equally condemned for its reality by the advocates of poetic speech. Acting is passion, not recitation, and the poetry of a play is created through the poetic harmony of the component parts that constitute the ephemeral art of the theatre. Passion and reality are not separate from poetic acting; they are essential components of it.

'I have been the advocate of poetry against the actor,' Yeats declared. But here he was speaking as a poet, and not as a dramatist—a poet who saw his theatre losing the passion of its early years and who feared the encroachment of naturalism, as opposed to the 'joy' that Synge demanded.

The word naturalism when applied to acting is illusive and deceptive. It can only be applied to a style of speech, behaviour and character interpretation that a given audience at a given time believes to be natural in a given type of play. Both Garrick and Edmund Kean were hailed as natural actors in their interpretation of Shakespeare. Antoine's naturalism which placed great emphasis on psychological interpretation of character, as well as upon 'natural' speech and behaviour held good for the social drama that constituted the main repertoire of Le Théâtre Libre, but his methods proved his undoing when he allied his naturalistic style to a classical repertoire at the Odéon. Otto Brahm whose Freie Bühne in Berlin followed in Antoine's footsteps equally failed when he applied the same methods of naturalism to a classical repertoire at the Deutsches Theater. In discussing the naturalistic actor's approach to the plays of Synge, Yeats and Lady Gregory, Fallon maintains that 'What the naturalistic actor calls "characterisation" cuts across the dialogue and clogs the rhythms of the speech.' He quotes Willie Fay's advice to Maire Nic Shiubhlaigh when she was rehearsing *The Shadow Of The Glen*: 'Be the *mouthpiece* of Nora Bourke, rather than Nora Bourke.' This may be fair enough advice to give to a raw amateur, but it is to deny to an actor the whole of his physical and spiritual contribution. Stanislavsky provided the answer to the question of acting style in relation to the style of the play and to the life-style of the audience when he spoke of the 'given circumstances' of a play. The 'given circumstances' include the 'language', be it poetry or prose, grand opera or variety. The 'given circumstances', he pointed out, have to be absorbed by the actor and become his own when he becomes the character, when he injects into it 'the life of the human spirit.' 'The human spirit' which is the 'self' of the actor exists in a living society and partakes of the style of its age. The actor will therefore so personalise his manner of expression in gesture, movement and speech that it relates directly to a contemporary audience.

When the Abbey actors first encountered Synge's language they found it strange, unusual and exceedingly difficult to speak. This is how Maire Nic Shiubhlaigh described her encounter with Synge's language:

> I found the part a difficult one to master for it was completely unlike anything I had played before. At first I found Synge's lines almost impossible to learn and deliver. Like the wandering ballad singer I had to 'humour' them into a strange tune, changing the metre several times each minute. It was neither verse nor prose. The speeches had a musical lilt absolutely different to anything I had heard before. Every passage brought some new difficulty and we would stumble through the speeches until the tempo in which they were written was finally discovered.[4]

This struggle with language, this 'humouring' of the lines 'into a strange tune' formed the basis of what was called the Abbey style. A style of speech that, combined with a natural behaviour, bred of an awareness of contemporary reality caused the eulogies that greeted the first performances of the young Irish company in London. The productions had the same effect on the London public as Antoine's company had upon the Parisian audience when Zola's *Jacques Damour* was presented in 1887, and Stanislavsky's company had upon the Moscow audience when *The Seagull* was performed in 1898. What happened in all three instances was that new acting styles were born of a fresh approach, untainted by theatrical tradition. The basic sincerity of the Irish actors was welcomed by an audience whose life-style had developed far beyond the rigid acting style of the time. On the stage there was 'reality.'

Synge's plays together with the plays of Lady Gregory and Yeats were largely influential in forming the acting style of the Abbey actors during the first two decades of the century. Just as Chekhov's and Gorky's plays influenced the acting style of the Moscow Theatre during roughly the same period. But the acting styles of neither theatre remained static. They developed in tune with their audiences; they were influenced by the changing ethos of those audiences; they were broadened by a growing professionalism and by contact with the work of new dramatists. O'Casey's plays in the early 'twenties were largely influential in developing the Abbey style, bringing to that style a greater identification between the actor's 'self' and the character.

This marriage between the 'self' and the character to which I referred earlier can be effected in two ways. The first is what Stanislavsky called 'living the part.' This is when the actor identifies himself so completely with the part that he lives the character in performance. His subconscious mind takes over the control of his action so that he is, as it were, possessed by the character and for a time at least loses the sense of his own identity. In fact every great actor has, from time to time, experienced this spiritual metamorphosis though he may not have consciously pursued any method or system. 'I cannot act Macbeth without being Macbeth,' Macready declared.

The other form of marriage between the 'self' and the character is that taught by Coquelin which Fallon maintains is closest to the style of the Abbey actors. In this form the actor consciously unites the 'self' with the part but stands apart from his creation in performance, observing and controlling the created character.

In my experience both forms of character creation are used by all actors, but for different purposes. In what might be broadly called psychological parts the actor is possessed by the character. In farce, comedy and highly stylistic drama the process of character interpretation follows the Coquelin method. This division does not necessarily exclude poetic drama from the former category where 'poetic and dramatic expression . . . are one and simultaneous' as they are in Synge. Where comedy predominates there is a need for the actor to be fully aware of audience reaction and hence there is a greater need for conscious control in performance, but the parts of Christy Mahon and Pegeen Mike in *The Playboy* must be 'lived' in performance, so too must the parts of Martin and Mary Doul in *The Well of the Saints*.

In fact those who have studied Stanislavsky's work as a whole, instead of basing their theories on the so-called System, will be aware that he used both methods; for he was not only a master of 'psychological' acting but of vaudeville and operatic acting. Whichever method is employed the actor must inject into the part 'the life of the human spirit.' He is not merely the *mouthpiece* of the dramatist's character. Perhaps the best description of this marriage of the 'self' with the part combined with the actor's interpretation of poetic speech can be found in Richard Flecknoe's tribute to Shakespeare's leading actor—Richard Burbage :

> he was a delightful Proteus, so wholly transforming himself into his part and putting off himself with his clothes, as he never (not so much as in the Tyring-house) assumed himself again until the play was done : there being as much difference between him and one of our common actors, as between a ballad-singer who only *mouths* it, and an excellent singer, who knows all the graces, and can artfully vary and modulate his voice, even to know how much breath he is to give every syllable.

I can think of no better advice to give to the interpretation of Synge's plays, nor a better tribute to the Abbey style at its best. It was when the actors ignored the basic principles of style that Yeats became disillusioned with the theatre he had created, and that led him to declare, 'I have been the advocate of poetry against the actor.' Basic principles must remain but time moves on.

As time moved on the search for identification between actor and character became more intense; speech assumed a different tempo; gesture and movement were more motivated, more 'real.' Art must be founded on reality, but reality itself is not static.

Nearly sixty years have passed since the actors of the Irish National Theatre 'stumbled through the speeches (of Synge's plays) until the tempo in which they were written was finally discovered.' Today new influences are developing the Abbey style. Scenic design has discarded naturalism. There are new technical aids, new lighting possibilities, new relationships between director and actor, between actor and audience. There are new styles of playwriting; above all there is a new style of living. We no longer regard the word 'shift' as outrageous. The management of the Abbey would not withhold the production of a play because a priest was tied up and gagged by a party of tinkers. As for Pegeen's allegation that Widow Quin had 'reared a black ram at (her) breast, so that the Lord Bishop of Connaught felt the elements of a Christian, and he eating it after in a kidney stew'—lines that Willie Fay had insisted on cutting—it is not beyond possibility that this cleric's remarkable perception might raise a laugh from the Lord Bishop himself!

Today the new stylistic influences—influences that are part of life—must be absorbed into the life of a living theatre. Tradition must be progressive, and for progress to take place experiment must be admitted. Theatre cannot live in isolation from the life around it, nor from contact with a rapidly contracting world. If I were asked how the passage of time affects the acting style of Synge, how far the style of performance must change, I would say, first, that whilst the verbal music that is at the heart of Synge's style must be preserved it must be played in a new tempo. The lines must not be intoned; they must be part of the character, not apart from the character. Secondly, interpretation of character must be deepened, made organically part of the actor's 'self.' When Willie Fay said to Maire Nic Shiubhlaigh: 'Be the *mouthpiece* of Nora Bourke,' he was speaking of an age before Stanislavsky's teaching had reached the ears of a new theatre. Thirdly, I would say that scenery must be less factual, more poetic. The nature imagery that modern critics have stressed as a distinctive ingredient of Synge's style must be felt as a physical presence. Mood must be created with the technical aids of light and sound; the darkness that envelopes the world outside Michael James's shebeen in the first act of *The Playboy;* the presence of the sea—that vital protagonist—in *Riders To The Sea;* the loneliness of Nora Bourke's cottage—the shadow of the glen. This is not a plea for scenic naturalism, but for the poetry of theatre. It demands from the designer something more than the box set. It calls for the technician, the designer and the director to be the creative interpreters of the dramatist's style, to *be* the play, not the *mouthpiece* of stage directions written for a theatre sixty years ago.

Finally, I would say that there is one aspect of Synge's style that today demands greater reality than was acceptable to audiences of the past. This is violence. Not only violence in action, but violence in the dialogue itself. Basically it was Synge's portrayal of the peasant as a person who had not lost the primitive instincts of man that infuriated those critics who sought to show that all Irishmen, and above all, all Irish women, were pure and beautiful and saintly. Ironically it was their rejection of Synge's literary violence that caused the violence of *The Playboy* riots.

In earlier productions violence in the dialogue was minimised by emphasising the poetic — non-realistic — qualities of Synge's speech, as well as by judicious cutting. The violence of the action was treated as lightly as possible. Willie Fay did his utmost to persuade Synge to cut the incident of Pegeen scorching Christy's leg with the burning sod. When I first saw *The Playboy* in the 1930's, the dragging of Christy to the peelers at the end of a rope was treated as high comedy. When I first directed *The Well Of The Saints* in the same period I would not have considered emphasising the full physical violence that is implicit in all three acts. Yet, when I directed the same play at the Abbey in 1969, the violence and cruelty of the people in stoning the blind Martin and Mary Doul broke out so spontaneously from the actors themselves that they dislocated the machinery of one of the stage lifts. When the Saint ordered the People to 'drag' Martin Doul off from his wife in the last act, and the actors responded with the lines: 'That's it. That's it. Come forward till we drop him in the pool beyond,' the response was such that the actor playing Martin was forced to ask me to control the actual violence with which he was handled.

Violence is a characteristic of our age. Violence was a characteristic of Synge's age. Synge's style reflects this violence. This was his 'reality.' The difference between the styles of Synge's audiences and of the audiences of today is that, whereas the former did not wish to recognise reality, today's audiences after two world wars, after the violence of the Irish struggle for independence, of the violence of Vietnam, of the racial riots in the U.S.A. and not least, the violence in the north of Ireland, have accepted Synge's 'reality' and have absorbed it within their style of living.

It is the rôle of the actor to reflect the reality and the style of the playwright in terms of the life-style of his audience.

NOTES

1 Una Ellis-Fermor, *The Irish Dramatic Movement* (London, 1939), p. 163.
2 (Dublin 1969), pp. 45-46.
3 *My Father's Son* (London, 1969), pp. 170-172.
4 *The Splendid Years, Recollections of Maire Nic Shiubhlaigh: As told to Edward Kenny*. (Dublin, 1955), pp. 42-43.

V: EIGHT NIGHTS IN THE ABBEY

HILARY BERROW

On Saturday 26 January 1907 Synge wrote to Lady Gregory, 'I do not know how things will go tonight. The day company are all very steady but some of the outsiders in a most deplorable state of uncertainty . . . I have a sort of second edition of influenza and I am looking gloomily at everything . . .'[1] That evening the small theatre in Abbey Street was full with a 'brilliant and discriminating audience.'[2] Lady Gregory, compact, black-clad and self-contained; Synge, tense, white and ill; Edward Martyn, his face 'round and large and russet as a ripe pumpkin;'[3] W. J. Lawrence, the theatre historian; Joseph Holloway, 'A stocky little man in middle age, with a long black overcoat, a bowler hat, a bushy moustache and hair that stuck out at all angles . . .;'[4] D. J. O'Donoghue, librarian of University College, Dublin; and MacNamara, the architect, filed into their usual seats in the stalls. The young literary set filled the cheaper seats: Mary Colum in white with blue and green embroidery, a blue *brath* and copper brooches, her girl friends equally ornate in gorgeous colours, gold Tara brooches and silver Claddagh rings; the young men wore Gaelic kilts of saffron or green with *braths* clipped to the shoulder of their jackets with silver or gold Tara brooches. But many of the audience were strangers to the Abbey, attracted by the gossip spread during rehearsals: 'reports spread through Dublin that there were improprieties in the play and that the womanhood of Ireland was being slandered, and these rumours were received with hilarity by some, with solemnity by others. At the opening night the attendance was far larger than usual—in fact the largest I had ever seen in the Abbey—and there were tenseness and expectation in the air.'[5] The set, 'the exact dimension of an Irish cottage—12 feet high in front, sloping down to 8 feet at the back wall, 20 feet long and 12 feet wide,'[6] was suitable for both the curtain raiser, *Riders to the Sea*, ("listened to attentively. The climax brought long and appreciative applause.")[7] and *The Playboy of the Western World*. '*The Playboy* scene, laid throughout in the main room of an inn on the western coast, was typical of Fay. He achieved the effect of brightness against the lime-washed walls of the set in a pleasantly unobtrusive manner. The fittings were a lovely deep brown, the colour of turf, and helped to show up the bright peasant costumes of the characters.'[8] The actual performance was not remarkable: Synge wrote to Molly, 'W. G. was pretty bluffy, and Power was very confused in places. Then the crowd was wretched and Mrs. W. G. missed the cue we gave, though she can hardly be blamed for that. I think with a better Mahon and crowd and a few slight cuts the play would be thoroughly sound.'[9] The nervousness of the actors seems to have stiffened their acting, and Maire Nic Shiubhlaigh has written, 'it was played seriously almost sombrely, as though each character had been studied and its nastiness made apparent.'[10]

The first act was applauded, and though there were protests in the second act, 'Faint calls and ejaculations like "Oh, no! Take it off!" came from various parts of the house . . .' " Lady Gregory was confident enough to send a telegram to Yeats, lecturing in Scotland, 'Play great success.' W. G. Fay says he felt hostility grow in the third act from the entrance of the Widow Quin; Padraic Colum blames Old Mahon's entry, 'That scene was too representational. There stood a man with horribly bloodied bandage upon his head, making a figure that took the whole thing out of the atmosphere of high comedy.'[12] There were hisses and cat-calls at the word 'bloody' and loud howls greeted Christy's words about a drift of chosen females standing in their shifts (an image made more real and shocking, according to Holloway, by Fay's substitution of 'Mayo girls' for 'chosen females.') The noise increased and 'by the time the curtain fell on the last act, the crowd was arguing and fighting with itself. People in front leaned over the backs of seats and demanded quiet—a lot of people seemed to be doing this—and those at the back responded by shouting and hissing loudly. The crowd which eventually emerged into the streets was in an ugly mood.'[13] Lady Gregory sent Yeats a second telegram, 'Audience broke up in disorder at the word shift.' She met Holloway in the vestibule and, he reports, asked him: 'What was the cause of the disturbance?'

And my monosyllabic answer was, 'Blackguardism!'

To which she queried, 'On which side?'

'The stage!' came from me pat.'[14] Holloway, ('he was worth his weight in gold as a sort of barometer by which to guage the public's reaction to our work . . .')[15] wrote in his diary that night, 'I maintain that . . . *The Playboy* is not a truthful or just picture of the Irish peasants, but simply the outpourings of a morbid, unhealthy mind ever seeking on the dunghill of life for the nastiness that lies concealed there . . .'[16] D. J. O'Donoghue and MacNamara agreed fervently that it was a good thing they left their wives at home, and Martyn hurried away feeling that 'he had heard enough blasphemy to keep him out of the theatre thenceforth . . .'[17] Synge, surprisingly, was more exhilarated than depressed with the reception of his masterpiece; he wrote to Molly the next day. 'It is better any day to have the row we had last night, than to have your play fizzling out in half-hearted applause. Now we'll be talked about. We're an event in the history of the Irish stage.'[18]

They were talked about, and written about. Most outspoken was *The Freeman's Journal,* which denounced the play as 'unmitigated, protracted libel upon Irish peasant men and, worse still, upon Irish peasant girlhood. The blood boils with indignation as one recalls the incidents, expressions, ideas of this squalid, offensive production . . . No adequate idea can be given of the barbarous jargon, the elaborate and incessant cursings of these repulsive creatures.'[19] The Directors' statement that they intended to keep the play on infuriated a public already embittered by the press reports. On Monday 28 January the house was full. A group of men in the centre of the pit was armed with tin trumpets, their din made the play inaudible, but the actors continued until near the end of the first act, when W. G. Fay announced that those who did not wish to listen to the play should leave; their money would be returned. Voices yelled 'We don't want the money . . . It is a libel on the National Theatre . . . We never expected this of the Abbey . . . Sinn Fein for ever . . . Irishmen don't harbour murderers . . . We respect Irish virtue . . .'[20] During the interval the audience sang 'The West's Asleep.' 'Hisses and boos greeted the uprising of the curtain, and the disorder of the gallery and pit prevented anyone in the other parts of the house from hearing what was said on the stage . . . Then Mr. Fay amid a storm of hisses came forward and announced that he had sent for the police and under their protection the comedy would be continued to the end. The orchestra played and directly six policemen entered the parterre while three made their way into the balcony.'[21] According to the *Daily Mail* reporter the Dublin Metropolitan Constabulary stood to attention like, 'nine big sticks with helmets on top' but, despite pleas from the stalls that they should silence the trumpets, they did nothing. Ellen Duncan wrote to the *Irish Times* that, 'many, like myself, were astonished that no use was made by the management of the able-bodied policemen who lined the walls of the pit. It seemed an extraordinary moment to choose for a policy of non-resistance . . .'[22] Towards the end of the second act Synge and Lady Gregory told the sergeant in charge that their services were no longer required. The protesters, in the belief that they had vanquished the police, broke into trimphant shouts and sang heartily, 'A Nation Once Again.' Lady Gregory told the sergeant to stay within call in case attempts were made on the actors or stage, and then cooly spent the interval cutting cake. Walter Starkie, a young boy at the time, was there, 'we joined the actors and their supporters gathered around Lady Gregory and J. M. Synge. While to me it seemed that all the players were wringing their hands, tearing their hair, and running hither and thither, Lady Gregory stood at the door of the Green Room as calm and collected as Queen Victoria about to open a charity bazaar. Seeing Paddy Tobin and myself, she beckoned us over and handed each of us a piece of the huge barmbrack . . .'[23] During the third act cries of 'Sinn Fein . . . Sinn Fein Amhain . . . Kill the author,' rent the air. The grand-nephew of Lord Edward, Lord Walter Fitzgerald, asked to be allowed to hear the play, but his request was refused. Synge, despite many calls, would not make a speech, 'his face was pale and shrunken . . . I watched him closely as he sat motionless through the dumb-show of his play, amidst the rioting and insults of the mob, but not a trace of emotion could I discern in his pale mask-like face that gazed unseeing at the raging auditorium.'[24] No more of the play was heard that night. After the final curtain Synge, Lady Gregory, and others, 'held animated conversation in the stalls . . . Small knots of people argued the situation out anything but calmly, and after about a quarter of an hour's clamour the audience dispersed hoarse.'[25]

Yeats arrived in Dublin the next morning. He blamed the Nationalists for an organised riot the previous evening and dealt with them in the traditional theatrical fashion : he organised his own claque. He and Lady Gregory distributed free tickets to undergraduates of Trinity College to support the play, and she told her nephew to 'bring a few fellow athletes, that we might be sure of some ablebodied helpers in case of an attack on the stage.'[26] She has admitted the shortsightedness of their policy: the sight of the Trinity students, 'was as a match to the resin of the pit, and a roar of defiance was flung back,—townsman against gownsman, hereditary enemies challenging each other as they are used to do when party or political processions march before the railings on College Green. But no iron railings divided pit and stalls, some scuffles added to the excitement, and it was one of our defenders at the last who was carried out bodily . . .'[27] It was one of their athletic defenders from Trinity who initiated the whole evening's proceedings : the student, referred to as 'Napoleon,' 'the man in the overcoat,' and 'the drunken Galwegian and the yelping pack from Trinity College,' by different press reporters, entered the theatre at eight o'clock with about twenty other students, all on free passes, and straight away issued a challenge to those in the pit, 'Come on, any of you;' the pit replied disdainfully, 'We would wipe the streets with you.'—or, as one of the audience understood the dialogue :

'Kindly come outside a minute,'
    Said Napoleon to the pit.
I'm anxious to begin it,
    But I cannot while you sit.
I know nothing about the play,
    But fain would 'pugilize'
So if you please will step this way
    I'll bung up both your eyes.'

A voice replied, 'You'd do it, mister,
    That is if yer fit'—
'I'd make yer face a blooming blister.'
    Echoed from the pit.
The balcony then seized the rail,
    And loudly did they thump it,
Above the din there rose the wail
    From out a penny trumpet.[28]

The student then pranced to the piano and commenced to play a waltz, announcing to the joy of pit and balcony, 'I am a little bit drunk, and don't know what I am saying.' After a few curses he shouted, 'Hurrah for Galway,' then, as the orchestra started up with an Irish jig he strutted to the balcony and gaily cut a few capers. At ten past eight Lady Gregory entered and talked to her nephew, Yeats followed her and the curtain raiser began. After the one act two students in the stalls began to shadow-box and continued until Yeats appeared before the curtain. Boos, hisses, cheers, and 'What about '98?' greeted him. He announced that a public debate on the comedy would take place the following Monday, proclaimed that no man should stop another from hearing the play and judging for himself, and threatened that the play would be repeated until a fair hearing was given it. The cat-calls, jeers and cheers which punctuated his speech rose to a crescendo at the end. The student from Galway tried to steal the lime-light again but was frustrated by his friends and bundled outside. During this shindy the orchestra players retreated clutching their instruments, and actors came to the footlights to watch the fun. Yeats returned and announced that a man, apparently intoxicated, had been removed, and appealed to those who were sober to allow the play to proceed. Sternly the pit replied, 'We are all sober here.' Noise abated only to reach new heights at Michael James' entrance. Pat Kenny, reporter for the *Irish Times,* stood up and asked that the management be allowed to fulfil their responsibility to him by letting him hear the play. A violent outbreak of stamping drowned his arguments and continued until the side door was thrown open and in strode Yeats followed by a long column of policemen. ('Know that I would accounted be, true brother of the D.M.P.,' as one wit commented in the next *Sinn Fein.)* The actors forgot their own drama; those on stage came to the footlights, and others peered through the set window and around the wings as the constables stoutly climbed over seats and placed themselves around the pit walls.

During the second act the police surrendered their inactivity and, seizing those members of the audience whom Yeats and Hugh Lane pointed out, hustled them outside and arrested them — actions which provoked a 'go to hell' from the pit, and 'Go home and kill your father' from the balcony. The welcome which Christy receives because of his crime drew shouts of, 'That's not the West . . . Get off the stage . . . Pull down the curtain . . .'[29]

Loud rhythmical stamping began. A smartly-clad gentleman in the stalls protested against Pegeen's description of the Widow Quin's poverty, and some of the audience, several ladies amongst them, walked out. Students and pittites heckled each other, and the suggestion was made that some of the policemen might be best occupied arresting Christy. Jeers and ironical applause greeted the end of the act. In the last act opposition reached its height in the rope scene and, according to one press report, 'The curtain was rung down amidst a pandemonium that reminded one of the Zoo at meal-time.' The drunken student returned to lend his voice to his companions' rendering of 'God Save the King,' and the pit replied with 'God Save Ireland' and 'A Nation Once Again.' Lights were lowered and raised, pipes and cigarettes lit up. The police eventually cleared the theatre 'whilst,' reads the *Herald,* 'Mr. William B. Yeats looked on, perched, like Poe's raven, upon a privileged staircase at the side of the stage.' The row was carried out into the streets as the students marched to Eden quay singing 'God Save the King,' and one of their fraternity was arrested for striking one of the constables in the face. So ended the third night; not more than six consecutive lines had been audible, and as one eyewitness states:

Our own opinion, we admit,
    Is rather—well—uncertain,
Because we couldn't hear one bit
    From rise to fall of curtain . . .
Part of the audience we may
    Term quite enthusiastic,
While others keen to stop the play
    adopted measures drastic.
With many a hiss and stamp and yell,
    Essayed to stop the action,
Which didn't in the slightest quell
    Cheers of the other faction.
And as these vocal gladiators—
    All of them—were stayers,
The stage became spectators
    And the audience the players.
Whether the play was good or bad,
    It didn't really matter,

Whether in comic vein or sad,
Beside the awful clatter,
We couldn't hear a single line
From rise to fall of curtain.
Our verdict, therefore, we opine
Is (as we said) uncertain . . .[30]

On Wednesday 30 January crowds waited outside the theatre for the doors to open, inside over fifty policemen lined the walls. The usual hisses and shouts interrupted the dialogue, but the presence of so many police, and the knowledge that those previously arrested had been charged and fined, subdued the audience. The remarks shouted out were more amusing than bitter and, 'at no time during the evening did the hostile demonstrations reach the magnitude of those witnessed on the previous night.'[31] The main incidents were Yeats's restlessness during the first act when he ran from stalls to stage so many times that the audience demanded, 'a cakewalk by Mr. W. B. Yeats' during the first interval; and the spontaneous burst of whistling of 'The Peeler and the Goat,' and the challenge from a small Englishman in the stalls to a big Irishman in the pit, their exit to the vestibule, followed by a couple of hundred persons, and the ensuing bout of fisticuffs during the second interval.

Thursday night was even quieter. The Abbey floor was padded with felt 'which frustrated the rhythmic stamping that had been the opposition's most effective device.'[32] As well as the police-padded walls, plain-clothes men were scattered in the pit, and a couple of hundred policemen stood on guard outside the theatre. Only two arrests were made, and during the third act a dozen or so young men arose from the pit and stamped out booing and hissing as they went. Lady Gregory admitted to a reporter, 'a few adjectives have been taken out, as have been most of the invocations of the Holy Name . . .' and Yeats commented, 'I think that gradually the audience are coming to understand what it means. We had tonight, for the first time I think, the majority of the pit on our side. We have always had the stalls, of course, if the previous disturbances are repeated tomorrow and Saturday we shall be compelled to give it again next week.' Holloway wrote bitterly in his diary that night, 'The police-protected drama by the dramatist of the dungheap . . . got a fair hearing . . .'

Friday night only one arrest was made. In the first act a young man hissed, and when the police warned him he asked if he was not entitled by law to express his feelings. (Mr. Wall, who tried those arrested that week for offensive behaviour in the Abbey, referred the case to the late Lord Chief Justice Bushe who in 1823, when hearing a case in reference to an alleged riot at the Theatre Royal, defined the rights of an audience : the audience was free to hiss or boo so long as it did not excite terror and was not 'riotous' but the expression of the feelings of that moment; hisses were not acceptable if they resulted from a pre-meditated determination to cause a disturbance, but a man had common law right to express approval or disapproval.) The young man then asked if he would have been interfered with if he had applauded. His question were left unanswered. He hissed again and was arrested. A voice called for three cheers for Mr. Wall and the audience cheered; at the end of the play there was more cheering for those who had been arrested during the production of *The Playboy;* then the audience quietly left the theatre.

Saturday night the police were still there, there were only a few hisses, no arrests and the play was applauded. In one of the intervals Synge was heard to say, 'The Irish seem to have lost all sense of humour; we shall soon have to establish a society for the Preservation of Irish Humour.'[33] But at least two products of that week belie his opinion : Cathal M'Garvey sang at a concert in Castleblayney, Co. Monaghan, 'The Playboy' to the air, 'Moriartee' :

Come all ye bogus Irishmen, and hear my
    Synge-y song;
In Abbey street my form you'll meet, 'mid
    peelers hundreds strong;
'Tis I'm the 'Man for Galway,' boys, so
    raise a joyful shout;
I'm the rattling lad that killed his dad—I'm
    the dirty stuttering lout.
    CHORUS

Then cheer, boys, cheer, for the Playboy here
    who knows not shame nor doubt;
For the lad, Hurrah ! ! that killed his 'Da'—
    For the dirty, stuttering lout !

I come to you to tell you true of Gaels I'm
not afraid;
In spite of all, you'll hear me call a spade a
bloody spade;
I understand the Western land, where life is
near the sod,
And potboys reign, with speech unclane—I'm
I'm one of them, by dad !
CHORUS.

Here girls galore my face adore; they think
my 'Da' is dead.
My deeds they tell, my boots they smell, and
hang around my head !
I curse and swear—they bring me fare :
eggs, fowl, and other gifts;
But all the same it is a shame to talk about
their — shirts! . . . .

and the following Saturday's *The Mail* included 'The Blushes of Ireland.'

You come, sir, with your English ways
Your morals of the Cockney cabby
Corrupting with unseemly phrase
The Abbey babby.

Unless we watch your wanton text,
And waken shame with boos and knockings,
You'll want that poor Miss Allgood next
To mention st-ck-ngs.

Unless we curb from hour to hour
This frenzied cult of Aphrodite,
You'll urge reluctant Ambrose Power
To name his n-ghty . . . . .

On Monday 4 February the Abbey Theatre was full for the public debate on *The Playboy.* The evening of frivolous banter seems best summed up in Lady Gregory's words to Synge, 'I was sorry while there that we had ever let such a set inside the theatre . . . ' No exchange of ideas or positive discussion was possible and, 'at half-past eleven, the audience were tired of speeches and their own noisy demonstrations, . . The audience went home after a night not so much tinged with rowdyism as with boisterous foolery.'[34]

Today it matters little whether the protests on the second night of the play were organised, or whether the main protesters were the Sinn Feiners and members of the Gaelic League as Yeats, Lady Gregory and Miss Horniman thought, or 'the middle class Irish Catholic, an ungodly ruck of fat-faced, sweaty headed, swine,'[35] whom Synge held responsible. Certainly much of the noise was spontaneous and was made by sincere Irishmen who thought that Synge was maligning the Irish character at a time when their image could least afford such misrepresentation. The grotesque Stage Irishman who had ruled the theatre for over a hundred years had been seen as typically Irish by most English and American audiences; Old Mahon and Michael James shared too many of his characteristics to be acceptable to patriotic serious-minded Irishmen. The protests against the language are equally understandable; most theatre audiences of that time would have been astounded by its rough realism. Before the production Jack Yeats had warned Synge : 'If you don't want to have to leave out all the coloured language in your play you'll have to station a drummer in the wings, to welt the drums every time the language gets too high for the stomachs of the audience. They used to do this in the old Music Halls,
Thus

get out of that ye son of a— — rub, a dub, dub, dub —'[36]

Yeats and Lady Gregory originally agreed to produce the play on the condition that the 'bad language' and 'violent oaths' were cut out during the rehearsal period, and it was due to a misunderstanding on their part that the cuts were not made until after the first night. W. G. Fay has pointed out that Synge was in advance of his time and that the theatrical sensation of the 1913 London season was Shaw's use of the word 'bloody' in '*Pygmalion*,' Since the eighteenth century drama had become divorced from the other arts and reduced to popular amusement; those who tried to reinstate drama, and show that a play could deal with life as seriously and as truthfully as any other art form, had hard battles to fight: Bjornson, Ibsen, Chekhov and Shaw all faced hostile audiences. Press attacks on Ibsen's plays were more brutal than

those on Synge's; Clement Scott thought '*Ghosts,*' 'an open drain; a loathsome sore unbandaged; a dirty act done publicly; a lazar-house with all its doors and windows open.' On the first night of '*The Seagull*' jeers and hisses rendered the play inaudible, and Chekhov left Petersburg in disgrace and disgust. 'The Playboy' riots were typical of their time, and, compared with Dublin theatre riots of the eighteenth and nineteenth centuries, they are a storm in a teacup. Their main significance today is that out of the conflict came some of the best dramatic criticism of this century,[37] and one very fine poem :
'On Those That Hated "The Playboy of the Western World," 1907'

> Once, when midnight smote the air,
> Eunuchs ran through Hell and met
> On every crowded street to stare
> Upon great Juan riding by :
> Even like these to rail and sweat
> Staring upon his sinewy thigh.[38]

NOTES

1 Lady Gregory, *Our Irish Theatre* (New York and London, 1914), p. 134.
2 *Independent.* Monday 28 January, 1907, in W. A. Henderson, *The Playboy and What He Did* (M.S. N.L.I.) p. 4.
3 George Moore, *Hail and Farewell! Vale* (London, 1914), p. 192.
4 Maire Nic Shiubhlaigh, *The Splendid Years* (Dublin, 1955), p. 66.
5 Mary Colum, *Life and the Dream* (Dublin, 1966), p. 119.
6 W. G. Fay and Catherine Carswell, *The Fays of the Abbey Theatre* (London, 1935), p. 200.
7 Maire Nic Shiubhlaigh, p. 82.
8 Maire Nic Shiubhlaigh, p. 82.
9 *J. M. Synge, Collected Works,* ed. Ann Saddlemyer (Oxford, 1968), IV, Book II, p. xxii.
10 Maire Nic Shiubhlaigh, p. 81.
11 Maire Nic Shiubhlaigh, p. 83.
12 Padraic Colum, *The Road Round Ireland* (New York, 1926), p. 368.
13 Maire Nic Shiubhlaigh, p. 83.
14 J. Holloway, *Diary,* Saturday 26 January, 1907, in *Joseph Holloway's Abbey Theatre,* ed. R. Hogan and M. J. O'Neill (Southern Illinois, 1967), p. 81.

15 Maire Nic Shiubhlaigh, p. 68.
16 *J. Holloway's Abbey Theatre,* p. 81.
17 George Moore, p. 192.
18 *J. M. Synge,* p. xxii.
19 *The Freeman's Journal,* Monday 28 January, 1907, *The Playboy and What He Did,* p. 1.
20 Dublin newspapers for Tuesday 29 January, 1907, W. A. Henderson, *Abbey Theatre and Irish Plays 1904 to 1907.* (M.S. N.L.I.)
21 Lennox Robinson, *Ireland's Abbey Theatre* (London, 1951), p. 53.
22 *Irish Times,* Thursday 31 January, 1907, p. 5.
23 *Irish Times,* Monday 7 October, 1963, p. 8.
24 *Irish Times,* Monday 7 October, 1963, p. 8.
25 *J. Holloway's Abbey Theatre,* p. 83.
26 Lady Gregory, p. 114.
27 Lady Gregory, p. 114.
28 P. L. Dickinson and J. M. Hone, *The Abbey Row,* NOT Edited by W. B. Yeats (Dublin, 1907), p. 1.
29 Dublin newspapers for Saturday 2 February, 1907, *Abbey Theatre and Irish Plays 1904 to 1907* (M.S. N.L.I.)
30 *The Abbey Row,* NOT Edited by W. B. Yeats, p. 10.
31 *Irish Times,* Thursday 31 January, 1907, p. 5.
32 W. G. Fay and Catherine Carswell, p. 216.
33 *Evening Telegraph,* Monday 4 February, 1907, *The Playboy and What He Did,* p. 44.
34 Lennox Robinson, p. 55.
35 Ann Saddlemyer, 'Synge To MacKenna: The Mature Years', *Irish Renaissance* ed. Robin Skelton and David R. Clark (Dublin, 1965), p. 74.
36 *J. M. Synge,* p. xx.
37 W. B. Yeats, *Explorations* (London, 1962).
38 W. B. Yeats, *Collected Poems* (London, 1965), p. 124.

VI: DEIRDRE OF THE SORROWS

LITERATURE FIRST . . . DRAMA AFTERWARDS

ANN SADDLEMYER

'My next play must be quite different from the *P. Boy.* I want to do something quiet and stately and restrained and I want you to act in it.' When Synge wrote these words to his fiancée Molly Allgood early in December 1906 he was ill, on the verge of disillusionment with the Abbey Theatre, and thoroughly fed up with Christy Mahon and the myth-making Mayoites. He was just recovering from his bitterest quarrel with Molly and was facing an even greater crisis with his mother, to whom, from a safe distance in England, he was at last breaking the news of his engagement. Opening night of *The Playboy of the Western World,* already postponed once, was less than two months away, but he was still dissatisfied with the third act and uncertain of the players' ability to fulfil his wishes. He was worried about his poverty and his ill-health, the two greatest obstacles to his marriage. No wonder he longed for peace, security and a change of pace, if only in his art.

But Synge was to face greater turbulence still. The shattering history of *The Playboy's* reception is well-known : on the first night actors were hooted from the stage, controversy raged in public and the press for months, his fellow-directors (one of whom disliked the play intensely) and the theatre suffered a serious loss of support for several years to come. Never a fighter, Synge retired to Kingstown with a bad cold, developed influenza and was not seen at the theatre for almost six weeks. However, he was not unduly depressed by the reaction to his comedy. 'I feel like old Maurya today,' he wrote to Molly after the first performance, '" It's four fine plays I have, though it was a hard birth I had with every one of them and they coming to the world." It is better any day to have the row we had last night, than to have your play fizzling out in half-hearted applause. Now we'll be talked about. We're an event in the history of the Irish stage.' He tended to blame part of the trouble on the actors' lack of preparation and inability to express the 'subtleties' his play required; he rejected well-meaning friends' criticisms of structure and mood, insisting that it was 'certainly a much stronger *stage-play*' than any of his other work; and he justified the offending 'Rabelaisian' note as an essential counterpoint to the romantic element in the play. As far as he was concerned *The Playboy* was an artistic success, if not yet one in performance; he was confident that he had achieved the sound comic structure, the precise patterning of characters and motifs, that he had worked for so painstakingly and so long. 'The story—in its *essence*—' he affirmed, 'is probable given the psychic state of the locality,' and in the preface to the published text he unashamedly compared himself to the greatest of Elizabethan dramatists.[1]

Now, confined to bed, he had time to recollect past experience and to dream of future plans. With *The Aran Islands* finally published, he planned two more travel books out of his raw material on Wicklow and Kerry; he made arrangements for *The Playboy* to be translated and produced in the continental theatres that had already seen *The Shadow of the Glen* and *The Well of the Saints.* He dug out old poems, re-worked them, and wrote new ones for Molly. In search of reading material for her, he rediscovered old favourites—R. L. Stevenson, George Meredith, Tolstoi, Walter Scott, the *Mabinogion,* the Arthurian tales. He delved further into his own past and re-examined portions of an old autobiography; he may even have attempted yet another revision of his first completed play, *When the Moon Has Set,* for notebook jottings of this period bear a close resemblance to some of the later drafts. Later that year he revised the unpublished, unproduced *Tinker's Wedding* and theorized further still about comedy, drama and literature. Then, during the summer months, he spent an idyllic convalescence in the Wicklow mountains with Molly.

It is impossible to say with any certainty when he decided to turn to ancient saga material for his next play, although it is apparent from his notebooks and published writings that he had been interested especially in the Deirdre story for at least five years. Even before he enrolled in de Jubainville's course in Old Irish at the Sorbonne in the spring of 1902 he had attempted his own translation of 'The Sons of Usnach' during a visit to Aran.

When he reviewed Lady Gregory's book *Cuchulain of Muirthemne* Deirdre's lament was cited as one of its finest passages, and he may well have had this story in mind when he wrote to Lady Gregory herself, 'What puny pallid stuff most of our modern writing seems beside it !'[2] A few years later he again singled out passages from the Deirdre story when reviewing A. H. Leahy's *Heroic Romances of Ireland;* but this time the translation was criticized as a 'deplorable misrepresentation of the spirit of these old verses' and the author was sternly advised to study Andrew Lang's translation of the medieval French *cante-fable, Aucassin and Nicolette,* a book he also recommended to Molly as 'filled with the very essence of literature and romance.'[3]

Following Lady Gregory's lead, other Abbey Theatre dramatists were exploring Ireland's past for fresh material. Æ's only play, *Deirdre,* was well-known and frequently revived by amateur companies throughout the country. In November 1906 Synge and Molly observed with some misgivings Yeats's one-act *Deirdre;* the same month he sent her *Aucassin and Nicolette* (which became their favourite book) and also recommended Lady Gregory's 'charming' translation of 'The Sons of Usnach.' Now, in March 1907 after the *Playboy* fracas, Yeats's earlier 'Cuchulanoid drama'[4] *On Baile's Strand* was revived, with Molly playing one of the musicians, followed two weeks later by Yeats's revised *Deirdre,* Molly again in the cast. At the same time, she was rehearsing the title role of W. S. Blunt's *Fand,* based on 'The Only Jealousy of Emer,' another story from Lady Gregory's *Cuchulain.* Spurred by this renewal of interest in saga material, and encouraged no doubt by his reading of Walter Scott, Synge revised an early poem, 'Queens,' and drafted an essay entitled 'Historical or Peasant Drama.' The poem ended with the questions,

> And are these ladies, I ask your pardon
> As dead as the doornail of Jim McCarden,
> Are all these queens of love and laughter
> As dry as Mahony's chimney rafter ?[5]

The essay concluded that historical fiction was now impossible and insincere, that modern poetry apart from a few lyrics was a failure, and again ended with a question: 'Is the drama—as a beautiful thing a lost art ? . . . For the present the only possible beauty in drama is peasant drama, for the future we must await the making of life beautiful again before we can have beautiful drama.'[6]

But if Synge was not yet ready to accept 'the drama of swords,' he could not deny the magnificence and tenderness of Ireland's popular imagination, which he had eloquently praised in the preface to *The Playboy* and out of which the saga material had grown. Other aspects of theory had also matured, for by now, too, he had reconciled the role of the artist with an earlier role, the lonely sensitive observer of nature's moods. Despite a reluctance to theorize, he found himself formulating an aesthetic creed and observing it in his prose works. The individual, he believed, could not achieve wholeness in himself until he was in harmony with nature and had attempted a wholeness within the entire cycle of experience. Just as the natural and the supernatural as he observed them on Aran are all part of the same spectrum of experience, so man must sound all the chords and moods of his own nature before he can hope to recognize and sympathize with the various moods and aspects of the universe of which he is a part. Life and nature at their most intense provide a sharpness to experience and hence greater joy in being and becoming; life at its most primitive provides the greatest opportunity for experiencing this sympathy between man and the natural world; therefore the hunter, the tramp and the poet, who are most free to roam and are constantly testing themselves are most receptive and sensitive to all of nature's moods. This is especially true of the artist, whose privileged position requires him to be not only sensitive but objective, openly sympathetic but inevitably alone. Loneliness became for Synge a necessary experience, balanced by a heightened exultation in the richness of 'what is superb and wild in reality,' and an inevitable part of the fully developed personality.[7]

But beyond this spectrum available to the 'prepared personality' is the evolutionary pattern of the universe itself, of which man's total experience is but one small part. For Synge had recognised in the twilights of Wicklow and the grey mists of Aran that nature too has a psychic memory, that time and place in turn range beyond the hours and seasons to include incidents from the distant past and hints of the future. His one-act tragedy *Riders to the Sea* had revealed this layering of events within the story of one family through the experiences of old Maurya, whose grief became at the same time personal and universal, encompassing the loss of three generations while centering on the last of six strong sons. Her final lament is for all mothers, everywhere, and for all who mourn, have mourned and will mourn the coming of death: 'No man at all can be living forever, and we must be satisfied.' Now he delved deeper into Ireland's past in an effort to identify and capture what is richest and most lasting in life, nature and time, and came at last to that meeting-place where man's story becomes part of the universal experience, to the fountain-head of all literature—folk history and primitive knowledge. In *The Well of the Saints* Synge had examined man's need for a myth out of which to carve the reality of his dreams; in *The Playboy of the Western World* he had explored the process of myth-making and celebrated its dangers and glories; now he turned to his most difficult task yet, the re-creation, in terms significant to modern man, of the myth itself. It was to lead him back through the unsophisticated peasant of Wicklow, Aran, and Kerry into the Irish folk spirit of legend, to the mingling of the immediacy of passion with those unyielding constants, Death and Time.

The starting-point on this journey must be the artist's personality and individual experience. For the first time the joy of a love returned matched Synge's exultation over beauty in the natural world, and his letters to Molly illustrate a fresh awareness of the sharp pain of intense emotion:

> All that we feel for each other is so much connected with this divine world, that our particular affection, in a real sense, must be divine also.
>
> You feel as fully as anyone can feel all the poetry and mystery of the nights we are out in—like that night a week ago when we came down from Rockbrook with the pale light of Dublin shining behind the naked trees till we seemed almost to come out of ourselves with the wonder and beauty of it all. Divine moments like that are infinitely precious to both of us as people and as artists . . . I think people who feel these things—people like us—have a profound joy in love, that the ordinary run of people do not easily reach. They love with all their hearts—as we do—but their hearts perhaps,

> have not all the stops that you and I have found in ours. The worst of it is that we have the same openness to profound pain—of mind I mean—as we have to profound joy, but please Heaven we shall have a few years of divine love and life together and that is all I suppose any one need expect.

Illness and exile had forced him also to a profound awareness of the brevity of man's span within the universal cycle:

> There is nearly a half moon, and I have been picturing in my mind how all our nooks and glens and rivers would look, if we were out among them as we should be! Do you ever think of them? Ever think of them I mean not as places that you've been to, but as places that are there still, with the little moon shining, and the rivers running, and the thrushes singing, while you and I, God help us, are far away from them. I used to sit over my sparks of fire long ago in Paris picturing glen after glen in my mind, and river after river—there are rivers like the Annamoe that I fished in till I knew every stone and eddy—and then one goes on to see a time when the rivers will be there and the thrushes, and we'll be dead surely.

Long before he had begun to write, Deirdre's lament at leaving Alban was part of his own experience.

But it would be a mistake to suggest that morbidity led Synge to the story of Deirdre. His first fears in tackling the theme were that 'the "Saga" people might loosen my grip on reality.' Diffidently, he expressed doubts as to his ability to write a satisfactory play. 'These saga people, when one comes to deal with them, seem very remote,' he complained to John Quinn; 'one does not know what they thought or what they ate or where they went to sleep, so one is apt to fall into rhetoric.' But he admitted it was an interesting and challenging experiment, 'full of new difficulties, and I shall be the better, I think, for the change.'

Many of those difficulties were inherent in the material itself, for the tale of Deirdre and the Sons of Usnach was the most familiar of all legends of the heroic cycle of Cuchulain and the Red Branch. Although manuscripts might differ in details, the general outline, the beginning and the end, were well known and the facts with which Synge worked were common to most versions. Even before Deirdre was born it was prophesied, so the story goes, that she would grow to be of great beauty and thereby cause the ruin of Ulster, the downfall of the House of Usna, and the death of many men. Hearing this, the High King Conchubor took her for his ward and placed her in a secluded place in the charge of a nurse and a tutor; but before he could claim Deirdre as his bride, she met Naisi and persuaded him to elope with her. The lovers, accompanied by Naisi's brothers Ainnle and Ardan, fled to Scotland where they took service with the King and won great honour by their feats of valour. Eventually they were found by Fergus, who as Conchubor's emissary brought pledges of forgiveness and a safe return to their beloved Ireland. Naisi, despite Deirdre's dreams foretelling disaster, agreed to return, but Conchubor had arranged to separate Fergus from his charges. With the help of magic, Naisi and his brothers were killed; Fergus sought revenge by pillaging and burning Emain, the seat of kings for many generations; and Deirdre, having fulfilled her unhappy prophecy, killed herself.[8]

But the problem remained : how to express the reality of this well-used myth 'in a comprehensive and natural form'? Yeats had chosen to concentrate on the last scene of the drama, using a chorus of musicians to explain events of the past and illuminate Conchubor's treachery. His two proud lovers remain frozen in their eagle-like passion until released by death. Synge followed Æ's earlier example and wrote his play in three acts, but with none of Æ's mysticism or unconscious bathos ('Thou art the light of the Ultonians, Naisi,' intones the druidess Lavarcham, 'but thou art not the star of knowledge.') From the beginning, although their story is foretold, Synge's characters remain true to their own natures; the action is the result of strong personalities clashing because they cannot do otherwise and still be themselves. Although he retained a hint of mysticism until very late drafts, eventually he rejected all dependence on prophecy or premonition; similarly the Sons of Usna meet their death not through druidic incantations but because they are tricked and outnumbered. But Synge's greatest originality remains the blending of theme and character, the shifting of emphasis and climax, in keeping with his developed theory of art and drama. He would not be satisfied until all was strengthened, 'made personal,' simple, intense, charged with his own vision of the world. In this experiment 'chiefly to change [his] hand,' he moves from the bright sunlit world of comedy and the melodramatic exaggeration necessary for the vividness of the amoral, to the moonlit world of tragedy and the patient anatomization of passion against a stark background of death and time. He wrote in his notebook, 'Sudden in the romance writer a real voice seems to speak out of their golden and burning moods, it is then they are greatest.'[9] He sought this same greatness in his dramatization of the saga of Deirdre of the Sorrows.

Synge completed his first draft of the play in November 1907. The ninth and final draft of Act I was completed four months later; but Act III, which ran to eleven drafts, was not in a finished state until mid-January 1909, and the second act was still unsatisfactory in its fifteenth draft, when Synge entered Elpis Nursing Home for the last time. During the fifteen months he was at work on the play there were many interruptions, but all contributed to his development of the story: theatre responsibilities — directing, managing, and coaching — made him more aware of heightened dramatic effect; publication of his poetry forced him to clarify further his thoughts on language and the artist; bouts of illness sharpened his sense of the beauty of this world and the urgent need to 'play all the stops'; comradeship with Molly intensified his belief in the purity of the passions; his mother's final illness served to remind him of the untidiness of a lingering old age and the reality of death. It is always intriguing to contemplate what might have been, but even in its unfinished state, with additional help from the notebook drafts, it is possible to see how closely Synge wove themes developed out of his personal view of the world through the framework of the established myth and, beyond the established text, to glimpse the shadowy pattern of the planned masterpiece. Had he lived to complete the play I believe it would have retained the same shape, but colour and theme would have been infinitely enriched through character and mood, the lyrical romanticism balanced by a tough fibre of the grotesque.

As it now stands, *Deirdre of the Sorrows* is a twilight play, beginning in the darkness of storm clouds and ending in the stillness of death.[10] Twilight for Synge, especially in Ireland, was a time filled with 'vague but passionate anguish,' when 'moments of supreme beauty and distinction' are possible, tinged with suggestions of death and loneliness. On such a night an ageing king will feel conscious of empty days and time passing, a young princess will become aware of her destiny, joyous young princes of their moment of triumph. It is the romantic hero Naisi who voices the tension already evoked by the forces of nature: 'At your age you should know there are nights when a king like Conchubor would spit upon his arm ring and queens will stick their tongues out at the rising moon. We're that way this night, and it's not wine we're asking only . . .' Distant thunder and threat of the worst storm in years are an appropriate background to the rare moment when the young child of nature sheds the duns and greys of her peasant world, lays aside nuts and twigs from the hillside, to don the jewels and robes and destiny of a queen. For Deirdre will be no ordinary queen, one rather who will be 'a master, taking her own choice and making a stir to the edges of the seas.' A woman of her like cannot deny the natural impulses within her, must in fact reach out and grasp what is hers, 'the way if there were no warnings told about her you'd see troubles coming.' She dreads Emain, the Dun of an ageing High King, because it is an unnatural resting place for one who has learned to be at one with the woods, the birds, the rivers, sun and moon. The threat of death holds less fear, being a natural part of nature's law; 'All men have age coming and great ruin in the end.' Just as nature has schooled Deirdre in the wisdom of time, so nature unites the two lovers: 'By the sun and moon and the whole earth, I wed Deirdre to Naisi . . . May the air bless you, and water and the wind, the sea, and all the hours of the sun and moon.' It is significant that Lavarcham, learned wise woman that she is, cannot wed them; she is committed to the rule of the High King, who is at war with time, careless of nature, and ambiguous in his feelings towards Deirdre. It is Ainnle, 'who has been with wise men and knows their ways,' yet is fellow huntsman and comrade-in-arms to Naisi, who performs the ceremony and thus initiates the Fate of the Children of Usna.

Seven years in Alban are happy and bright, with love as pleasing as 'the same sun throwing light across the branches at the dawn of day.' But it is at the beginning of the darkness of winter that the lovers choose to leave, 'the time the sun has a low place, and the moon has her mastery in a dark sky.' Twilight now is the foreshadowing of death and the end of love: 'It's this hour we're between the daytime and a night where there is sleep forever.' Earlier the woods promised fulfilment of love; now they deny hope of safety, for independently both lovers confess their awareness that in the course of nature nothing can stand still. 'There are as many ways to wither love as there are stars in a night of Samhain, but there is no way to keep life or love with it a short space only.' The quiet woods below Emain Macha hide the promised grave, open to receive them 'on a dark night.' When Deirdre at last mourns the death of Naisi and prepares for her own death, she bequeathes the strange dignity of her loneliness to the little moon of Alban, left 'pacing the woods beyond Glen Laid, looking every place for Deirdre and Naisi, the two lovers who slept so sweetly with each other.' Lavarcham's final speech underscores this sympathy with the natural world, but at the same time assures the permanence of a universe in which their story can be told forever: 'Deirdre is dead, and Naisi is dead, and if the oaks and stars could die for sorrow it's a dark sky and a hard and naked earth we'd have this night in Emain.'

Against this background of the natural passage of time, Deirdre and Naisi's decision to return to Emain becomes much more significant and meaningful. Just as they had earlier chosen life in the woods and exile from Ireland, now they choose to accept the harsh facts of nature and go gladly forward to meet fate in an effort to retain the fullness and freshness of their love. 'Isn't it a better thing to be following on to a near death, than to be bending the head down, and dragging with the feet, and seeing one day a blight showing upon love where it is sweet and tender?' For seven years they have had perfection of love and comradeship; but the dread of the natural course of life and love, heretofore unspoken, has now fallen like a shadow across that perfection of passion. Unlike Lavarcham, who speaks for the unfolding of the full course of nature, they prefer to cut their time short. Nor do they wish to fight off or distort the true course of nature like Conchubor, who sees Deirdre as surety against old age and death, or Owen, who attempts to seduce Deirdre from her natural mate. But their decision has far-reaching implications, for Ainnle and Ardan, who have been satisfied with comradeship and fraternal loyalty, are pulled along with them; 'four white bodies' will share the grave chosen by Deirdre and opened by Conchubor.

But if the lovers' decision prepares the way for joy and triumph in myth, where love reigns supreme over death, it introduces a contrasting leitmotif, the pain of love in the real world, with the ultimate irony of the grave's victory. As the moment of nature's perfection can never be isolated, so the dream of perfect love in this life proves impossible. The climax of their story occurs not in Act II, at the decision to return to Emain—that is a continuation of their acknowledgment of the inexorable laws of nature—, but here in Act III at the edge of the grave prepared for Naisi by Conchubor. Panicking at the realization of what they must lose to retain their place in the saga, Deirdre reneges on that pact in the woods and seeks an unnatural compromise with Conchubor. She pleads for the very right to age and withering mortality that she had earlier rejected: 'I'll say so near that grave we seem three lonesome people, and by a new made grave there's no man will keep brooding on a woman's lips, or on the man he hates. It's not long till your own grave will be dug in Emain and you'd go down to it more easy if you'd let call Ainnle and Ardan, the way we'd have a supper all together, and fill that grave, and you'll be well pleased from this out having four new friends the like of us in Emain.' But it is too late, for Conchubor is helpless to break the chain of events earlier forged by the two lovers; Ainnle and Ardan are attacked. Now Deirdre, for the first time, forces Naisi to choose between his brothers in battle and complete absorption in her love. Because he can no longer follow his whole nature (foreshadowed in the brothers' quarrel at the end of Act II), Naisi breaks under the strain and bitterness erupts, cracking the perfection he and Deirdre had risked everything to attain. Hurt by the threat of loss, the lovers quarrel and in a stroke of painful irony lose the safety of the grave.

But Naisi's death in the shadow of Deirdre's mockery heightens his role at the end of the play; Deirdre's grief is intensified by the memory of their quarrel: 'It was my words without pity gave Naisi a death will have no match until the ends of life and time.' The story told forever threatens to be one of pain, not comfort; not only have they lost their love—their own choice—but they have lost their triumph as well, and Deirdre is left truly desolate. The only way to retain the fullness of their story and thus preserve their love is for Deirdre to grow even further in stature, until Conchubor becomes 'an old man and a fool only,' and a greater High King, Death, marks her for his own. To regain a sense of her own strength and retrieve the dignity of her loss, she must turn her thoughts back from this night 'that's pitiful for want of pity' to the splendour of their life in the woods. Her lament must embrace not only the glory of the past but also the future, where palaces fit for queens and armies become again the haunts of weasels and wild cats, crying on a lonely wall below a careless moon. Finally, sorrow itself must be cast aside to make room for the cold pity of prophecy and the impersonal triumph of the myth. Only then, by giving up all claims to this world, can Deirdre be assured of her joy with Naisi forever. Exulting in her loneliness, she stands imperious and triumphant over the grave of the Sons of Usna, free at last of all demands both of man and time itself:

> I have put away sorrow like a shoe that is worn out and muddy, for it is I have had a life that will be envied by great companies. It was not by a low birth I made kings uneasy, and they sitting in the halls of Emain. It was not a low thing to be chosen by Conchubor, who was wise, and Naisi had no match for bravery . . . It is not a small thing to be rid of grey hairs and the loosening of the teeth . . . It was the choice of lives we had in the clear woods, and in the grave we're safe surely.

Not only do the characters represent various stages on the spectrum of choice and reaction to time, they also indicate the full range of the passions of love and loneliness. While on Aran Synge had observed the simplicity of primitive man's judgment, 'that a man will not do wrong unless he is under the influence of a passion which is as irresponsible as a storm on the sea.' Now, using material 'filled with the oldest passions of the world,' he set out to construct through his various characters a chord which would sound all the notes of love and longing, ranging from Naisi's romantic defiance of destiny to Lavarcham's wise acceptance of the passing of love. In contrast to the character development of his comedies, here he must start with persons already fully developed, infinitely themselves, 'types' in a special sense. It might not be too fanciful, in fact, to trace this simplification of character and emphasis on individual ruling passions back to his earlier studies of music and French literature. The currents or leitmotifs of destiny (as well as the consuming fire at the conclusion) are expressed in a grand Wagnerian manner, while the starkness and grandeur of passion and the inevitability of its consequence are reminiscent of French classical theatre, in particular the dramas of Racine.[11]

When he reviewed Lady Gregory's *Cuchulain of Muirthemne,* Synge remarked,

> Everywhere wildness and vigour are blended in a strange way with impetuous tenderness, and with the vague misgivings that are peculiar to primitive men. Most of the moods and actions that are met with are more archaic than anything in the Homeric poems, yet a few features, such as the imperiousness and freedom of the women, seem to imply an intellectual advance beyond the period of Ulysses.[12]

Now in the character of Deirdre, written especially for Molly, he sought to convey the same imperious freedom, strength of will, and maturity of passion. The full responsibility of action rests finally on Deirdre alone; the intensity and purity of her love must be above question, and matched by greatness of soul in both herself and her lover. But Deirdre must also be sufficiently realistic to be 'probable,' perhaps like the young girl he admired on Aran: 'At one moment she is a simple peasant, at another she seems to be looking out at the world with a sense of prehistoric disillusion.'[13] By using nature not as atmospheric background only but as the living standard by which Deirdre determines her actions, Synge attempted to combine the present with the past and emphasize the inevitability of her decisions. The framework and scope of her personality are fully developed in the first act: although caught in the web of prophecy, she is eminently herself. Wild with the wildness of nature, she has spent her days on the hillside or alone in the woods, 'gathering new life . . . and taking her will.' It is 'wilfuller she's growing these two months or three,' Lavarcham complains to Conchubor, and Deirdre echoes the warning: 'I'm too long watching the days getting a great speed passing me by, I'm too long taking my will, and it's that way I'll be living always.' The 'like of her' is not for Conchubor, blind to the ways of nature, and careless of Deirdre's schooling in freedom, greedy for a comrade to ease the weight and terror of time. In place of nuts, twigs, birds and flowers, he offers her dogs with silver chains, white hounds, grey horses, symbols of the constraints of his role. However, Deirdre seeks not her opposite, but 'a mate who'd be her likeness,' whose high spirits will match her wildness, and who in the violence of youth will wrench love from its hiding place and taste 'what is best and richest if it's for a short space only.'

Like Deirdre, Naisi has been a long time in the woods and dreads neither death nor 'the troubles are foretold.' Challenged by Deirdre, he accepts his destiny, 'and it earned with richness would make the sun red with envy and he going up the heavens, and the moon pale and lonesome and she wasting away.' Perhaps he has more to lose, for he and his brothers have 'a short space only to be triumphant and brave.' A warrior as well as a hunter, he knows long before Deirdre the untidiness of death, 'a tale of blood, and broken bodies and the filth of the grave.' And in Act II, although Deirdre first voices her dread of the passing of love, 'wondering all times is it a game worth playing,' it is Naisi who acknowledges responsibility for that dread and tries to protect Deirdre from the advance of time. But after seven years the safety he offers in the woods is as ineffective as the security of Conchubor's High Chambers; reluctantly he must acknowledge the justness of Deirdre's decision to return. Just as Naisi had more to lose in their flight to Alban, now he has greater troubles to bear: the prophecy foretells the ruin of the Sons of Usna, while Deirdre's fate is left undetermined. He must carry with him the memory of their love and the bitter possibility of being superseded by another; and he stands to lose not only Deirdre's love but the perfect comradeship of his warrior brothers, a double loneliness in the grave.

On either side of the two young lovers stand Conchubor and Lavarcham, representing two aspects of love tempered by age. Again their characteristics are clearly identified in the first act. Lavarcham, wise in the ways both of man and the natural world, combines the function of chorus (in the Elizabethan sense) and the tolerance of age. She has taught Deirdre nature's lore and recognizes her pupil's affinity with the life of the woods: 'Birds go mating in the spring of the year, and ewes at the leaves' falling, but a young girl must have her lover in all the courses of the sun and moon.' Reminding us constantly of the troubles foretold, she recognizes also that Deirdre too has the right to a life of her own choosing. And it is she who counsels Conchubor, in vain, not to meddle where he has no natural right: 'Fools and kings and scholars are all one in a story with her like.' But in spite of her role as wise teacher, Lavarcham is vulnerable in her love for Deirdre: anxiety gives way to insolence and bitter anger when the sons of Usna discover Deirdre's hiding-place in Act I; grief at the prospect of Deirdre's sorrow in Act II forces her again to defy fate in a desperate attempt to keep the lovers in Alban. Owen tells us that Lavarcham too has had her share of love and happiness, but in contrast to Deirdre, she has chosen to accept the limitations of old age. 'There's little hurt getting old, saving when you're looking back, the way I'm looking this day, and seeing the young you have a love for breaking up their hearts with folly.' Yet there is room in her pity for Conchubor as well; it is she who remains at the end to mourn the deaths of Deirdre and Naisi, and to offer comfort to the broken, desolate old king.

Conchubor on the other hand refuses to accept age and its consequences. Defying the course of nature, he claims Deirdre for his bride although his role in her upbringing makes him more father than lover. In Act III he remains stubbornly tied to the remnants of passion, asserting again his unnatural right: 'It's little I care if she's white and worn, for it's I did rear her from a child should have a good right to meet and see her always.' Bewildered, he at last recognises he will never deserve the grief Deirdre holds for Naisi, and having lost the right to both love and kingship in his last desperate fight against time, he is led away by Deirdre's old nurse, a pathetic, broken old man. 'There's things a king can't have . . .'

Where Ainnle and Ardan give support to Naisi's role as hunter and warrior and through Naisi's desertion of them highlight the relationship between the two lovers, Fergus gives support to Conchubor's cause and shares in Conchubor's blindness. In Act II he too speaks from the vantage point of age and serves to underline one other aspect of the natural world—love of one's country. But his early arguments originate in the alien society of Conchubor's world as opposed to the universe of the lovers: he emphasises the loneliness of the exile's lot, especially with encroaching old age and separation from their children; he mocks the warrior brothers for paying heed to 'a timid woman'; he taunts Deirdre, 'It's a poor thing to see a queen so lonesome and afraid.' When traditional eloquence will not suffice, he turns to

Naisi with more success, voicing the threat of love-weariness. But Fergus makes no impressive impact on the two lovers; their decision is made on grounds beyond his understanding, and his role remains that of emissary until the third act. Even then, as avenger against Conchubor's treachery, his reasoning comes from the world Naisi and Deirdre had rejected seven years earlier, his final lament reminding us only that neither force nor love can halt the passage of time and the inevitability of fate.

Conchubor's folly arises out of ignorance; alone and defeated, he deserves our pity at the end. But with Conchubor sole rival to Naisi the spectrum of love was not complete, nor despite the omnipresence of death was the reality of love sufficiently rooted in the clay and the worms. Almost desperately, Synge sought for a foil to Conchubor, for another aspect of the distortion of love. At first he contemplated developing Ainnle's role so that he became his brother's rival, but that would upset the delicate balance he had achieved through the lovers' quarrel. A harsher, grotesque element was necessary, underscoring the ugliness of time and the violence of unfulfilled, unseemly passion. Finally he introduced Owen, the ragged, wild messenger of Act II who rudely and brusquely reminds Deirdre of the passing of time and inevitability of old age. Coldly rejected by Deirdre, he returns to startle Naisi and finally commits suicide as first casualty of Deirdre's beauty. Synge died before he could work Owen fully into the fabric of his play, but from his notebooks and Yeats's diaries it is possible to ascertain the role this grotesque figure was to carry. In Act I, Yeats reported, 'He was to come in with Conchubor, carrying some of his belongings, and afterwards at the end of the act to return for a forgotten knife—just enough to make it possible to use him in Act II'. 'When Owen killed himself in the second act, he was to have done it with Conchubor's knife.'[14] Synge therefore intended Owen to serve as spy for Conchubor and, succumbing to the fatal charm of Deirdre, thus serve as contrast also to Conchubor's other servants, Lavarcham and Fergus. But here passion exceeds all restraint and form, introducing an entirely new note and emphasising a different kind of loneliness. For Owen is an outsider, the freak or madman of nature, perhaps the fool. He may have his origin in Trendorn of the early saga, the stranger hired by Conchubor to kill Naisi; like Trendorn, Owen hates Naisi because Naisi killed his father. He has some affinity also with the tramp of Synge's earlier plays, especially Patch Darcy, the herd of *The Shadow of the Glen* who runs mad in the hills from loneliness. But in *The Aran Islands* we can find further clues. Standing on the shore of the south island Synge noticed among the crowd 'several men of the ragged, humorous type that was once thought to represent the real peasant of Ireland . . . there was something nearly appalling in the shrieks of laughter kept up by one of these individuals, a man of extraordinary ugliness and wit.' Commenting on 'this half-sensual ecstasy of laughter,' he reasoned,

> Perhaps a man must have a sense of intimate misery . . . before he can set himself to jeer and mock at the world. These strange men with receding foreheads, high cheek-bones, and ungovernable eyes seem to represent some old type found on these few acres at the extreme border of Europe, where it is only in wild jests and laughter that they can express their loneliness and desolation.[15]

Here I believe we have the source for Owen's disjointed passion, his wild fits of laughter and sudden action, perhaps even for the folly of his hopeless love for Deirdre. Had Synge finished the play, Owen would perhaps have taken on also more of the character of the Elizabethan fool, who speaks in riddles of great sense and carries with him a haunting reminiscence of another world. But here, in his unfinished state, Owen tells Deirdre nothing she does not already know, nor does the grotesqueness of his imagery rouse in her anything but momentary contempt and a slight uneasiness at the vehemence of his tone. Owen's impact is directed instead towards the audience, lest they overlook the seriousness of Deirdre's earlier confession to Lavarcham, require further assurance of the perfection of the love Deirdre and Naisi have shared for seven years, or seek to identify a climax of action too early in the play. The reality of old age is already a threat to Deirdre, but we may not have grasped its full horror: 'Well go take your choice. Stay here and rot with Naisi, or go to Conchubor in Emain. Conchubor's a swelling belly, and eyes falling down from his shining crown, Naisi should be stale and weary.' And, in contrast to the lonesomeness of happiness fulfilled, there is the loneliness of love unfulfilled: 'It's a poor thing to be so lonesome you'd squeeze kisses on a cur dog's nose.'

There is something more terrible in this mad folly than in the mistaken folly of Conchubor's solitude. Love can also lead to madness and an undignified death.

Deirdre of the Sorrows was, Synge had claimed, chiefly an experiment to change his hand. In the range of character, depth of passion, and evocation of atmosphere, the play even in its unfinished state proved once again the originality of his genius. At the same time, however, he remained true in treatment of subject and development of theme to the task he originally set himself. As early as April 1904 he had written to Frank Fay, 'The whole interest of our movement is that our little plays try to be literature first—i.e. to be personal, sincere, and beautiful—and drama afterwards.' And a later jotting in his notebook unconsciously traces his own development as a dramatist: 'Dramatic art is first of all a childish art—a reproduction of external experience—without form or philosophy; then after a lyrical interval we have it as mature drama dealing with the deeper truth of general life in a perfect form and with mature philosophy.'[16] It would be naïve not to recognise that the pathos of *Deirdre of the Sorrows* is intensified by our knowledge that while Synge was here celebrating both his love and his mature art he was himself close to death. But pathos should not block our awareness of the artistry behind the play, the careful blending of all the notes celebrating love and the glories of the natural world, 'the rich joy found only in what is superb and wild in reality.' Perhaps the greatest irony lies in our realization that, like the two lovers who just missed perfection of life and love, the artist did not quite achieve perfection of the work. *Deirdre of the Sorrows* remains a superb fragment, a lyric tragedy, in the words of Una Ellis-Fermor, 'nobly planned and all but greatly carried out.'[17]

NOTES

1 All quotations concerning Synge's comments on *The Playboy of the Western World* and the writing of *Deirdre of the Sorrows* are taken from my introduction to *J. M. Synge Plays Book II* (Oxford University Press, 1968).

2 From a letter dated April 1902 in the possession of Major Richard Gregory.

3 See *J. M. Synge Prose,* ed. Alan Price (Oxford University Press, 1966), p. 371; all quotations from Synge's letters to Molly are taken from *Letters to Molly: J. M. Synge to Maire O'Neill,* ed. Ann Saddlemyer, (Belknap Press of Harvard University Press, 1971).

4 In a letter to Stephen MacKenna, January 1904, Synge rejected the concept of 'a purely fantastic unmodern, ideal, breezy, springdayish, Cuchulainoid National Theatre,' describing a recent production of Yeats's *The Shadowy Waters* as 'the most *distressing* failure the mind can imagine', see 'Synge to MacKenna: The Mature Years', *Massachusetts Review* (Winter 1964). p. 281. He wrote of Yeats to Molly on 21 August 1907: 'I saw a book copy of *Deirdre* at Roberts' yesterday at 3/6. There is an extraordinary note at the end giving a page of the play that he had cut out, and then found that it was necessary after all. He makes himself ridiculous sometimes.'

5 This draft occurs on the back of an unfinished letter to Agnes Tobin dated 8 March 1907; for the final version of 'Queens' see *J.M. Synge Poems,* ed. Robin Skelton (Oxford University Press, 1962), p. 34.

6 See *Plays Book II,* pp. 393-94, for the complete essay.

7 I have traced the development of Synge's aesthetic theory in 'Art, Nature and the Prepared Personality: A Reading of *The Aran Islands* and Related Writings,' to be published in 1971 in *Sunshine and the Moon's Delight* a volume of centenary essays edited by Suheil Bushrui and published by Colin Smythe. Two quotations from Synge's notebooks are of particular interest here: *Prose,* p. 35: 'All art that is not conceived by a soul in harmony with some mood of the earth is without value, and unless we are able to produce a myth more beautiful than nature — holding in itself a spiritual grace beyond and through the earthly — it is better to be silent.' *Prose,* p. 14: 'A cycle of experience is the only definite unity, and when all has been passed through and every joy and pain has been resolved in one passion of relief, the only rest that can follow is in the dissolution of the person.'

8 In addition to Lady Gregory's and Leahy's translations of the cycle, Synge was also familiar with a manuscript written about 1740 by Andrew MacCruitin, and published in 1898 by the Society for the Preservation of the Irish Language; with the work done on the legend by his professor at the Sorbonne, H. d'Arbois de Jubainville and doubtless knew countless other recent translations, including the cantata by T. W. Rolleston and his friend the composer Michele Esposito. See Appendix C of Maurice Bourgeois, *John Millington Synge and the Irish Theatre* (London: Constable, 1913), Adelaide Duncan Estill,

The Sources of Synge (Folcroft Press, 1969), pp. 34-41, and Herbert V. Fackler's article on the Deirdre legend in *Eire-Ireland* (Winter 1969), pp. 56-63.

9 Notebook 47, in the possession of Trinity College Dublin.

10 William Empson in *Seven Types of Ambiguity* (London: Chatto and Windus, 1947), pp. 38-42, traces the imagery of the storm and the grave throughout the play.

11 As early as *Riders to the Sea,* Synge developed his themes musically; this can be seen more clearly in his later scenarios where 'current' or 'motif' is paralleled by character development and plot. Synge tended to choose examples from Elizabethan and French classical dramatists; there are among his papers scene analyses of both *l'Avare and Phèdre,* and he attended lectures on French literature by Petit de Julleville, whose monumental *Histoire du Théâtre en France* he knew well. Synge also acted as advisor for the Abbey Theatre productions of Lady Gregory's translations of Molière, even writing to the *Comédie Française* for copies of their prompt books.

12 See *Prose,* pp. 368-69, also his article 'La Vieille Littérature Irlandaise', *ibid.,* pp. 352-55.

13 *Prose,* p. 114, also p. 143 note: 'They have wildness and humour and passion kept in continual subjection by their reverence for life and the sea that is inevitable in this place.'

14 W. B. Yeats, *Autobiographies* (London: Macmillan, 1955), p. 457 and Yeats's Preface to the published play, *Plays Book II,* p. 179.

15 *Prose,* pp. 140-42.

16 See *Plays Book I,* p. xxvii and *Prose,* p. 350.

17 'John Millington Synge', *The Oxford Companion to the Theatre,* 3rd ed. (London: Oxford University Press, 1967), p. 931.

VII: THE PROSE OF JOHN MILLINGTON SYNGE

T. R. HENN

I

It is not easy, at this point of time in the Twentieth Century, to say much that is meaningful about prose style. If we are historians or teachers of literature we can make some show of recognising and cataloguing the great traditional styles. We know the mannered and formal complexity of Euphuism, the so-called Senecan and Ciceronian styles of the Seventeenth Century, the cadenced Latinities of Sir Thomas Browne; the strength and simplicity of Swift; the urbanity of the 'model' Addison; the 'sweet reasonableness' of Goldsmith. The work of Dr. Johnson, Gibbon, Burke is signed as surely as is a picture by Raeburn or Gainsborough . . . We might prolong such a list indefinitely : weaving the threads back and forth between Sir Thomas More and Sir Walter Scott. It was once true to say, with Buffon, 'Le style c'est l'homme même' : the moral qualities of each writer stand out with some clarity against the background of the tradition, the civilization, in which they are set. We can as it were gesture towards their special qualities; at times we can even discourse about them with some effect. But we are left with the knowledge that there are no sharp critical tools available to us for the analysis of the technical qualities of prose. Saintsbury's great *History of English Prose Rhythms* has few readers today. Nor have I found that any writer on prosody sheds more than the palest of light on the nature of poetry; for all the vast bibliography of that subject.

As we look back on history we may think that there was a kind of fragmentation, as of a bomb bursting, in style as well as in certain qualities of the creative imagination : that becomes apparent in the first three decades of the Nineteenth Century. At the beginning of this period the majority of writers are still manipulating prose with leisure and a strong and graceful premeditation. They still have the power of controlling the sentence, and a concern both for decorum and good manners produces, in sentence and paragraph, patterns that seem to come full-moulded from the pen. Then individuality begins to reassert itself, and prose seems often to attempt to approximate to some of the emotional qualities proper to poetry; in Carlyle, in Ruskin, in the pre-Raphaelite work that so often is flavoured with 'the back-tolled bells' of the writers' medieval proclivities. The prose poem has indeed its temporary fashion at the end of the Century, and we can trace something of its incidence on the prose translations —often admirable—that Synge made of Petrarch and Villon.

Yet three Irishmen are working in a firmly-rooted tradition, marked by a concern for elaborate craftsmanship that can at times become precious. We remember Flaubert's saying, that a perfect sentence is the crowning achievement of mankind. The pages of *The Yellow Book* and *The Savoy* bear witness to this ideal. The doctrine received as it were a benediction from the work of Pater, to whom Yeats looked for his 'sacred book'; and it is from him, and particularly from *Marius the Epicurean,* that the prose style of the early and middle Yeats seems to derive. But the most carefully-wrought critical work of the period is to be found in Oscar Wilde, who is only now receiving his due consideration at the hands of scholars. The third writer is George Moore, once acclaimed as the greatest prose-stylist of his generation, and now almost forgotten in the twin whirligigs of taste and time. Perhaps he is one of those on whom the current fashion for sociological criticism has scattered its poppy.

II

We may turn now to Synge, and remind ourselves first of the traditional qualities of any prose style. *Prosus* means (as every schoolboy and journalist should know) a straightforward progress, a march without the returning patterns, in prosody or in linguistic energies, of verse. We should probably demand of it, above all things, adequacy : that is a vocabulary and control of vocabulary, fitted to deal with the subject propounded. Then there must be clarity, in which meaning is never obscured except for a definite purpose; variety, of which the main object is to keep alive the reader's attention; and 'pleasantness' which we should all recognize but be hard set to define, being a delicate and subtle compound. Our ideal prose should be economical. It should avoid the 'vices' which the Greek or Sicilian critic 'Longinus' found in the false 'sublime', and which Yeats considered to be the rhetoric which arises 'when the will tries to do the work of the imagination'. Among these vices is turgidity; tumidity (that which is hollow, swollen, pretentious) common to many journalists and politicians; and frigidity, that over-ingenuity in straining after effect, as in bad metaphysical verse, and in imitations of Joyce.

The organization, the patterning should in the main obey the logic and tradition of clause, sentence, paragraph as units of thought: it also contains a rhythmic element which should, in theory, correspond to the emotional pressure or activity that underlies it. We might (again in theory) construct a sort of graph in which this rhythmic content, and the emotional pressure, might seem to suggest points on some rising curve. On it would lie, say, *Henry V,* the debate on the responsibilities of kingship between Henry, Bates and Williams on the night before Agincourt, which is low tension; set against Mistress Quickly's great speech that describes the death of Falstaff. Towards the top of our curve we might set, for example, the Tramp's speech at the end of *The Shadow of the Glen;* Maurya's three speeches at the end of *Riders to the Sea;* Deirdre's defiance of old age and death. Yet when the curve is at its summit we seem to reach a level of consciousness where rhythmic intensity is no longer relevant, and we fall back on extreme simplicity which alone can bear and refract the pressures, can embody the authority of the greatest statements:

> . . . 'and immediately the cock crew.'
> . . . 'he then having received the sop went immediately out, and it was night.'
> 'Prithee, undo this button.'

Most famous of all, perhaps, is 'Longinus's' quotation from *Genesis:*

> 'Thus too the Lawgiver of the Jews, no common man, said—What did he say ?—'Let there be light, and there was light.'

III

I have lingered thus on the simple qualities of prose because I want to propose as it were a series of norms for Synge's use of language. Let us consider first his *Introduction* to *The Aran Islands:*

> 'In the pages that follow I have given a direct account of my life on the islands, and of what I met with among them, inventing nothing, and changing nothing that is essential.'[1]

This is a noble statement, and it has many precedents among the great writers. Like all good artists his narrative is selective. His unit is not the controlled paragraph, and its architectonics and his reflections on the life about him are desultory, almost in the nature of asides. For an example we might quote his version of the words of the old man who spoke with him on Kilronan:

> 'He went on to complain in curiously simple yet dignified language of the changes that have taken place here since he left the island to go to sea before the end of his childhood.
>
> ' "I have come back," he said "to live in a bit of a house with my sister. The island is not the same at all to what it was. It is little good I can get from the people who are in it now, and anything I have to give them they don't care to have." '[2]

This is utterly plain, direct, with three idiomatic usages, and a subtle cadence in the last sentence. Like most of his prose, but especially that major part which floats on the rhythms of the Gaelic, it has that slight but precise hesitancy with which Gaelic speakers—even if they are 'travelled men'—respect their second language. This is seen at its clearest in his translation of the poem *Rucard Mor*,[3] and in the letters which he received from his friends.[4]

Under the stress of the operation and the ether, this might have been written by de Quincey, and the mode is wholly foreign to Synge's normal usage:

> 'The next period I remember but vaguely. I seemed to traverse whole epochs of desolation and bliss. All secrets were open before me, and simple as the universe to its God. Now and then something recalled my physical life, and I smiled at what seemed a moment of sickly infancy. At other times I felt I might return to earth, and laughed aloud to think what a god I should be among men. For there could be no more terror in my life. I was a light, a joy.
>
> These earthly recollections were few and faint, for the rest I was in raptures I have no power to translate. At last clouds came over me again. My joy seemed slipping from my grasp, and at times I touched the memory of the operation as one

gropes for a forgotten dream . . .'[5]

Such psychedelic experiences are not uncommon, whether under anaesthesia or invoked by drugs. There are, perhaps, echoes of Wordsworth, Keats. Few have the discipline and sensitivity to record them with such honesty.

IV

There are certain subjects that move Synge strongly and which seem to me to act powerfully as determinants of his style. The 'pressure' behind his writing is perceptible, not in reliance upon 'poetic' patterning, but upon a carefully-wrought laconic structure, achieving its effects out of simplicity and, often, out of contrasting brush-work. Among those subjects of primary importance are his response to the moods of nature; which are adumbrated derivatively and without distinction in the *Poems*, but often with great subtlety and sensitivity in the prose.

One such example is his delineation of the muted and oppressive effect of fog and mist, familiar in the background of *In the Shadow of the Glen*:

> 'A week of sweeping fogs has passed over and given me a strange sense of exile and desolation. I walk round the island nearly every day, yet I can see nothing anywhere but a mass of wet rock, a strip of surf, and then a tumult of waves.
>
> The slaty limestone has grown black with the water that is dripping on it, and wherever I turn there is the same grey obsession twining and wreathing itself among the narrow fields, and the same wail from the wind that shrieks and whistles in the loose rubble of the walls.
>
> At first the people do not give much attention to the wilderness that is round them, but after a few days their voices sink in the kitchen, and their endless talk of pigs and cattle falls to the whisper of men who are telling stories in a haunted house.'[6]

There are notable things in this passage. The statement is even-toned, predominantly monosyllabic. It has a circular structure: *exile, desolation,* carry over through the *mournful* connotations of the limestone that has grown *black,* the *obsession* of the fog, the sounds of the winds, the *wilderness,* the *sinking* voices, the *haunted* house : even the *narrow* fields contribute to our sense of uneasiness, we notice the predominance of the words associated with death. But the whole is anchored to reality by the accuracy of observation; the *slaty* limestone, the talk of pigs and cattle in the kitchen, the dramatic structure brought back to earth and yet intensified, by that last clause. And we may remember Lady Gregory's description in *Poets and Dreamers :*

> 'When a sea-fog blots out the mainland for a day, a feeling grows that the island may have slipped anchor, and have drifted into unfamiliar seas.'

I have found it necessary to quote at some length to draw attention to these habitual patterns of Synge's thought. Here again is the brilliance of observation, the laconic tone, the melancholy, and the final touch of drama, suspended until the last sentence :

> 'The daylight still lingered but the heavy rain and a thick white cloud that had come down made everything unreal and dismal to an extraordinary degree. I went up a road where on one side I could see the trunks of beech trees reaching up wet and motionless with odd sighs and movements when a gust caught the valley—into a greyness overhead, where nothing could be distinguished. Between them there were masses of shadow, and masses of half-luminous fog with black branches across them. On the other side of the road flocks of sheep I could not see coughed and choked with sad gutteral noises in the shelter of the hedge, or rushed away through a gap when they felt the dog was near them. Above everything my ears were haunted by the dead heavy swish of the rain. When I came near the first village I heard a loud noise and commotion. Many cars and gigs were collected at the door of the public-house, and the bar was filled with men who were drinking and making a noise. Everything was dark and confused yet on one car I was able to make out the shadow of a coffin, strapped in the rain, with the body of Mary Kinsella.'[7]

Consider the brushwork, the calm use of contrast-values, in this passage; the literal accuracy of the word *commotion,* the sounds of the *coughing* sheep (potentially sinister, but so familiar on a sheep-farm) that appear again in *In the Shadow of the Glen.*

Again, Synge is waiting in a public-house at Kilronan for a reply to a telegram to Galway about the sailing of the steamer:

> 'The kitchen was filled with men sitting closely on long forms ranged in lines at each side of the fire. A wild-looking but beautiful girl was kneeling on the hearth talking loudly to the men, and a few natives of Inishmaan were hanging about the door, miserably drunk. At the end of the kitchen the bar was arranged, with a sort of alcove beside it, where some older men were playing cards. Overhead there were the open rafters, filled with turf and tobacco smoke.'[8]

This is vivid description, as of a Jack Yeats painting; the very smell and texture of the shebeen. Then follows what the medieval world would have called the *meditatio* upon it:

> 'This is the haunt so much dreaded by the women of the other islands, where the men linger with their money till they go out at last with reeling steps and are lost in the sound.' (Synge notes elsewhere that most of the fishermen met their deaths when drunk.) 'Without this background of empty curaghs, and bodies floating naked with the tide, there would be something almost absurd about the dissipation of this simple place where men sit, evening after evening, drinking bad whiskey and porter, and talking with endless repetition of fishing, and kelp, and of the sorrows of purgatory.'[9]

The words, only faintly coloured *(haunt, dreaded)* lead up to the shock of the last sentence; which confronts us, as it is meant to do, with Synge's observed blend of paganism and Christianity, of Horace and the drowned sailor, that underlies the life of the islands. Again there is the technique of the sudden unexpected drama of the final phrase.

V

Synge's morbid preoccupations are sufficiently apparent in the Plays and in the Poems. We may remember the astonishing passage in *The Aran Islands* where he describes the funeral,[10] and the digging up of an earlier grave (this I have seen)

> Some second ghest to entertain.

And he describes, with vivid imagination, his own fate if he should die on the island; hurriedly nailed up in a box and 'thrust into some wet crevice in the rocks.' The same thought occurs again in the poems. Many writers have been

> Half in love with easeful death

and those over whom some shadow of disease is hanging in their youth are those who have often dwelt upon it most lovingly in their despair. With Synge it comes near to being obsessional : the descriptions of hanging (so also Hardy and Housman; was it in the air in the 1890's, perhaps, because of *The Ballad of Reading Gaol ?)* and of the skeletons that a Mayo man saw in a Dublin church :[11]

> 'Every day some new morbid idea strikes through my brain like the thrust of a poisoned dagger. How long can it continue ? I have no delusion, no definite mania, yet I watch myself day and night with appalling apprehension.'[12]

The mood is translated into lyricism in his contemplation of Mutability, the loneliness of beauty that passes so swiftly, that perennial subject of all poets; and as we should expect it produces lyric prose of a kind that is not common in his prose writings. This is from *Vita Vecchia :*

> 'A week ago the lilacs flowered in the Luxembourg, but it rained yesterday and there is nothing left but a mass of withered petals. Do flowers mourn like women for their briefness ? In the Luxembourg I see also girls from eighteen to twenty in the blossom of their beauty, and women with a few babies who are withered.
>
> Are men durable by contrast? A young man cannot express; a man who has passed thirty is not able to experience. We go out among the woods and mountains and kiss the lips of girls in wild efforts to remember. We are less fortunate than women. The frailest suckling is robust beside the offspring we have borne in travail darker than a woman's, and all our honour and glory is in the shadow of a dream.'[13]

I have quoted this because it is of a type of prose unusual for Synge. There is indeed little in the thought that is new. We could trace almost every thought to Horace, the Psalms, Shakespeare, Montaigne, Herrick, Shirley, Marvell . . . and countless others.

But it is direct, sincere: and the final cliché is redeemed by the unusual '*in* the shadow.'

VI

Synge's passion for music, his mystical absorption in it, provides some of the best writing:

> 'I am trying to co-ordinate the inner life of this monk' (he has picked up by sheer accident a copy of the *Imitatio*)—'and my own inner life as a musician. It seems as I read him that his joy in its essence was identical with my own. As all thirst is quenched by liquid, so perhaps the inner longing of the personality is only assuaged by an ecstasy which is as multiform as the varieties of liquid, and exists as essentially in prayer as in the sound of the violin. Even in the preparatory discipline there is much that is similar in the saint's life and in the artist's.'[14]

But later he repudiates the saint: as Yeats did, with vacillation. Music remains. His response to it produces his most 'poetic' prose, with the mark of the Nineteenth Century Romantics indelibly impressed upon it:

> 'Symbols of things beyond my comprehension cloud through the waving of the inward light. Strange stars shine upon me with prophetic rays. Purple feathers float in my hands, and choral symphonies wind themselves about me. Two divine children haunt the twilight of my sleep: Are they souls that would create their lives in my passion for the Chouska?'[15]

These are matters of particular interest here. Coleridge or 'Æ' or Yeats would have understood the Neo-Platonism in the reference to the divine children waiting for re-birth; Synge may well have read MacKenna's *Plotinus*. Wordsworth (who is always close to him) would have understood the *waving* of the light, which seems to mingle with *The English Mail Coach*: the prose-rhythms are not unlike that of *Per Amica Silentia Lunae*.

His passionate absorption in his music is apparent in one of the dreams he suffered on Aran: which, he suggests, 'gives strength to the opinion that there is a psychic memory attached to certain neighbourhoods.'[16] Again, we may find traces of Plato's music, of Wordsworth, perhaps of *Kubla Khan*:

'Last night, after walking in a dream among buildings with a strangely intense light on them, I heard a faint rhythm of music beginning far away on some stringed instrument.

It came closer to me, gradually increasing in quickness and volume with an irresistibly definite progression. When it was quite near the sound began to move in my nerves and blood, and to urge me to dance with them.

I knew that if I yielded I would be carried away to some moment of terrible agony, so I struggled to remain quiet, holding my knees together with my hands.

The music increased continually, sounding like the strings of harps, tuned to a forgotten scale, and having a resonance as searching as the strings of the 'cello.

Then the luring excitement became more powerful than my will, and my limbs moved in spite of me.

In a moment I was swept away in a whirlwind of notes. My breath and my thoughts and every impulse of my body, became a form of the dance, till I could not distinguish between the instruments and the rhythm and my own person or consciousness.'[17]

VII

The best prose, which is subtly varied, is beyond doubt to be found in the descriptions of natural scenery. Let us examine some examples in differing kinds. The first works by deliberate brush-strokes :

'It has cleared, and the sun is shining with a luminous warmth that makes the whole island glisten with the splendour of a gem, and fills the sea and sky with a radiance of blue light.

I have come out to lie on the rocks where I have the black edge of the north island in front of me, Galway Bay, too blue almost to look at, on my right, the Atlantic on my left, a perpendicular cliff under my ankles, and over me innumerable gulls that chase each other in a white cirrus of wings.

A nest of hooded crows is somewhere near me, and one of the old birds is trying to drive me away by letting itself fall like a stone every few moments, from about forty yards above me to within reach of my hand.

> Gannets are passing up and down above the sound, swooping at times after a mackerel, and further off I can see a whole fleet of hookers coming out from Kilronan for a night's fishing in the deep water to the west.
>
> As I lie here hour after hour, I seem to enter into the wild pastimes of the cliff, and to become a companion of the cormorants and crows.'[18]

There are several things to be aware of here. The eye moves over the sea and landscape in a leisurely panoramic movement; and this is aided, as a matter of technique, by the use of very light punctuation. The cliff 'under my ankles'—we might have expected 'feet'—gives a sense of actuality; the 'white cirrus' of wings an unexpected precision of focus, with, perhaps, a submerged onomatopoeic assertion; as does the episode of the hooded crow. The eye moves over the scene in four stages, returning to the observer and his participation in the 'wild pastimes of the cliff'; these are the aerobatics, and the cries of the birds, which he develops in the next paragraph. In the phrase

> As I lie here hour after hour

we may think that our ear detects an echo of Browning's 'The Bishop Orders His Tomb in St. Praxed's.'

> 'As here I lie
> In this state-chamber, dying by degrees,
> Hours and long hours in the dead night, I ask
> Do I live, am I dead ?'

(The thought is twice repeated in the poem.) And certainly in the final cadence

> to become a companion of the cormorants and crows

there is a Biblical echo : perhaps a conflation of Job's

> I am a brother to dragons, and a companion to owls . . .[19]

with

> But the cormorant and the bittern shall possess it :
> the owl also and the raven shall dwell in it . . .[20]

Consider next a passage in which the sense of landscape images, as it were, with his sense of the community of the people :

'When night comes on after a day spent among these people one is faced again by questions no one can answer. All day in the sunshine in the glens where every leaf sparkles with peculiar lustre, and where air, foliage and water are filled with life, one has inevitable sympathy with vitality and with the people that unite in a rude way the old passions of the earth. Then twilight comes, and the mind is forced back to the so-called spiritual mood when we cry out with the saints. Often after these hot days I have spoken of a peculiar fog rises in the valleys of Wicklow so that the whole land seems to put [a] white virginal scarf about it to meet with the stars and night. Then through the mist lights come out in a few places from the cottages, and the [person] who knows their interiors . . . can [sense] the life of each separate group. How can one reconcile the often coarse liveliness of healthy men with the rapt mood that comes with the night ? It is one of the endless antinomies . . .[21]

Here are several facets of Synge's style and thought. The vocabulary is, as usual, sparse, monosyllabic, the sentences lightly-punctuated even to the point of ambiguity. There is a sense of the underlying paganism—'the old passions of the earth,' which is like that of 'Æ'—perhaps as in *The Earth Breath.* There is the tension, already apparent in the autobiographical writings, between belief and unbelief : the carefully-guarded reluctance of 'the mind is *forced back* to the *so-called spiritual mood*'. 'When we cry out with the saints' recalls his early reading of them, and his rejection, in Paris; but which underlines the tendency towards the mysticism which never left him. And this yearning is emphasised by the 'virginal' scarf of the mist, and the almost banal 'meet with the stars and night'.

Very often the descriptions of nature lead him to this sense of the numen of place. Again and again he returns to it : the common words are 'isolated', 'desolate', 'solitary'. This is the stuff out of which *In the Shadow* is made; in *Deirdre* it seems as if the Wicklow Glens are transported into Argyll. In the main the prose is simple; every so often we are brought up short by the precision of a single word.

We can throw some light on Synge's characteristic methods by comparing a piece of his prose with a somewhat similar passage from Yeats's early tale, *Dhoya.* Both concern a fight with a giant. Synge's is taken down from 'Old Pat' on Aran:

> 'He got up on to his feet and he caught the giant round the legs with his two arms, and he drove him down into the hard ground above his ankles, the way he was not able to free himself. Then the giant told him to do him no hurt, and gave him his magic rod, and told him to strike on the rock, and he would find his beautiful black horse, and his sword, and his fine suit.
>
> The young man struck the rock and it opened before him, and he found the beautiful black horse, and the giant's sword and the suit lying before him. He took out the sword alone, and he struck one blow with it and struck off the giant's head. Then he put back the sword into the rock, and went out again to his cattle, till it was time to drive them home to the farmer.'[22]

This is straight-forward disjunctive prose in the manner of Malory: it has hints of *Morte d'Arthur* as well as of *Sir Gawain and the Green Knight.* By contrast—

> 'For a long while they fought. The last vestige of sunset passed away and the stars came out. Underneath them the feet of Dhoya beat up the ground, but the feet of the other as he rushed hither and thither, matching his agility with the mortal's mighty strength, made neither shadow nor footstep on the sands. Dhoya was wounded, and growing weary a little, when the other leaped away, and, crouching down by the water, began: "You have carried away by some spell unknown the most beautiful of our bands—you who have neither laughter nor singing. Restore her, Dhoya, and go free". Dhoya answered him no word, and the other rose and again thrust at him with the spear. They fought to and fro upon the sands until the dawn touched with olive the distant sky, and then his anger-fit, long absent, fell on Dhoya, and he closed with his enemy and threw him, and put his knee on his chest and his hands on his throat, and would have crushed all life out of him, when lo! he held beneath his knee no more than a bundle of reeds.'[23]

The second passage is manièré prose, in the Pre-Raphaelite traditions, with repeated archaisms, inversions, and the nearly dead clichés of Nineteenth Century medievalism. The instances are too many to need quotation. By contrast the fairy tale from the Irish is simple and direct. Its 'flavour' from the Gaelic is pronounced, but never ostentatious, and derives as much from the tone and intonations as from the syntax. There is no attempt to write 'fine' prose; the vocabulary has something of the naiveté of the Scottish Ballads. We may note also the greater force of the first by contrasting two hyperboles:

> . . . 'he drove him down into the hard ground above his ankles'
> 'underneath them the feet of the Dhoya beat up the ground'

VIII

Synge's critical writing is limited in bulk and in intention. It rests mainly on the *Prefaces* to *The Playboy, The Tinker's Wedding* and the *Poems*. The second is in the nature of an apology, a plea for a sense of humour, an ability to understand and to relish the satire implicit in the play, which was for so long unactable in Ireland for reasons that are only too evident. The centre of his pleading is in the final paragraphs :

> 'Of the things which nourish the imagination humour is one of the most needful, and it is dangerous to limit or destroy it. Baudelaire calls laughter the greatest sign of the satanic element in man; and where a country loses its humour, as some towns in Ireland are doing, there will be morbidity of mind, as Baudelaire's mind was morbid.'[24]

The appeal was a vain one. Perhaps it is always so when nations consider that their national pride or morality has been offended. There are sufficient *exempla* in our own time : let Shaw, O'Casey, Joyce bear witness. The Ireland of the first decade of the Twentieth Century was peculiarly sensitive as to its reputation for sanctity, woman's chastity, and pride of its past. Yeats had laboured to build up its image by his invocation of history, of its archetypal imagery 'that marries us to rock and hill'; and, like 'Æ', extolled the ancient spirits of the high places.

Beyond that we have *The Playboy Preface.* This was another apologia for the extravagant language of what Yeats called 'that wild laughing thing', a defence of the phrases of the country-folk overheard and remembered, and heightened : as every dramatist must do. That language is to be 'rich and copious;' we remember Lady Gregory's attempt to censor some of the 'outrageous' phrases in *The Playboy.* It is a repetition of another attack (this Yeats also made) against Ibsen and Zola, their 'joyless and pallid words'. Synge is pleading for 'what is superb and wild in reality'. (It is not easy to explain, either to ourselves or to English readers, the overtones of the word *wild.)* 'In a good play every speech should be as fully flavoured as a nut or an apple' : he had found this richness in Aran, Wicklow, West Kerry, born out of the wealth of the Gaelic substratum that underlay the Elizabethan precision and profusion.

Of the prose preface to the *Poems* there is little to say. We may perceive the common tenets of the Romantic revival, and of its late flowering in the medievalism of William Morris. The 'timber' of poetry—is he thinking of Ben Jonson?—must have 'strong roots among the clay and the worms' . . . 'It may almost be said that before verse can be human again it must learn to be brutal'. So we can set 'The Haystack in the Floods' against 'Danny'; some of *The Princess* in contrast with the 'Queens' that derives from Villon. I believe that Yeats's later work is much influenced by this polarity : consider 'The Three Bushes', 'The Wild Old Wicked Man'. Synge's literary tact led him to perceive unerringly what was pretentious and false : witness his reviews of Fiona Macleod's *The Winged Destiny.*

> 'This style has met with a good deal of admiration, and, in many passages it has, there is no doubt, an elaborate music that can only be attained with a fine ear and a good command of the vocal elements of language. Yet unfortunately, while many of the sentences she delights in are so constructed that they can only be read slowly, their form and meaning do not satisfy when dwelt on.'[25]

And he proceeds to quote an instance of emotive sea-description which contrasts strongly with his own economical, even drab descriptions of the same subject.

IX

We may now consider his views on a highly controversial subject, that of the Irish language. He is almost alone among the major Irish writers in his competence to handle this theme: competent because of his knowledge of Irish and of the Irish people; competent also because he is a European, and has some command of three cultures which influenced his dramatic and lyrical art.

He is not a proponent of the Irish language as a universal solution to the problems of emergent Irish nationalism:

> 'Some of this new Irish work has very considerable value, but what, one cannot but ask, will be its influence on the culture of Ireland? Will the Gaelic stifle the English once more, or will the English stifle the new hope of the Gaels?
>
> The Gaelic League with the whole movement for language revival is so powerful that it is hard to think it will pass away without leaving a mark upon Ireland, yet its more definite hope seems quite certain to end in disappointment. No small island placed between two countries which speak the same language, like England and America, can hope to keep up a different tongue. English is likely to remain the language of Ireland, and no one, I think, need regret the likelihood. If Gaelic came back strongly from the West the feeling for English which the present generation has attained would be lost again, and in the best circumstances it is probable that Leinster and Ulster would take several centuries to assimilate Irish perfectly enough to make it a fit mode of expression for the finer emotions which now occupy literature.'[26]

However heterodox the sentiments they seem to have been approved by time. Synge's realistic view is echoed by Shaw; and, less vocally but practically, by the majority of writers. Synge is, like most great Irishmen, a co-inheritor of a European tradition as well as of the Irish one. He had the supreme advantage of tradition: not merely in the Irish that he had learnt in the hard and pure school of the spoken language, but in his contact, however perfunctory, with Breton culture. I do not think that we can better the list of his masters that he himself gives: Villon, Ronsard, Cervantes, the Pleiade; Petrarch and Dante: the great Elizabethans and Jacobeans; Burns, Wordsworth, Shelley; and some exposure (I use the word deliberately) to the work of his contemporaries in the 1890's. But he was too reserved, too proud, to own any master; and when he tried to use the Wordsworthian voice the failure was absolute. He had more in common, from the point of view of technique, with Villon, Ben Jonson, Burns.

X

Let us attempt, at this final stage, some kind of summary of Synge's achievement in prose : always excepting that of the Plays and the Translations.

As prose, it is informed, given shape, by Synge's own personality. Yeats's categorization of his qualities in *The Death of Synge* is, I think, substantially valid but by no means inclusive. He is the 'solitary man', the 'enquiring man'. We remember that the old Cumberland farmer once characterized Wordsworth as 'a desolate-minded mon, ye knaw' : he had watched the poet walking over the hills with his dejected family trailing behind him. So, in a common mood, Synge was 'desolate-minded'; the victim of his own preoccupation with death and corruption and violence; the victim—perhaps like most poets, and especially one of his favourites, Burns—of his own pity for the starving, the lonely, the oppressed. And indeed few places in Europe offered more opportunities for the study of those bound in the iron misery of poverty than the West of the 1890's. Today if we wished to stir the springs of sorrow we should perhaps consider an unpackaged tour of the peasantry of Southern Italy, Portugal, Spain.

Between pity for others and for himself he is torn between two great loves : that of music, which has the power for him of the most profound mystical experiences of rhythm, of order, of intermittent glimpses of a Platonic *phusis*. This music is integral with that other love, of country; of the many moods of the changing landscapes, of the drama of rain, fog and storm; of man's exaltation and loneliness in those dramatic settings.

Among—not 'between'—these antinomies the prose runs its course. Much of it, perhaps the greater part, is direct and wholly honest *reportage :* the recording in laconic, drab and wholly honest prose the impact of the life which (Yeats thought) no writer had yet chronicled. When the drama of some particular event appeals to his own sense of the theatre—for this is seldom wholly absent—he sets it down with unfailing tact and his own peculiar kind of power. We remember the descriptions of the Aran funeral, the Wicklow coffin, in the rain, outside the public house. The dialogue which he records are (to my ear) honest and 'unimproved' by that besetting temptation to give pattern to a reporter's language. Lady Gregory fell into this trap. Only in the occasional exactitude of a word, the rare cadence, does he show the artistry that is to give life and energy to the prose of the *Plays*. This is what we should expect of any dramatist: the heightening, selection, the imposition of pressure; the quest for 'the speech as fully flavoured as a nut or an apple'. We may, if we wish, pursue that metaphor to its depths; the fierce desire for 'the bright and glorious words', the 'high astounding terms,' of Spenser or of Marlowe.

Behind the mask of the prose we can perceive (as in the Plays) a quiet ironic observant temperament: that is aware of the burden of the mystery with an agonizing clearness. The vision is informed by a great and profound pity, only to be made bearable by that laughter which is so near to tragedy.

The pressure, the capacity of the spirit to be finely touched, is only intermittently apparent in the prose. He is moved by death and its pity; by music in many forms; by landscape; by the sense of the supra-natural, and above all the supra-natural of place. The evil thing in the night may be countered by the *De Profundis,* or by the steel of needle or knife. Strange presences—these too are Wordsworthian—haunt the hills; older than Christianity, and often perceived at the roots of the hair.

The common accusation, that he did not know the hidden Ireland, that he was in part inhibited by his inheritance and race, is, I think true. One would reply (if a reply were needed) that no single writer has succeeded, or ever will, in encompassing that immense and self-contradictory world. He himself realized this:

> 'In some ways these men and women seem strangely far away from me. They have the same emotions that I have, and the animals have, yet I cannot talk to them when there is much to say, more than to the dog that whines beside me in a mountain fog.'[27]

His achievement in prose was to be ruthlessly honest within

the limits, and the genius of his own personality. His vision included, as in the plays, the Shakespearean extremities of the life he had seen. It was a vision that was joyous, 'wild', extravagant, morbid, mocking. It is informed, given shape, by the interweaving of compassion and irony with a delicacy and integrity that is the reflection of his own complex personality.

NOTES

Except when stated otherwise all the references are to J. M. Synge Collected Works, Volume II (Prose), edited by Alan Price, Oxford University Press, 1966.

1 P. 47: 'The Aran Islands', Introduction.
2 P. 53: 'The Aran Islands, I'
3 P.172: 'The Aran Islands, IV'
4 Greene, D. H. and Stephens, E. M.: *J. M. Synge* New York, 1959. p. 102ff.
5 P. 42: 'Under Ether'
6 P. 72: 'The Aran Islands, I'
7 P. 192: *In Wicklow, West Kerry and Connemara:* 'An Autumn Night in the Hills'
8 P. 145: 'The Aran Islands, III'
9 *Ibid.*
10 P. 160ff: 'The Aran Islands, IV'
11 The church in question is St. Michan's.
12 P. 29: 'Etude Morbide'.
13 P. 23: 'Vita Vecchia'
14 P. 31: 'Etude Morbide'.
15 P. 34: 'Etude Morbide'.
16 P. 99: 'The Aran Islands, I'. This was also the opinion of Yeats.
17 Pp. 99-100: 'The Aran Islands, I'. We may recall Yeats's 'Among Schoolchildren':

> O body swayed to music, O brightening glance,
> How can we know the dancer from the dance?'

18 P. 73: 'The Aran Islands, I'
19 *Job:* 30:27
20 *Isaiah:* 14:11.
21 P. 199: *In Wicklow, West Kerry and Connemara:* 'People and Places'
22 P. 95: 'The Aran Islands, I'
23 W. B. Yeats, *John Sherman and Dhoya,* Ed. R. J. Finneran. Wayne University, 1967. (p. 121).
24 *Collected Works Vol. IV,* p. 3: Preface to *The Tinker's Wedding.*
25 P. 388: 'Reviews'
26 P. 385: 'The Old and the New in Ireland'
27 P. 113: 'The Aran Islands, II'

VIII: SYNGE'S POETIC USE OF LANGUAGE

SEAMUS DEANE

I would straightaway call attention to the title. My subject is not Synge's use of poetic language but his poetic use of language. The difference is important. To say a man uses language poetically is to say that he chose not to use it in some other way—e.g. scientifically. To say he uses a poetic language is to say that he chose not to use another *kind* of language—e.g. prosaic language. In other words, simply by shifting the word 'poetic' in this instance we reveal a shift in our attitude towards language itself. We are thinking of language as a matter of different modes of usage, or as a matter of different kinds of usage. If we think of it as a mode—i.e. of language as something we deploy in different ways for different purposes, we admit its subjectivity. As Roland Barthes has argued, no language is innocent.[1] We could paraphrase this further and say literary works are distinguished more by intent than by content. This is to a lesser degree true of all other forms of writing. Even the scientist who pretends to objectivity is simply using objectivity as a mode, a major device for the expression of what is in fact his own subjectivity. But if we take the other alternative, and say that we don't have different modes so much as we have different kinds of language, we leave ourselves in the rather puzzling situation in which certain arrangements of words are agreed to be prosaic and others to be poetic; and we differentiate between them by pointing out how ornamental one is, how lacking in ornament the other. But in the end, isn't it true that we must admit that lack of ornament is as deliberate a choice as the presence of ornament? The choice is for different kinds of device, but the notion of device is always present. No one is any closer to the 'real' than the other; each is artificial.

Insofar as these alternatives exist in our minds, to that extent we have adopted an attitude towards the nature, and, inevitably, the function of language. One attitude declares that Content is All—the language is the glass through which the object or experience is perceived. The cleaner the glass the more clearly perceived the object. That is, or has been until fairly recently, the scientific notion of language which displaced the old system of rhetoric. Rhetoric, as a university discipline, was grounded in the belief that language was an embodiment of truth and not a means towards the expression of a truth which exists in some other non-verbal realm.[2] The Biblical and the Classical traditions each in their different ways emphasise the intimacy between truth (or virtue) and eloquence. The various classical schemes for relating the cardinal virtues to the art of rhetoric are best exemplified in the story of the pilgrim soul arriving at the city of rhetoric and learning there about the cardinal virtues at the same time as he is learning eloquence, and from the same teacher.[3] And Isaac Rabinowitz has pointed out that Hebrew Scriptures were not meant as a means of transmitting ideas or feelings to their hearers, 'but to constitute the very factors and forces that determine and create reality.'[4] Where the scientist divorces language from truth, the old rhetoric insists on their indissolubility. So too does the new rhetoric which was so aggressively defended by the Romantics. Mallarmé has said in his own elliptic way that

> La Poésie est l'expression, par le langage humain ramené à son rhythme essentiel, du sens mystérieux des aspects de l'existence.[5]

The parenthetic phrase there looks back to Wordsworth and forward to Synge. Roman Jakobson supplies a more analytic comment on this attitude to language when he remarks that 'poetic language takes as its object, not its content, but its own form.'[6] Or, to come directly to Synge, in his Preface to *The Playboy of the Western World,* 'In a good play, every speech should be as fully flavoured as a nut or apple, and, such speeches cannot be written by anyone who works among people who have shut their lips on poetry.'[7] Speech for the sake of speech, yes; because 'words are our only good.' Truth exists insofar as it is spoken. Truth is therefore a matter of linguistic structure. Criticism is devoted to making the various kinds of structure intelligible.

A peculiar barrenness has afflicted the various investigations into the relation between thought and language. As L. S. Vygotsky has pointed out:

> . . . all the theories offered from antiquity to our time range between identification, or fusion, of thought and speech on the one hand, and their equally absolute, almost metaphysical disjunction and segregation on the other.[8]

Neither position is philosophically tenable. Worse, neither is particularly useful except in giving a certain polemical emphasis to a writer's theoretical stance. But what is useful in this respect to the writer is useless to the critic. If thought and speech are one, there is no problem of relationship. If they are totally independent, the same is true. Since they are neither, the need is to find a means of describing their relationship, not doctrinally, but as it manifests itself in practice. Vygotsky found a way out, via Piaget and Stern, in his concept of 'word meaning.'

For Vygotsky, recent advances in linguistics have been largely brought about by a concentration on the psychology rather than on the physiology of speech. This is indicated in the replacement of single sound by the phoneme as the unit of analysis. For the purposes of literary criticism, these linguistic methods can be applied with some tact and delicacy. It is obvious, for instance, that there are kinds of lyric poem in which the reader's attention will very properly and naturally dwell on the small phonemic variations which together help to form the poem's total pattern of sound and meaning. Equally, there are other kinds of poem, there are novels and plays in which the linguistic focus has to be lengthened to conform to the different demands for different kinds of proportion which each genre makes. In such cases, the basic unit of analysis will vary with the genre. In the case of a play, for example, I would think it inevitable that the morpheme rather than the phoneme be the smallest available unit for useful analysis. It is true that there are passages in any work which can be described in terms of their phonetic structure alone. Such a description is not always or even often illuminating since it may simply reduce the text to a number of discrete elements without acknowledging that the aura and resonance of the whole piece depends upon a combination of the affective and intellectual in a system of meaning the physiological basis of which, described as a system of sounds, does not help to explain its psychological force.

The psychological force of Synge's language is very largely determined by its self-conscious assertion of its own peculiarly stylised qualities in opposition to the utilitarian mode of language then prevalent in the theatre. The 'theatricalist' movement of the late nineteenth century included practitioners of poetic, expressionist and surrealist drama bonded together by their rejection of stage realism and by their advocacy of deliberately heightened forms of stylization in the theatre. Moredecai Gorelik gives this useful summary of their objections. We can see that Synge would have been in full sympathy with them :

> Do not bring on the stage your carcase of reality . . . Do not exhibit your vanloads of bricabrac, your butcher shops with real meat, your restaurant walls of cement and tile, your street paved with real cobblestones. These collections of materials do not tell us of the nature of the world : rather they confess your inability to define the nature of the world. If you really wish to give us an illusion of life, you must seize upon the essence of life. Forget the body; give us the soul.[10]

This is what Synge attempts for Irish life : a stylised representation of its inner essence in a drama of a new magnificence and splendour made possible by the existence of a society where, in Mallarmé's words, '. . . aurait sa place la gloire dont les gens semblent avoir perdu la notion.'[11] This notion of glory still existed in Ireland; it exhibited itself above all in the language of the peasantry.

So, we experience the works of Synge (or of any other writer) as language, not as a system of ideas or as a collection of themes. We read the language by first identifying the stance it has assumed towards its culture. If we have a culture which has espoused the scientific notion of language then a self-consciously literary language like Synge's has to be understood as assuming a revolutionary stance. He describes this very plainly in the *Playboy* preface. On the one hand we have language as joy and richness; on the other we have language 'dealing with the reality of life in joyless and pallid words.'[12] This is a basic opposition—Synge perceives that language can be dehydrated if it is thought of as medium rather than as its incarnation : the word made flesh. If we are to understand his language we must recognise this underlying tension, and recognize further how that tension creates a number of subsidiary binary oppositions which ramify throughout his work. We read the language by identifying the recurrent signs of opposition, and in doing so, we experience the conflict between them. Experience and language in a state of fission are transmuted by his effort into a state of fusion.

Ireland was particularly important to Synge because it retained the faith linguistically. In its oral Gaelic traditions it had preserved that joy in words which Europe seemed to him to have very largely lost. He perceived what Marshall McLuhan has since charted as a fact of twentieth century literature; that 'only people from backward oral areas had any resonance to inject into the language—the Yeatses, the Synges, the Joyces, Faulkners and Dylan Thomases.'[13] Synge recognised this; but he also recognised that a place like the Aran Islands epitomised the conflict between a native language of richness and joy and a cosmopolitan language of pallid joylessness—one fading, the other encroaching. His work is an assertion of the vitality, not of the Gaelic language as such, or any Anglo-Gaelic hybrid, but of the attitude towards the connexion between language and truth which characterised the Gaelic.

This brings us to the problem of the folk (or folksy) element in Synge's language. I think it pointless to argue about the presence or absence, the vulgarisation or the transcriptive accuracy in Synge's English of the Gaelic idioms and indeed of the Gaelic tales which he heard from the people among whom he lived. Folklore, committed to paper, is radically transformed, even if it is written down by a collector. The oral ceases, the written begins. The new context changes the function of the words. How much more deeply, then, is it transformed when an artist like Synge deploys it for his own particular purposes—especially when we remember that those purposes were revolutionary? He was going against the grain of his time. Pushkin had done something similar with Russian folk-tales and idioms. Again, to quote Roman Jakobson: 'A writer may create in opposition to his milieu, but in folklore such an intention is inconceivable.'[14] Synge's language is not stage-Irish; it is Irish language staged for polemical purposes which his Dublin audience totally misunderstood. The speech of the Irish peasants gave him a linguistic model for which he had been vainly searching in Paris, a model adaptable by virtue of its range and power to his own urgent sense of life. The model language was poetic in the sense already spoken of; it was Synge's achievement to use it for his own purposes by exploiting its own nature.

He used it, but he did not abuse it. For the joy implicit in that language was to him a sacred joy, just as Ireland became to him a sacred place. At one point in his *Autobiography,* speaking of his teenage loss of faith in Christianity, he says:

> Soon after I had relinguished the Kingdom of God I began to take a real interest in the kingdom of Ireland. My politics went round from a vigorous and unreasoning loyalty to a temperate Nationalism. Everything Irish became sacred.[15]

A glance at the page from which this quotation comes reveals a whole series of references which indicate the emergence of a personal language that was to find its social home in the language of the Irish peasantry. In a short space we have the following sequence of words: radiance, beauty, intangible glory, transfigured, pilgrim, divine ecstasy, puberty, primitive people, adoration, divinity, kingdom, God, Ireland, sacred, human, divine, goddess. Synge's personal language is innovatory and his search was for a public language with which it could fuse. Ferdinand de Saussure, the founder of the modern school of linguistics, speaks of this phenomenon in other terms; their relevance to Synge's case is striking. De Saussure spoke of this innovatory, private idiom as *la parole,* the public institutionalised language as *la langue* and the two together as forming *le langage.*[16] Synge's language can thus be understood as a merging of his own idiom of erotic joy and pagan ecstasy with the Gaelic tongue's long-learned capacity to embody such experiences.

It may perhaps be already clear how this intermarriage between the artist and his chosen society was going to produce a language tensed by oppositions. We have already noticed the opposition between joy and joylessness which Synge detailed; we can also see how that opposition breeds others. Anyone who reads *The Aran Islands* will quickly become aware of Synge's emphasis on the pagan quality of the people as it is expressed in sexual candour, stoicism, or in a nude and terrifying grief at the fact of death—all of these impressions reinforced by the antiquity of their stories, their rudimentary way of life, the exposure of the human to the natural forces of land and sea. This paganism has of course been overlaid by Christianity. So we have pagan energy expressing itself in a Christian idiom: the language of the peasants, redolent of the language of the great myths which a man like Pat Dirane relays to them, is braided in with the language of Christianity, producing a colourful combination in which, for example, pagan Irish idioms of respect for royalty, nobility and fame blend in with Catholic idioms of respect for sainthood, the Papacy and salvation. The language, in its richness, expresses a tension between two traditions; and again one can see how this public tension was characteristic of Synge's own private experiences. In the *Autobiography,* he describes how, at the age of ten, he wandered in the woods at Rathfarnham with his first girl friend, after hearing of the death of an aunt:

> The sense of death seems to have been only strong enough to evoke the full luxury of the woods. I have never been so happy. It is a feeling like this makes all primitive people inclined to merry making at a funeral.
>
> We were always primitive. We both understood all the facts of life and spoke of them without much hesitation but [with] a certain propriety that was decidedly wholesome. We talked of sexual matters with an indifferent and sometimes amused frankness that was identical with the attitudes of folk tales. We were both superstitious, and if we had been allowed, . . . we would have evolved a pantheistic scheme like that of all barbarians . . . The monotheistic doctrines seemed foreign to the real genius of childhood in spite of the rather maudlin appeal Christianity makes to little children . . .[17]

If we remember these two major oppositions in Synge's language, joy and joylessness, paganism and Christianity, we can find them suddenly crystallising in those of his poems which manage to avoid a wan derivative tone typical of the aesthete traditions to which most of them in fact belong. Take, for instance, the poem editorially titled *Abroad:*

> Some go to game, or pray in Rome
> I travel for my turning home
>
> For when I've been six months abroad
> Faith your kiss would brighten God!

This was written in 1908 and may, as Robin Skelton says, be a deliberate variation upon a Gaelic original which Frank O'Connor has translated thus:

> To go to Rome
>   Is little profit, endless pain;
>
> The master that you seek in Rome
>   You find at home, or seek in vain.[18]

Note that Synge has only retained the opposition between the rhymes Rome and home; otherwise his poem turns on a different axis. There is the opposition between 'Some' and 'I'; the opposition between 'game' and 'pray,' the different associations of these words linked by the similarity of their central vowel sounds; the opposition between simple 'go' and the more purposive 'travel,' one which is extended to the prepositions 'to,' 'in' and 'for' which are controlled by these verbs. 'For' emphasises the purposiveness of the movement of 'travel;' it arouses wider expectation which the final lines fulfill. The cross rhymes obviously confirm the oppositions—Rome/God, home/abroad; Rome is abroad, home is with God. But God is naturally associated with Rome; so 'God' is a religious term that has to be converted to the poem's secular purpose; this is done by the kiss (phonally anticipated in the precision of 'six') given the returned lover who uses the word God as a condescending metonomy for the world abroad, the world of Rome which he repudiates for the kiss. The condescension is amused: the word 'Faith' stands at the poem's heart, a pun embracing the secular and the sacred together. The poem is, then, a series of verbal pirouettes, some sexual and consonantal, some sacred and open vowelled. Taken together they form a total choreographic figure. That figure is the poem. We know it by its oppositions and balances.

The notion of God, the divine, brightened by the human, is one which Christy Mahon exploits in his courtship of Pegeen Mike. Synge has it in another poem, *Dread,* written between 1906 and 1908 in which the final line runs

> The Lord God's jealous of yourself and me.

And in the early sequence *Vita Vecchia,* written in 1896 and revised in 1907, we have the four line poem *In Dream:*

Again, again, I sinful see
    Thy face, as men who weep
Doomed by eternal Hell's decree
    Might meet their Christ in sleep.[19]

This once more is a love-poem, or a poem of lost love, in which the religious idiom is converted to secular purposes. The phonal basis of the poem is simple and effective; we have the homophonous words 'see, weep, decrees, sleep;' the soft alliteration of 'sinful see,' 'who weep,' harder alliterations of 'might meet,' 'doomed . . . decree' all creating a pattern which is suddenly entranced into unexpected shape by the voiced sibilant 'Christ.' The balance between opposites like 'I' and 'thy face,' 'men' and 'their Christ,' is struck suddenly so that the dream's private whisper, couched in the first and second person singular, is suddenly amplified into the poem's public language couched in the third person plural. So the dream of the beloved, lost love and moment of sleep are transposed to the public idiom of the beatific vision, hell and death. All are harmonized by the simile which poses an opposition between an 'I' and 'men,' and then resolves it. In the other poem, *Abroad,* 'I' and 'some' had the same function.

Even in poems as short as these we can see that Synge is fond of retarding the experience by sponsoring its opposite and then converting that opposite into a culmination. If we remember this principle of retardation is a governing device in his language then a great deal of its inversions and figurative delays can be understood as something more than stage-Irishry or untrained exuberance. When we turn to the plays the oppositions already noticed are heard in a more fully orchestrated language, written, as the dramatic form demands, for many voices, but audibly in one dominant key.

Synge's poetic use of language depends for its effects particularly in his plays, upon a system of verbal oppositions which recur periodically throughout a text. These oppositions are to be found rooted in certain base words or morphemes which then breed derivatives or allomorphs. In *The Playboy of the Western World,* for instance, the two basic words which form one part of the pattern of opposition are 'lone' and 'fear,' and all their allomorphs. The word 'lonesome' occurs as often as twenty-five times in the course of the play; 'fear,' 'fearing,' 'afeard' and 'fearless' occur almost as often, and almost always in the company of an only slightly less important morpheme 'dark' or its allomorph 'darkness' or its cousin 'night.' The orchestrations on these basic words are founded upon a natural connexion—lonesome-fear-dark-night. The orchestration can be understood as a series of variations upon a basic sentence pattern or what in transformational grammar is known as a kernel.[20] That basic pattern in Synge is a noun phrase plus a verb phrase plus a participial modifier. Shawn Keogh gives an early and simple example when he says 'It was a dark lonesome place to be hearing the like of him.'[20] Pegeen gives an orchestrated version, or, if you like, a transform of this basic pattern, when she says

> If I am a queer daughter, it's a queer father'd be leaving me lonesome these twelve hours of dark, and I piling turf with the dogs barking and the calves mooing, and my own teeth rattling with fear.[21]

The basic pattern is contained in the phrase, 'it's a queer father'd be leaving me lonesome;' the transform on that pattern is achieved by the four participial modifier clauses which bring us from one base word 'lonesome' to another 'fear.' We do not therefore simply have an idiom, a characteristic kind of language in Synge; we have also a characteristic structure of language. Further, we can notice the strength of the participial clauses because the main verb is so often a variant of the verb 'to be.' The frequency with which Synge begins a sentence with a phrase like 'It is,' 'It's,' 'It is not,' 'It's I,' 'It is not I,' or 'That is,' 'There is' lends to his language a certain ritual or, in Alan Price's word, 'liturgical'[23] quality. Each statement which begins in this assertive manner is invested with the grandeur of conviction, a conviction which is either amplified or modified by the inevitable participial clauses which follow. The conviction of the statement is extended by its being launched into a context which gives that conviction a continuity, a pathos and a landscape in which it can operate. To be lonesome is to hear the dogs barking, the cows mooing, etc. while one is piling turf. The word takes flesh, the morpheme begins to reverberate in a syntax carefully constructed to give full acoustic effect.

Yet, in *The Playboy,* I have so far only given one part of the dual pattern it possesses. The morphemes 'lone' and 'fear' which are cast in those sentence structures I have just tried to describe, are opposed throughout the drama by the morphemes 'decent' and 'sainted.' Each of these has its own genealogy—'Christian' and 'sacred' are the first cousins and the connection expands from them to include God, Pope, Cardinals, Bishops, Father Reilly, Justices of the Peace, peelers, police. We have, in other words, a social idiom set against an idiom of loneliness. Yet the oppositions stated initially in this form do not remain static. As the play progresses we begin to see the opposition resolved; and then after an intermediate resolution branch out again, but now with a renewed power and a different meaning. I am arguing therefore that it is precisely through the opposition between the basic morphemic units of the play that they each, in the end, suffer a semantic change. The change comes about in this way.

Lonesomeness and decency are not, as far as Christy Mahon is concerned, necessarily opposites. Decency indeed is what the lonesome man craves. Shawn Keogh and Christy, the two orphans in the play (even if they are orphans in different senses) have this much in common—they want to get married, settle down and be acknowledged in the social world. They want to leave the dark of anonymity and come into the light, even if only the turflight, of identity and respectability. This is a turning point in the play. In what way do their respective notions of decency differ? Pegeen has, of course, from the beginning made that difference plain. At an early point in the play she compares Shawn Keogh and the society generally to the great heroes there used to be in the past. Christy appears to her and, more belatedly, to himself, to be their reincarnation :

> . . . and I a proven hero in the end of all.[24]

Or again, this time to Pegeen :

'. . . you're setting me now to think if it's a poor thing to be lonesome, it's worse maybe to go mixing with the fools of earth.'[25]

Here lonesomeness rejects decency and respectability. The opposition which had appeared to be offering one as the alternative to the other is repudiated completely. Christy is at first involved in and finally transcends that opposition by his gift for language. And his gift for language is related to the fact that he is not an actual but a symbolic murderer. He transforms the actual into a myth. The real murderer in the play is the Widow

Quin, who killed her husband. She offers herself to Christy as an alternative to Pegeen. In doing so she reveals what the decent has to offer the lonesome. As the main figure in the play's sub-plot, a witch woman who nevertheless speaks the social language of shrewd materialism as against Christy's heraldic lyricism, she represents the obverse of decency which is notoriety. And notoriety, for an actual murder, is the provincial form of fame; and fame, for a symbolic murder which is a matter of words, is what Christy finally seeks and finds. So the progression of the play's key-terms, lonesome and decency, finally yields in the end to a semantic shift whereby the decent is identified with the anonymity which the lonesome had once known, and notoriety is rejected for the sake of fame. The contrapuntal rhythms of loneliness and decency define the village society : the speech of the villagers is caught between those two poles. The tension between them is resolved in terms of gossip and notoriety. Christy goes beyond the village sphere because he speaks a large mythic language of heroic deeds, a language which embraces the great wide vistas of the world beyond. When he first appears Michael James, Philly and Pegeen try to guess what terrible deed he has done; but their imaginations cannot rise to the occasion. Christy dismisses them peevishly. His imagination is already making a myth out of his action : 'You'd see the like of them stories on any little paper of a Munster town.'[26] Only Christy can get beyond the stock liturgical responses of the village speech to the point where the base words 'lonesome' and 'decent' begin to give way to the others—the others being 'wonder' and 'madness.' Wonders belong to the great world beyond; they are associated with travel and the exotically distant. Madness belongs to the village which is divorced from that world, a world represented for it primarily by Catholicism in its hierarchial, colourful aspects : Pegeen says to Shawn :

> It's a wonder Shawneen, the Holy Father'd be taking notice of the likes of you; for if I was him I wouldn't bother with this place where you'll meet none but Red Linahan, has a squint in his eye, and Patcheen, is lame in his heel, or the mad Mulrannies were driven from California and they lost in their wits. We're a queer lot these times to go troubling the Holy Father on his sacred seat.[27]

The world, envisaged as geography or history shrinks to provincial idiocy in the impoverished village frame. Shawn Keogh, of course, is completely subjugated by the notions and the language of respectability and decency. As regards the pagan past, he can only think of Father Reilly's 'small conceit' for heroes; and the Christian present centres itself in the dispensation Father Reilly is reputed to be receiving from Rome. Christy, on the other hand, subjugates the Christian idioms of respect to the purposes of his joyfully pagan love-making; despite their names he is less Christian and more pagan than Pegeen; religion is only a metaphor of human love; if he takes it literally it is to condescend to it. We noted this same feature in Synge's poetry:

> till I'd feel a kind of pity for the Lord God is all ages sitting lonesome in his golden chair.[29]

The base-word 'lonesome' is now related, not to darkness or fear, but to splendour and condescension. Christy's next outburst has the Christian mitred bishops and holy prophets peering through the bars of paradise for a glimpse of the pagan Lady Helen of Troy. Similarly, the word 'darkness' begins in the course of Christy's lovemaking to release itself from the binding oppositions which have trapped poor Shawn Keogh.

> ... and I abroad in the darkness spearing salmons in the Owen, or the Carrickmore.[30]

'Abroad' and the sonority of the exotic place names again identify Christy, as he identifies himself, with a world beyond the one in which the villagers, like Pegeen, are living. Christy's language opens out in a series of geographical, liturgical and historical references to the western worldly horizons of fame. Fame is the theme which swivels on the axis formed by anonymity and notoriety. It is the language of the poet-vagrant who speaks of travelling abroad in the dews of night while Shawn Keogh speaks of staying safely at home. The play's theme is incarnate in the language. Christy's emergence from the unreal opposition between lonesomeness and decency to the new world of wonder (which the village thinks of as madness) is the emergence of a Gaelic pagan myth hero from a Christianised, anglicised and therefore impoverished community. Lonesomeness is not finally a condition but a choice. Christy goes through a series of evolutionary mutations from the sub-human to the heroic; each stage of his evolution is marked by an intensification of language, and finally by the release of language from the oppositions which had compressed its force.

Synge is by no means extraordinary in his use of a rural or isolated community as a metaphor of vanishing value. This is an old romantic and even utopian tradition—Wordsworth and Hardy are two names that come readily to mind. Further, the Catholic idioms of Irish peasant speech, although they had their own uniqueness, were to be met with in different forms in the tradition of French literature represented in Synge's mind primarily by Baudelaire and Jean-Karl Huysmans in particular. The literary roots of his language and preoccupations are there—in the rural nostalgia of the English romantic tradition, the Catholic decadence, so-called, of the French tradition. The roots flowered in Irish air, because the Irish oral tradition was still sufficiently alive to give Synge's language the resonance of myth.

The County Mayo village which was briefly paganized by Christy Mahon loses its myth and its joy—as Pegeen too late realizes—because it clung too slavishly to Christianity and fact. The elaboration of the language is such that we can see various triadic movements operating on a number of levels—anonymity via notoriety to fame, Christianity via superstition to pagan myth, loneliness via decency to triumphal wonder, flight via stability to chosen vagrancy. All of these facets of the play swing into view as it turns on its central linguistic axis.

This is even more clearly true of the short play, *In the Shadow of the Glen.* All of Synge's dramas involve a transformation in which the infinite nature of human desire, confronted with the finite nature of reality, converts the limits of that reality to the infinity of its desires. Thus we have at the centre of the plays conversion motifs like mock-deaths, hallucinations, a marriage; and in the tragedies the symbolic and actual deaths fused together. Through these conversions the natural overcomes the deficiencies of the social, the human triumphs over the deficiencies of the actual. The transformation has to take place in the language itself, and there it almost always takes a triadic form. *In the Shadow of the Glen* offers us two morphemes as base words—again we have 'lonesome' and its opposing word 'queer,' each occurring more than a dozen times in the brief text. The opposition is again resolved by an intermediate term 'afeard' which occurs with the same frequency. We can then read the play as showing that the queer (which may mean mad or wonderful) are the victims of loneliness which they fear, the loneliness of lost beauty, for a lost hero like Patch Darcy, the loneliness of old age and of death. Again, the play transforms that fear and loneliness into an act of choice—the choice epitomised in the tramp and his chosen vagrancy, his freedom, his promise of youth and mobility being set against the solidifying forces of social respectability and old age. The spinelessness of Michael Dara and the old age of Dan Burke are finally accommodated at the expense of the vital Nora and the fine-talking tramp. The basic figure of the play is the movement from heroism and myth to convention and impoverished realism. One other way of tracing this development would be to trace the interactions between the basic morphemes of the play and the multiple references to mountain ewes, sheep and mist. The interaction reveals the structure which gives the play its compact form.[31]

Similarly, in *The Well of the Saints,* a traditional opposition between sight and vision is expressed in terms of an opposition between the word 'fine' and all its many derivatives (beautiful, splendid, grand, great, nice), and the word 'pitiful' with all its cognate words (wretched, poor, cold, etc.). 'Fine' undergoes a semantic change as a result of this opposition. At first it refers to illusory beauty; after the conflict with the world of ugliness it refers to imaginative beauty. Again, we have the triadic rhythm, again we have the symbolic truth defined in a language which embraces and goes beyond fact. The various forms of colour symbolism which distinguish *Deirdre of the Sorrows* and *Riders to the Sea* could be similarly seen in the light of this technique of conversion through opposition.

It is obvious that Synge's drama is more truly seen as a severe critique of the defects of Irish peasant society than a glorification of it. He found in the richness of the language of the Irish peasants an inbuilt critique of the poverty of their social conditions. He transformed the language into a code, elaborate in its complication, simple in its principle. The code was deeply indebted to the oral tradition from which it emerged. But it differed from it in that the code took the image of an heroic language living in an impoverished environment as its basic metaphor of human vitality fading under the pressure of institutional forces. But it was a metaphor of decay which he transformed into an assertion of vitality. Synge's linguistic code finally highlights in dramatic terms the myth of heroism which impregnated the language of the peasantry. He radically transformed the oral tradition and simultaneously transformed the modern tradition of the Ibsenite-Shavian problem play. In the Preface to *The Tinker's Wedding,* he said 'The drama, like the symphony, does not teach or prove anything.'[32] The simile is apt. His drama incarnates its meaning in its language and like the symphony that language can be understood in terms of various devices of composition. My concern here has been to show what some of those devices are, and how they operate as linguistic structures.

NOTES

1 Roland Barthes, *Writing Degree Zero,* trans. A. Lavers and C. Smith (London, 1967), *passim.* See also his *Elements of Semiology* (London, 1967) especially p. 21.

2 K. G. Hamilton, *The Two Harmonies: Poetry and Prose in the Seventeenth Century* (Oxford, 1963), p. 105: 'Put briefly, the 'scientific' style of the later seventeenth century attempted to communicate through words knowledge achieved by non-verbal methods; the earlier 'philosophic' style was primarily an attempt to arrive at knowledge through words.' See also the much more ambitious and tendentious study by Walter J. Ong, S. J., *The Presence of The Word* (Yale University Press, 1968) and compare Roland Barthes, 'Science Versus Literature', *Times Literary Supplement* (28 September, 1968).

3 See Helen F. North, 'Canons and Hierarchies of the Cardinal Virtues in Greek and Latin Literature' in *The Classical Tradition,* ed. Luitpold Wallach (New York, 1966), p. 183.

4 Isaac Rabinowitz, 'A Theory of Biblical Literature' in *The Classical Tradition,* p. 322.

5 Stéphane Mallarmé, *Propos sur la Poésie* (Monaco, 1953), p. 134.

6 *Structuralism, A Reader*, ed. and introd. by Michael Lane (London, 1970), p. 411.

7 *J. M. Synge: Collected Works,* General Editor, Robin Skelton, 4 vols. (London, 1962-68), IV, 54.

8 L. S. Vygotsky, *Thought and Language,* ed. and trans. E. Hanfmann and Gertrude Vakar (Cambridge, Mass., 1962), p. 2.

9 *Ibid,* p. 5: 'A word does not refer to a single object but to a group or class of objects. Each word is therefore already a generalization. Generalization is a verbal act of thought and reflects reality in quite another way than sensations and perception reflect it. Such a qualitative difference is implied in the proposition that there is a dialectal leap not only between total absence of consciousness (in inanimate matter) and sensation but also between sensation and thought. There is every reason to suppose that the qualitative distinction between sensation and thought is the presence in the latter of a generalized reflection of reality, which is also the essence of word meaning; and consequently that meaning is an act of thought in the full sense of the term. But at the same time, meaning is an inalienable part of the word as such and thus it belongs in the realm of language as much as in the realm of thought.'

10 Mordecai Gorelik, *New Theatres for Old* (New York, 1940), p. 197.

11 Stéphane Mallarmé, *Oeuvres Complètes,* texte établi et annoté par Henri Mondor et G. Jean-Aubry (Paris, 1956), p. 869.

12 cw IV 53.

13 'Marshall McLuhan', paper read at Berkeley by Richard Kostelanetz.

14 *Structuralism, A Reader,* p. 191.

15 cw II 13

16 Rulon S. Wells, 'De Saussure's System of Linguistics' in *Structuralism, A Reader,* p. 102. See also Roland Barthes, *Elements of Semiology,* pp.13-25 and L. Hjelmslev, *Essais Linguistiques,* Travaux du Cercle Linguistique de Copenhague, vol. XIII (Copenhagen, 1959), p. 69 ff.

17 cw II 7

18 cw I 2

19 cw I 18

20 See Noam Chomsky, *Syntactic Structures* (The Hague, 1957) and 'A Transformational Approach to Syntax' in *Classics in Linguistics,* ed. D. E.Hayden, E. P. Alworth, G. Tate (London, 1968), pp. 337-371.

21 cw IV 61.

22 cw IV 63.

23 Alan Price, *Synge and Anglo-Irish Literature* (London, 1961), p. 205.

24 cw IV 167.

25 cw IV 165.

26 cw IV 71.

27 cw IV 59.

28 cw IV 59.

29 cw IV 147.

30 cw IV 149.

31 Nora tells the tramp that she is 'afeard' of: death, the passage of time, the loss of heroism. He in turn recollects the hallucinatory effects of fog on the hills and Patch Darcy's death. The multiple references which follow show the opposition between lonesome

and queer operate at close range. Ewes are 'a queer breed', Patch went 'queer in his head' but was also 'a Great Man' although a dead one; 'and he mad dying'. Patch's real death is compared with Dan's fake death (Dan is dressed in 'queer white clothes') just as his expertness with ewes is contrasted with Micheal Dara's inability to handle them. The tramp brings the various references to sheep, old age and the lady of the house together in his account of what he saw and heard the night Patch died.

32 cw IV 3.

IX: THE POETRY OF SYNGE AND YEATS

JON STALLWORTHY

'Those who want to know what he was in himself,' Masefield wrote of Synge, 'should read the poems. The poems are like the man speaking. They are so like him that to read them is to hear him.'[1] Since Synge only cared for modern poetry that was personal and lyrical,[2] Masefield's judgement testifies to the success of his friend's intentions and suggests that the poems may deserve more attention than they have so far received.

The first of which we have any record was written when Synge was seven and later described in an autobiographical fragment as 'a poem intended to be a satire on an aunt who had slightly offended me,'[3] an appropriate debut for the author of *The Playboy of the Western World* and 'The Curse,' that Swiftian squib dedicated 'To a sister of an enemy of the author's who disapproved of *The Playboy*.'[4]

The seven-year-old satirist was not, however, apprenticed to what Yeats was to call his 'sedentary trade' for some years yet, being then chiefly interested in natural history. Even before he went to school he was, in his own Wordsworthian phrase, 'a worshipper of nature,' and the frequent illnesses that subsequently kept him at home gave him time to wander round the fields near his house. From keeping 'a large establishment of pets—rabbits, pigeons, guinea pigs, canaries, dogs—' he and a small girl-friend, who lived near-by, graduated to reading books on ornithology and bird-watching with a ten-shilling telescope bought with their shared resources, 'which led to trouble afterwards.' He began a collection of birds' eggs, with a view to writing a book on birds one day, and remembered 'telling—or intending to tell her—that each egg I found gave three distinct moments of rapture: the finding of the nest, the insertion of [the] egg successfully blown in my collection, and, lastly, the greatest, exhibiting it to her.' He was a founder-member of the Dublin Naturalists' Field Club, but resigned in his sixteenth year when, as he wrote, 'everything changed. I took to the violin and the study of literature with wild excitement and lost almost completely my interest in natural science although the beauty of nature influenced me more than ever.' In May 1886 he went on a field trip with the club to the Howth peninsula, and the first sight of Criffan's Cairn and the dolmen in the grounds of Howth Castle appears to have sown the seeds of an interest in Irish antiquities that was to supersede natural science.[5]

At the age of eighteen—the age at which Yeats had entered the Metropolitan School of Art—Synge enrolled in the Royal Irish Academy of Music and entered Trinity College, Dublin, which, Yeats tells us, 'does not, as a rule, produce artistic minds.' The summer vacation of 1892 Synge spent in County Wicklow, tramping the hills in search of archaeological and historical remains, delighting in the beauty of the countryside and the rich dialect of its inhabitants. Returning to Dublin in September, he produced a number of musical compositions, some of which have survived, and a sonnet, 'Glencullen.' The diction of the opening lines is markedly Keatsian, but as the poem's single sentence unfolds itself, Synge's voice breaks through. Warming to his subject —the contrast between Ireland's past and present—he moves from such an eighteenth-century formula as 'a charm of birds' to the result of his own observation:

> Yet on the bank still sings the merry wren
> And in thy stream the frolic ousels dive
> While old traditions linger in thy name.

The 'merry wren' and 'the frolic ousel' are the first of a great procession of birds and animals that passes through Synge's poems. It was in character that almost the last question he put to his brother Edward, the day before he died, should be whether he had heard any blackbirds singing yet.

'Glencullen' was published in 1892, when Synge was twenty, the same age at which Yeats, in 1885, had published his first poem, 'A man has the fields of heaven.'[6] In this 'the wisest owls' and 'dreaming water-fowls' lead off a feathered procession even larger and more varied than Synge's. The *Concordance* to Yeats's poems lists, among many other species, 8 hawks, 2 kites, 6 falcons, 15 eagles, 8 ospreys, 5 kingfishers, 2 robins, 13 peacocks, 2 peahens, 10 herons, 10 doves, 3 flamingoes, and 6 cuckoos. A similar roll-call can be made of the lions, leopards, weasels, foxes, and most other species of the animal kingdom known to Noah. Yeats's schooling had been as interrupted as Synge's and he, too, acquired an early interest in natural history that gave his first poems a richness and precision of natural detail not to be found in his later work.

Synge's Wicklow summer of 1892 produced a second poem, 'A Mountain Creed,' which is, one might irreverently say, by Wordsworth out of *Hymns Ancient and Modern* (a book, incidentally, that also influenced Yeats, who always 'took pleasure in the words of the hymn, but never understood why the choir took three times as long . . . in getting to the end'[7]). Synge's poem opens with a distinct echo of 'Good King Wenceslas' :

A mountain flower once I spied,
A lonely height its dwelling,
Where winds around it wailed and sighed
Sad stories sadly telling.

'Fair flower,' said I, 'thou all alone
Thy days up here art spending,
Now listening to the sad winds' moan
And now before them bending.

'When clouds and mists infold thee round
For many days together
And o'er thee weep until the ground
Is murky as the weather, . . .'

The poem ends with the flower replying in hymnal vein :

'Yet cloud and storm can hurt me not,
My joy it is not pleasure,
But 'tis to be, no humble lot,
One jewel 'mid God's treasure.'

Fortunately, the influence of Wordsworth, who had long been his favourite poet, proved stronger than that of *Hymns Ancient and Modern.* In his notebook, echoing *The Prelude,* he wrote :

> the presence of furze bushes and rocks and flooded streams and strange mountain fogs and sunshine gave me a strange sense of enchantment and delight but I think when I [rested] on a mountain I sat quite as gladly looking on the face of a

> boulder as at the finest view of glen and river. My wish was that nature should be untouched by man, whether the view was beautiful or not did not interest me.

A Wordsworthian pantheism is preferred to the God of his fathers —or, to be more exact, his mother—in another poem of this period:

> For my own soul I would a world create,
> A Christless creed, incredulous, divine,
> With Earth's young majesty would yearning mate,
> The arms of God around my breast intwine.

I have the impression that Wordsworth's 'Lucy' poems were particular favourites at this time. There is no mistaking the rhythm of

> She dwelt among the untrodden ways
> Beside the springs of Dove,
> A maid whom there were none to praise
> And very few to love . . .

behind the last stanza of Synge's poem 'In a New Diary':

> I start upon a stoney way
> Untrod by feet of men
> My strength or weakness to display
> Until these leaves are sealed again.

Such later poems as 'His Fate' and 'The Alteration' would seem to owe something to the same source.

Of more significance in the history of Synge's development as a writer is his 'Ballad of a Pauper,' a dramatic dialogue 'between an old man of the roads on his way to the poorhouse and the speaker, a young man from one of the big houses in Wicklow, presumably Synge himself.'[8] An extension of Wordsworth's experiments with 'the language of conversation in the middle and lower classes of society,' Synge's lyrical ballad moves with a good deal more pace and vigour—particularly in its passages of Dublin dialect—than do many of his early traditional poems. It should also be said that it carries more force and dramatic authenticity than certain of the original Lyrical Ballads, and is a better poem than such of Yeats's experiments in the same genre as 'The Ballad of Moll Magee.'

Though the latter exhibits an already formidable technical control, this cannot disguise the fact that its sprinkling of dialect, like the religious imagery of its penultimate stanza, has been added like seasoning. One is left with the impression that the poem owes more to literary than peasant sources and, no less than Yeats's later pre-Raphaelite verse, justifies Susan Mitchell's satire :

> But W. B. was the boy for me—he of the dim, wan clothes;
> And—don't let on I said it—not above a bit of a pose;
> And they call his writing literature, as everybody knows.

In the summer of 1894 Synge decided to abandon his plans for a musical career in favour of the study of foreign languages; a decision paralleled by Yeats's to abandon art for literature. Music, however, was to play as important a part in determining the nature of Synge's writing as art was to play as a continuing source of poetic inspiration for Yeats. On New Year's day 1895 Synge left Oberwerth, where he was studying German, for Paris, and there wrote his farewell to music :

> For thee I would have led my life,
> Have braved a breadless, barren strife.
> I was not destined for the glee
> True musicians find in thee.
>
> Now I am poor but poor alone,
> No music answers to my moan,
> My heart is hard as hardest stone.[9]

Music, however, would seem to have been at the back of his mind when he sat down to plan his first substantial literary undertaking, the *Vita Vecchia* cycle. We know that he once 'started words and music of an opera on Eileen Aruine;'[10] also that he was aware that 'most of the early Irish romances are written in alternating fragments of prose and verse.'[11] It is hardly surprising, therefore, that he should be attracted to a conception hallowed by both musical and literary tradition : a cycle of poems linked, as arias, by a prose recitative.[12] The narrative is autobiographical, with the female cast—Cherry Matheson, Hope Rea, and 'the Celliniani'—heavily veiled in the approved fashion of the nineties. They are seen as *princesses lointaines,* at a window across a street (on three separate occasions), across the aisle of a church, or with the inward eye of memory; and their detachment is further increased by the dream in which they are frequently enfolded. The poet dreams of his love in a third of the linking prose passages and in two of the poems.

Yeats was at this time even more dream-absorbed and a good deal more at ease in his dream vestments than Synge. As The Happy Shepherd, he ends the introductory poem of 'Crossways' on a typical note:

> I must be gone : there is a grave
> Where daffodil and lily wave,
> And I would please the hapless faun,
> Buried under the sleepy ground,
> With mirthful songs before the dawn.
> His shouting days with mirth were crowned;
> And still I dream he treads the lawn,
> Walking ghostly in the dew,
> Pierced by my glad singing through,
> My songs of old earth's dreamy youth :
> But ah ! she dreams not now; dream thou !
> For fair are poppies on the brow:
> Dream, dream, for this is also sooth.

Yeats's dream in *The Wanderings of Oisin and Other Poems,* like Synge's in 'Glencullen,' is most frequently of 'old Eire and the ancient ways,' but thereafter Cathleen-ni-Houlihan's features become more and more recognizably those of Maud Gonne :

> The wrong of unshapely things is a wrong too great to be told;
> I hunger to build them anew and sit on a green knoll apart,
> With the earth and the sky and the water, remade, like a
>   casket of gold
> For my dreams of your image that blossoms a rose in the deeps
>   of my heart.

At the other end of his life he was to write in retrospect :

> I thought my dear must her own soul destroy,
> So did fanaticism and hate enslave it,
> And this brought forth a dream and soon enough
> This dream itself had all my thought and love.

The *Concordance* to his poems lists twice as many appearances of the word 'dream' in one form or another, noun, verb, or compound adjective, in poems published over the twenty-five years up to 1910 as in the twenty-eight years that remained of his writing life.

In his 1907 revision Synge drastically cut *Vita Vecchia,* and it is easy to understand his dissatisfaction with its full 'operatic' form. Quite apart from its weaker poems that he was later to excise, the linking narrative makes little contribution and is not even well written. Passage after passage ends 'In the morning I wrote these lines,' 'I made these lines,' 'After many months I find these lines in my notebook.' The sections of recitative grew shorter and shorter, as if in recognition of their dispensibility, shrinking finally from two words before the penultimate poem to none at all between it and the last. This, 'A Dream,' opens under the influence of Keats :

> Mid rush, rose, lavender, luxuriant piled,
> Low melodies I marked a soul to sing . . .

but moves to a Wordsworthian vision :

> A woman from the shadow passed to sight
> And I beheld drowse on her drooping breast
> A babe that breathed with bliss of bland delight
> Till both a dual joy self-solaced seemed
> As some calm incarnation soul of seraph dreamed.

By sudden contrast, in a final quatrain we hear the voice of Synge himself :

> Then I awoke.—The morn was cold and keen,
> I viewed the grey-faced, straggling Paris street
> Where fouler sight in life hath sorrow seen
> Than starved disease in bitter rains and sleet?

This poem leads into a questioning prose meditation on mortality, answered with a Wordsworthian celebration of nature—'Every leaf and flower [and] insect is full of deeper wonder than any sign the Cabbalists have invented'—and an injunction: 'We must live like the birds that have been singing or will soon be singing over the way . . . . The world is an orchestra where every living thing plays one entry and then gives his place to another.'

In 1907, when Synge took up again the cycle he had set aside in 1897, he must have realized the confusion of themes and their lack of organized development. He abandoned the prose recitative, the first three poems (which had contributed nothing to the narrative), the eighth, and the last two. Those that remain are numbered 1 and 3-9. If a number 2 ever existed, it is now not known and would seem to be unnecessary, in that 'In a Dream' follows on naturally enough from 'At a Funeral Mass.'

> I saw a woman bend,
> Bowed in saintly prayer,

can even be regarded as a rhetorical preparation for :

> I saw thee start and quake,
> When we in face did meet . . .

The 'grassy grave' envisaged in this poem anticipates the 'death-tortured' speaker in the third poem, 'In Rebellion,' who curses the God that sits 'weaving woes' for him, and in the fourth poem curses

> . . . my bearing, childhood, youth
> I curse the sea, sun, mountains, moon,
> I curse my learning, search for truth,
> I curse the dawning, night, and noon.

He resolves—in bitterness and sexual frustration—that

> Cold, joyless I will live, though clean,
> Nor, by my marriage, mould to earth
> Young lives to see what I have seen,
> To curse—as I have cursed—their birth.[13]

Abandoning after this a feeble two-stanza poem about the country-side to which he flees 'from all the wilderness of cities,' he entitles the next poem 'In the City Again,'

> Where no one wayfarer I meet
>   That I have loved or known.

At this point appears a *dea ex machina,* who upbraids him for the sinful life into which he has apparently fallen :

> 'How canst thou to all lowness turn thee near,
> With loathsome life, how meditate, endure?'

This poem in its first version was more explicit about the speaker's temptation by that classic nineties' figure, the prostitute :

> Through ways I went where waned a lurid light,
> While round about lewd women wan did glide,
> Yet none to my lone weeping I allied,
> But will-less went, held from the earth my sight . . .

That first quatrain Synge excised in 1907 as he excised a stanza with a similarly explicit reference from the poem 'Rendez-vous Manqué dans la rue Racine.' Like most poets of any quality he tended to prune his poems in revision rather than add to them, and certainly these two are improved by his pruning knife.

After his vision of the Beatrice-like 'woman white,' the poet sees her again and again 'In Dream,' and concludes his revised cycle with a perception of mortality that was to be many times repeated in such later poems as 'On an Anniversary' and 'I've Thirty Months.' All of these include specific numbers; indeed, throughout his poems the constant repetition of such numbers and such temporal units as morning, day, night, week, month, provide a moving index of his obsession with time and death. Yeats's poems, early and late alike, also show a marked concern with time,[14] but it tends to be historical Time rather than the lengthening shadow of mortality that fills Synge's poems with a bitterness and despair more immediate than the 'sorrow' of *The Wind among the Reeds.*

When, in 1907, Synge came to draft a Preface for the Cuala Press edition of his poems, he wrote that 'they were written from five to eight years ago and, as is obvious enough, in Paris among all the influences of the so-called decadent and symbolist schools.' In the published version of his Preface he alludes to these influences only by implication—when he states that 'In these days poetry is usually a flower of evil or good.' The odours of Baudelaire's *Fleurs du Mal* are unmistakable and Greene and Stephens make, I think, an uncharacteristic error of judgement when they say that 'Synge's indebtedness to French literature is negligible' and that critics are wrong in attributing 'the combination of the tragic and the grotesque in Synge's work to the influence of Baudelaire.' While it would be equally wrong to see nothing but 'the influences of the so-called decadent and symbolist schools' in *Vita Vecchia,* there are elements in this cycle common to the city poems of Baudelaire and Verlaine, in particular, not to be found in Synge's earlier, rural verses. To take an obvious example, 'In the City Again':

> Wet winds and rain are in the street,
> Where I must pass alone,
> Where no one wayfarer I meet
> That I have loved or known.
>
> 'Tis winter in my heart, the air
> Is wailing, bitter cold,
> While I am wailing with despair,
> As I have wailed of old.

This surely owes something of its subject, tone, and style to Verlaine's

> Il pleure dans mon cœur
> Comme il pleut dans la ville.
> Quelle est cette langueur
> Qui pénètre mon cœur?
>
> O bruit doux de la pluie
> Par terre et sur les toits !
> Pour un cœur qui s'ennuie,
> O le chant de la pluie ![15]

Verlaine's '*langueur*' is Synge's 'bitterness,' just as the cursing and blasphemy of Baudelaire's *Fleurs du Mal* showed Synge how to express the explosive sentiments of 'In Rebellion' and 'Execration.' His 'Autobiography' testifies to the undoubted fact that these *were* genuine sentiments, the result of a grimly religious upbringing:

> While still very young the idea of Hell took a fearful hold on me. One night I thought I was irretrievably damned and cried myself to sleep in vain yet terrified efforts to form a conception of eternal pain. In the morning I renewed my lamentations and my mother was sent for. She comforted me with the assurance that the Holy Ghost was convicting me of sin and thus preparing me for ultimate salvation.... the well-meant but extraordinary cruelty of introducing the idea of Hell into the imagination of a nervous child has probably caused more misery than many customs that the same people send missionaries to eradicate.

His own brother, Sam, became such a missionary, and there was a family crisis when John refused to be present at his first sermon, having lost his faith as a result of reading Darwin at the age of fourteen. Yeats's experience was almost identical: led by his interest in natural history to 'Darwin and Wallace, Huxley and Haeckel,'[16] he too renounced the Bible Story, although less vehemently than Synge. Gentler and wiser parents spared him the other's obsession with sin, and perhaps with death as the wages of sin. Indeed, long after Yeats's faith in the Old Testament had been undermined, his poetry and plays—notably *The Countess Cathleen*—remained rich in Christian symbolism. For all its decorative value, however, this usually carries less conviction than Synge's anti-Christian sentiments, crudely though these are sometimes expressed. In the same way, Yeats's early sexual frustrations are reflected in his poems with nothing like the violence that prompted Synge to blame God for his predicament and write a play in which a writer woos a nun and persuades her to renounce her life of celibacy.[17] This last would seem to be a wish-fulfilment revenge on the God who had won Cherry Matheson from him; she being unable to bring herself to marry an unbeliever. The many tender and observant references to women in Synge's prose reinforce the impression left by the poems that he was a man of strong physical passions.

The poems of *Vita Vecchia* are principally a record of his frustrations at this time; frustrations not only sexual but artistic. At heart a countryman, he was no more at home in 'the wilderness of cities' than he was at ease in the borrowed robes of Baudelaire and Verlaine. A man who, as Yeats said, was 'in love with reality,' preferring daylight to dreams (or *rêves),* objects to abstractions, people to personifications, he was not the stuff out of which symbolist poets are made. *Vita Vecchia* in its revised form has a definite dark power, but its exaggerated alliteration and syntactic contortions betray not only a lack of technical expertise, but the awkward stance and strained accents of a poet cramped by metrics ill-suited to the natural rhythms of his voice.

Much though in retrospect Yeats and Synge may be seen to have in common, one must resist the temptation to represent this as more than it was, and certainly at their famous first meeting on 21 December 1896 few writers can have seemed less alike.[18] The one had published a single neglected poem in a college magazine, while the other had a reputation already reaching beyond the shores of England and Ireland as the author of *The Wanderings of Oisin and Other Poems, The Countess Kathleen and Various Legends and Lyrics,* and *The Celtic Twilight.* His friend Arthur Symons, whose book *The Symbolist Movement in Literature,* wrote Yeats,[19] 'I cannot praise as I would, because it has been dedicated to me,' had exposed him also to 'the influences of the so-called decadent and symbolist schools.' The theories of Mallarmé, to whom Symons had introduced him, were then leading him to revise his own theories of poetry and remodel his style accordingly. Abandoning the comparative clarity and momentum of his earliest poems, in those that were to be collected in *The Wind among the Reeds* he sought for a rhythm:

> To prolong the moment of contemplation, the moment when we are both asleep and awake, which is the one moment of creation, by hushing us with an alluring monotony, while it holds us waking by variety to keep us in that state of perhaps real trance, in which the mind liberated from the pressure of the will is unfolded in symbols.[20]

Yeats's slight knowledge of French, coupled with a personality already strongly formed and in closer contact with ordinary life than his manner sometimes suggested, prevented him from swallowing Mallarmé's doctrine whole.[21] Characteristically, he took only what he wanted, and with it formulated a new poetry involving, among other things, 'A return to the way of our fathers, a casting-out of descriptions of nature for the sake of nature.' Henceforth, 'fish, flesh, or fowl' would seldom appear in his poems —as in Synge's—in a natural so much as a symbolic role.

While Yeats moved deeper into a dream of love, a dream of Ireland's past and Ireland's future, Synge two years later took his advice to 'Give up Paris . . . . Go to the Aran Island. Live there as if you were one of the people themselves; express a life that has never found expression.' In 1898 he exchanged dreams for realities, city for country, the Gallic twilight for bright mornings in the West of Ireland. His transformation was as dramatic as the change of scene. 'Is not style,' he once asked Yeats, 'born out of the shock of new material ?' That is to say, is a man not born out of the shock of new experience ? Certainly, it was a new man who, only a year later, wrote 'In Spring' :

Buds are opening their lips to the South
Sparrows are pluming their mates on the sill
Lovers are laying red mouth to mouth
Maidens are marging their smocks with a frill

Yet I lie alone with my depth of desire
No daughter of men would I choose for my mate
I have learned loving and lived to require
A woman the Lord had not strength to create

All sense of strain has gone, the syntax is relaxed, and the diction is natural. Though the poems of this period still record an aching heart, they move with a new confidence and an unmistakable delight in the country detail feeding the countryman's trained eye again. In so far as he thought of French literature at all, Ronsard and Villon seem to have suited his mood rather than Baudelaire and Verlaine.

Sometime between 1895 and 1898 Synge wrote in his notebook: 'Lyrics can be written by people who are immature, drama cannot. There is little great lyrical poetry. Dramatic literature is relatively more mature.'[22] Though, as the French say, all generalizations are untrue including this one, there is a good deal of truth in Synge's statement, and certainly it applies to his own work. In Aran, spoken language—and not only conversation but spoken poetry—made an impact on his ear stronger, it would seem, than ever literary language made on his eye. He sought to capture its more relaxed cadences in prose. Part of the manuscript of *The Aran Islands* he left with Lady Gregory, who read it aloud to Yeats. They found it 'extraordinarily vivid,' but amusingly urged 'that the book being solid and detailed, as it is, would lose nothing but would rather gain by the actual names of the islands and of Galway not being given. Borrow always left his localities vague in this way, which gives a curious dreaminess to his work.'[23] Synge, however, had abandoned dreams for reality and was no more attracted to this suggestion than to their proposal that he add 'some more fairy belief.'

The unhappily self-absorbed poet of 1896 learnt in 1898 to look beyond himself and find happiness in observing other people. It was natural then that he should turn to the writing of drama, and in even the first speeches of his first play one can detect an ease and freedom seldom to be sensed in the earlier poems.

> COLM [*looking round the room*]. Sister Eileen has gone to bed ?
> BRIDE. She has not, your honour. She's been in a great state fearing you were lost in the hills, and now she's after going down the hollow field to see would there be any sound of the wheels coming.[24]

Even in this play, *When the Moon has Set,* which Synge never liked well enough to publish, his language has a vitality that seems to betray a sense of relief at having escaped from the restrictions of self and metre. This lends support to Yeats's belief 'that all happiness depends on the energy to assume the mask of some other self; that all joyous or creative life is a rebirth as something not oneself.'[25] He learnt this doctrine from his remarkable father, who 'exalted dramatic poetry above all other kinds,' and under whose influence he invented his first 'fantastic and incoherent plots.' 'The Island of Statues,' 'The Seeker,' and 'Mosada' had been followed by poems in many personae other than his own, so that his verse drama of the 1890s was occasioned by nothing like the imaginative liberation in which Synge discovered himself and his true medium. When he awoke to the reality of Ireland—a reality in which he rejoiced, for all that his detractors might say—Yeats was still pursuing his dream of a heroic Ireland.

The difference in imagination between these two men is well reflected by the personalities of the two women who possessed their respective imaginations and to some extent there symbolized Ireland : Maud Gonne and Molly Allgood, whom Synge met in 1905. He was thirty-five and she not yet twenty-one, but in her company his life broke into its late flowering and he returned to poetry :

> Beside a chapel I'd a room looked down,
> Where all the women from the farms and town,
> On Holy-days, and Sundays used to pass
> To marriages, and Christenings and to Mass.
>
> Then I sat lonely watching score and score,
> Till I turned jealous of the Lord next door . . . .
> Now by this window, where there's none can see,
> The Lord God's jealous of yourself and me.

No longer does he dream of a *princesse lointaine* or, looking up from the street, see his love at a window. No longer does he curse God for his sexual and artistic frustrations.

> Now by this window, where there's none can see,
> The Lord God's jealous of yourself and me.

The poem has the confidence and authority of the man himself, its situation is dramatic, its language colloquial ('I'd a room;' 'there's none can see'), and its irony beautifully turned. No longer does he see

> A God, inhuman, great,
> Sit weaving woes for me.

God is now an equal to be pitied rather than a monster to be feared :

> Some go to game, or pray in Rome
> I travel for my turning home
>
> For when I've been six months abroad
> Faith your kiss would brighten God !

And again :

> Then in the hush of plots with shining trees
> We lay like gods disguised in shabby dress.
> Making with birches, bracken, stars and seas,
> Green courts of pleasure for each long caress;
> Till there I found in you and you in me
> The crowns of Christ and Eros—all divinity.

Synge's love for Molly irradiates the world he sees,[26] but its colours are intensified by a contrasting darkness that he can never entirely exclude from the back of his mind. So, with perhaps a subconscious recollection of Marvell's 'To His Coy Mistress,' he speaks 'To the Oaks of Glencree' as to his love:[27]

> My arms are round you, and I lean
> Against you, while the lark
> Sings over us, and golden lights, and green
> Shadows are on your bark.
>
> There'll come a season when you'll stretch
> Black boards to cover me :

Then in Mount Jerome I will lie, poor wretch,
With worms eternally.

In poem after poem, bird-song and silence, light and darkness, the living and the dead keep company, and whenever they come together Death has the last word. Molly told Yeats that Synge 'often spoke of his coming death.' This prevision was so strong that it communicated itself to her in dreams. 'He used,' she said, 'often to joke about death with me and one day he said, "Will you go to my funeral ?" and I said, "No, for I could not bear to see you dead and the others living."' Her reply prompted 'A Question,' though it is Synge's voice that answers for her in the poem :

I asked if I got sick and died, would you
With my black funeral go walking too,
If you'd stand close to hear them talk or pray
While I'm let down in that steep bank of clay.

And, No, you said, for if you saw a crew
Of living idiots, pressing round that new
Oak coffin—they alive, I dead beneath
That board,—you'd rave and rend them with your teeth.

This struggle on the brink of the grave, the convulsive violence of an unusually reserved man raging 'against the dying of the light,' recurs in two of the four ballads Synge wrote between 1905 and 1908, 'Danny'[29] and 'The 'Mergency Man;' while a calmer death is the subject of a third, 'Patch-Shaneen.' All four ballads move with a wild vitality and show an abundance of specific detail, numbers and places named, that are the marks of a man in love with life, but looking his last on all things lovely. These are unmistakably the poems of a sick man. As Yeats said : 'What blindness did for Homer, lameness for Hephæstus, asceticism for any saint you will, bad health did for him by making him ask no more of life than that it should keep him living, and above all perhaps by concentrating his imagination.'

With Synge's later poems should be read his translations, to which I suspect he turned, as many poets before and since, by way of relief when the writing of his own poems proved too much of a strain. And, as is usually the case, the choice of poems to be translated is highly significant. Their themes are his own themes, with the result that the voice is his own voice. Synge is speaking to Molly, not Walter Von Der Vogelweide to *his* love:

> I never set my two eyes on a head was so fine as your head, but I'd no way to be looking down into your heart.
>
> It's for that I was tricked out and out—that was the thanks I got for being so steady in my love.
>
> I tell you, if I could have laid my hands on the whole set of the stars, the moon and the sun along with it, by Christ I'd have given the lot to her. No place have I set eyes on the like of her, she's bad to her friends, and gay and playful to those she'd have a right to hate. I ask you can that behaviour have a good end come to it?

We know that Synge was reading Petrarch in 1895, but his decision to try his hand at translating the sonnets from 'Laura in Death' would seem to have been prompted by seeing the translations by Agnes Tobin, whom Yeats, in an unguarded moment, described as the greatest American poet since Whitman. How much Synge's translations owe to Agnes Tobin one brief comparison will show. Her version of Sonnet XII begins:

> I do not think that I have ever seen
> So many times in one short afternoon
> The Lady they call dead: I did nigh swoon
> When she came running towards me through the green . . .[30]

Synge's version has the cadence of his plays:

> I was never anyplace where I saw so clearly one I do be wishing to see when I do not see, never in a place where I had the like of this freedom in my self, and where the light of loving making was strong from the sky.

When, in 1907, he decided to assemble his poems for publication, he drafted a Preface and, among some notes made about the same time, wrote:

> Poetry roughly is of two kinds—the poetry of real life—the Poetry of Burns, and Shakespeare, Villon, and the poetry of a land of the fancy—the poetry of Spenser and Keats and Ronsard. That is obvious enough, but what is highest in poetry is always where the dreamer is leaning out to reality or where the man of real life is lifted out of it . . . . In Ireland Mr Yeats

> one of his poets of the fairyland has interests in the world and for this reason his poetry has had a lifetime in itself ...[31]

He duly sent his poems to Mr Yeats with a covering letter that explored these themes further:

> If I print them I would possibly put a short preface to say that as there has been a false 'poetic diction' there has been and is a false 'poetic material.' That if verse, even great verse is to be alive it must be occupied with the whole of life—as it was with Villon and Shakespeare's songs, and with Herrick and Burns. For although exalted verse is the highest, it cannot keep its power unless there is more essentially vital verse at the side of it as ecclesiastical architecture cannot remain fine, when domestic architecture is debased.[32]

Robin Skelton, in a useful discussion of these passages,[33] examines the essentially domestic character of Synge's poetry so different from what might be described as the ecclesiastical manner of Yeats's. He says that Synge's poetry 'is used in the cause of living, and in the furtherance of living.' Certainly, as we have seen, it was Synge's belief that 'if verse, even great verse is to be alive it must be occupied with the whole of life.' To a larger or a lesser extent the poems of Villon, Shakespeare, Herrick, and Burns, fulfil this condition, but Professor Skelton is surely too partisan in claiming for Synge that 'he left behind a couple of dozen poems that will last out centuries, and that will always keep his name in mind as one of the great renewers of tradition.' The truth of the matter, I am inclined to think, lies midway between this view and Denis Donoghue's equally extreme verdict that 'the poems are not very important, except inasmuch as one can, studying them, learn something about poetry and language.'[34]

Synge was a reticent man. He reveals himself more in his poems, it is true, than in his plays and most of his prose, but there is scarcely a poem written before 1905 in which he breaks through his reserve for more than a sentence or two. After meeting Molly he speaks more directly, more urgently, 'and words obey [his] call,' as they did not before. These later poems give us vivid glimpses of the whole man, but in only a handful—such as 'Dread,' 'To the Oaks of Glencree,' and 'A Question'—are we brought face to face with him. Professor Skelton finds the persona of these poems 'partly that of the Cavalier, ... partly that of the poet who saw his vocation as a social function.' One need not look to 'the tribe of Ben,' however, for the ancestry of a twentieth-century Irish poet passionate in his loves and hatreds, who wrote praise poems and curse poems; a poet in whose work a 'romantic' and an 'earthy' diction meet 'not in crude conflict but in a relationship of mutual restraint and modification;'[35] a poet morbidly aware of the passing of time, tenderly aware of all living things. These have been distinguishing marks of the Celtic imagination since, and before, Irish monks thronged their illuminations to *The Book of Kells* with animals, birds, and fishes; and, in the same century, an Irish poet wrote :

> A wall of forest looms above
> and sweetly the blackbird sings;
> all the birds make melody
> over me and my books and things.
>
> There sings to me the cuckoo
> from bush-citadels in grey hood.
> God's doom ! May the Lord protect me
> writing well, under the great wood.[36]

By temperament and imagination Synge was unmistakably an Irish poet, but he did not aspire, as Yeats did, to a place in the grand tradition of the old Irish *fili,* national poets 'wont to quaff wine from the hand of kings or knights.'[37] Synge, in fact, expressly turns his back on the faded trappings of this tradition in 'The Passing of the Shee.' One wonders whether he gave this its sub-title, 'After looking at one of Æ's pictures,' lest it should be thought to have been written after reading one of W.B.Y.'s poems.

Robin Skelton has pointed out 'how much all the poems that Yeats had first printed after September 1908 and that appeared in *The Green Helmet* of 1910 differed from the poems printed before this date.' He attributes this striking fact to the impact of Synge's poems, and undoubtedly these played a major part in the reshaping of his style. It should not be forgotten, however, that the 'brusque hardness of tone which emerges so clearly in the 1910 collection' is to be found in 'Adam's Curse' written in 1902;

and that between 1902 and 1908 Yeats had written almost no poetry, his time being taken up with

> plays
> That have to be set up in fifty ways, . . .
> Theatre business, management of men.

He wrote in *Autobiographies* that 'I did not see, until Synge began to write, that we must renounce the deliberate creation of a kind of Holy City in the imagination, and express the individual.' This renunciation was reflected in the changing style of the plays he wrote between 1902 and 1908, and it is to these that we must look for stepping stones between the poems of *In the Seven Woods* and those of *The Green Helmet and Other Poems.* When Synge the poet showed Yeats the way forward into his later style, he was but redirecting him along a road he had already taken under guidance from Synge the playwright. Yeats profited from Synge's example, because he understood the nature of the man and his achievement. He repaid him with the most perceptive and influential assessment of his work yet written, and his judgement on the poems stands: 'I think this book . . . has certain sentences, fierce or beautiful or melancholy, that will be remembered in our history, having behind their passion his quarrel with ignorance, and those passionate events, his books.'

NOTES

1 *John M. Synge: A Few Personal Recollections, with Biographical Notes* (Dublin, 1915), p. 20.
2 David H. Greene and Edward M. Stephens, *J. M. Synge 1871-1909* (New York, 1961), p. 261.
3 Alan Price, ed., *J. M. Synge: Collected Works,* vol. II (London, 1966), p. 5.
4 Robin Skelton, ed., *J. M. Synge: Collected Works,* vol. I (London, 1962), p. 49. Unless otherwise stated, all poems by Synge cited in this essay are taken from this edition.
5 Greene and Stephens, p. 20.
6 Peter Allt and Russell K. Alspach, eds., *The Variorum Edition of the Poems of W. B. Yeats* (New York, 1957), p. 643. Unless otherwise stated, all poems by Yeats quoted in this essay are taken from this edition.

7 W. B. Yeats, *Autobiographies* (London, 1955), p. 24.
8 Greene and Stephens, p. 50.
9 *Ibid,* p. 50.
10 *Ibid,* p. 45.
11 Price, p. 371.
12 *Ibid,* pp. 16-24.
13 For an autobiographical gloss on this poem, see Greene and Stephens, p. 17.
14 The *Concordance* lists over 100 appearances of the word.
15 *Romances Sans Paroles,* III. Awareness of this debt may have been one reason why Synge re-wrote this poem in 1907. See Skelton, p. 63, for the later version.
16 *Autobiographies,* p. 60.
17 *When the Moon has Set.* See Ann Saddlemyer, ed., *J. M. Synge: Collected Works,* vol. III (London, 1968).
18 Yeats gives three accounts of this: *Autobiographies,* pp. 343-5, pp. 567-70, and *Essays and Introductions,* pp. 298-9. See also Ann Saddlemyer, 'A share in the Dignity of the World: J. M. Synge's Aesthetic Theory,' *The World of W. B. Yeats* (Dublin, 1965).
19 In his important essay on 'The Symbolism of Poetry' (1900), *Essays and Introductions,* pp. 153-64.
20 *Essays and Introductions,* p. 159.
21 On the nature of Yeats's debt to the French Symbolists, see C. M. Bowra, *The Heritage of Symbolism* (London, 1943); Graham Hough, *The Last Romantics* (London, 1959); and Richard Ellmann, *The Identity of Yeats* (London, 1964).
22 Price, p. 350.
23 Greene and Stephens, p. 127.
24 Saddlemyer, p. 157.
25 *Autobiographies,* p. 503.
26 That Molly's love was, at least at this time, less intense is indicated by a poem quoted in Elizabeth Coxhead's *Daughters of Erin,* p. 187. This is one of three poems, together with a version of 'The Masque of May', not included in vol. I of *J. M. Synge: Collected Works,* edited by Robin Skelton.
27 To my mind there is an element of deliberate — and dramatically effective — ambiguity in the poem, which Robin Skelton denies when he writes that it 'begins with an arm around a girl and ends with the worms' ('The Poetry of J. M. Synge', *Poetry Ireland,* I, 1962, p. 35.).
28 W. B. Yeats, *Autobiographies,* p. 519. See also pp. 509-10 and 517.
29 See Greene and Stephens, pp. 174-5, for a useful account of the background to this poem, which Elizabeth Yeats refused to include in the Cuala Press edition of Synge's poems because of its brutality.
30 Agnes Tobin, *Letters, Translations, Poems* (San Francisco, 1958), p.85.
31 Skelton, pp. xiv-v.
32 *Ibid.* pp. xv-xvi.

33 'The Poetry of J. M. Synge', *Poetry Ireland,* I, 1962, pp. 32-44.
34 'Flowers and Timbers,' *Threshold,* I, 3, 1957, pp. 40-7.
35 Denis Donoghue, *ibid.*
36 'Writing Out of Doors,' trans. from the Irish. James Carney, *Medieval Irish Lyrics* (Dublin, 1967), p. 23.
37 See Jon Stallworthy, *Vision and Revision in Yeats's Last Poems,* (Oxford, 1969), pp. 25-38.

X: SYNGE AND MODERNISM

THOMAS KILROY

Within the history of the modern drama the Irish Dramatic Movement up to the death of Synge (from which point it may be said to lose its peculiar historical meaning) is remarkable chiefly in its rejection of what is central to European drama of the same period. In its excellences as in its defects the Movement of that first decade, up to 1907, is an example (one of several within the ambit of Modernism)[1] of an exuberant, determined provincialism. All assessments of Synge and of the early Yeats have to take into account this fact, that terms which are indispensable to an understanding of the best of modern literature are often irrelevant when applied to theirs. The question is especially urgent in the case of Synge because Yeats had still a long way to go after Synge's death. The issue is not simply a preference for all that is embraced by the complex idea, Modernism; it is more a matter of finding a way of seeing Synge's plays or of reading the early Yeats poems and plays which will do justice to their intrinsic worth while remaining loyal to the kind of discrimination which Modernism has insisted upon, above all its assertion that the art-work be independent of considerations of a purely local or provincial nature.

When Yeats came to reflect upon the early Abbey Theatre in a stanza of 'The Muncipal Gallery Revisited' he described it in a way which must serve as a primary text in any discussion of the matter:

> John Synge, I and Augusta Gregory, thought
> All that we did, all that we said or sang
> Must come from contact with the soil, from that
> Contact everything Antaeus-like grew strong.
> We three alone in modern times had brought
> Everything down to that sole test again,
> Dream of the noble and the beggar-man.

Yeats says nothing here of Edward Martyn's Ibsenism, of the

unsuccessful attempt of George Moore to open the Movement to what was happening in the theatre elsewhere. Nor does Yeats refer to the Movement's own version of Ibsenite realism which came to dominate the repertoire after the death of Synge. With Colum, T. C. Murray, Lennox Robinson and George Shiels the theatre of Synge, Yeats and Gregory was to become, as Moore noted with acerbic glee, a version of the realist theatre, dedicated to the simulation of the ordinary, the mundane, with its own version of the Ibsenite problem-conflict and its attention to what Ibsen called 'the difficult art of writing the genuine, plain language spoken in life.'[2]

Instead Yeats writes of the exclusiveness, in modern terms, of a theatrical idea based on heroic legend and peasant life which would combine in some way the two extremes of the social scale, the aristocratic and the humble, the poetic and the demotic, 'dream of the noble and the beggar-man.' Synge's plays are central to all of this in that they might almost have been designed to meet the requirements of the Movement. Firstly, they unite in several ways and often within the one theatrical image, the aristocratic and the humble, imposing an heroic mould on common life, as in *Riders to the Sea* and a peasant mould on heroic myth as in *Deirdre of the Sorrows*. And Synge's theatrical language, a highly stylised, artificial medium, combined some of the properties of formal poetry with the rooted vernacular of spoken language. Finally, the truth of Synge's dramatic action, the truth of his dramatic language is a poetic truth, not a social truth, it conforms only to the laws of a shaping imagination, it is apolitical, its folk setting virtually removes it from the social anxiety which is so characteristic of much modern drama. What social comment there is in Synge is oblique and I will refer to it again, later.

What was manifestly excluded by the early Abbey Theatre was the articulate life of the bourgeoisie, the drama of social man, of the human figure within the evolution of the modern, middle culture. In effect this was the kind of drama which Synge attempted in his first play, *When the Moon Has Set,* with its modish ideas of emancipation, Nature-worship and anarchic individualism. Yeats wrote disparagingly of that piece, 'It might have had a slight stage success with a certain kind of very modern audience.'[3] It might indeed, but the Abbey Theatre would have nothing of it. 'What we wanted,' Lady Gregory explains in words which recall Yeats's stanza, 'was to create for Ireland a theatre with a base of realism, with an apex of beauty.'[4] But her notion of dramatic realism cannot be construed as the phrase was habitually understood elsewhere at the beginning of this century; elsewhere it is synonymous with the radical assault upon bourgeois morality through a painstaking representation of its destructiveness, its desiccation of the human spirit.

What Lady Gregory means by realism is, of course, peasant drama. And peasant drama for Lady Gregory, Yeats and even Synge (with important qualifications) is, strictly speaking, idealist, a sophisticated, external view of primitive life, a celebration of the Natural Man which is shared by drama and poetry alike of the period, identifying the whole literature of the Anglo-Irish Revival as a late phase of European Romanticism. The literature which emerged suffered many of the defects of late Romanticism in the imprecision of its language, its escapism and its undiscriminating observation of peasant life.

This leads us to the first of several qualifications that have to be made if Synge is to be considered merely as part of the early Irish Dramatic Movement. He simply stands apart from his contemporaries in the way he avoids the excesses of Romanticism which bedevilled so much writing of the time, especially on peasant themes. There is a hard centre to Synge which would accept no compromise. If modern dramatic realism proceeds as much from a conviction that inhibition or compromise subverts the truth, as much as from sociological detail, then Synge has one of the fundamental attitudes of the realist. In language he had solved the problem of giving romance a hard foundation and in this he deeply influenced the development of Yeats's poetry. In dramatic characterisation he was attracted principally by the tough individualism, the wild, Rabelaisian spontaneity of his people. Through deep association over a relatively short time he had shrewdly penetrated below the splendid surface charm, the delightful speech of the West of Ireland which bemused and distracted so many other outsiders. There is an amusing passage somewhere among his writings where he tells of the visitor to the cottage, the charm with which he is received and the ironical humour with which his visit is dissected when he has gone. Synge observing all of this is Synge the dramatist.

The position of Synge, then, within the Irish Tradition, is rather a special one, he cannot be simply accommodated within the early Abbey Theatre Movement and left there. There is a similar discomfort for those who try to associate him with the standard anthology of modern drama, however much his stature as an artist may be recognised. Eliot's well-known comments in *Poetry and Drama* on Synge's language might serve as a model of the uneasy treatment that Synge has had from modern criticism. His case, it is said, is special, the circumstances of his achievement are local, they do not apply beyond this. 'The language of Synge,' Eliot writes, 'is not available except for plays set among the same people.'[5] The same might be said, and has been said, of his plots, his sense of place and so on. Yet this cannot be the whole of the matter for Synge, with Shaw, Yeats, Joyce and Beckett is one of the artists of permanent, major significance born in this country in modern times.

In his Prefaces to *The Tinker's Wedding* and *The Playboy,* as elsewhere in his occasional writings, Synge deliberately rejects modernist drama and makes an appeal on behalf of a vital regionalism in literature, uncontaminated by the sterility, as Synge saw it, of modern urban life. Yet the sensibility behind the plays is one which constantly evokes the kind of aesthetic values that inform the best of modern writing. This is exactly the kind of problem which faces the modern student of Synge's work. I try to describe this sensibility as private, intensely preoccupied with the nature of human freedom, which is here but another way of saying human privacy, secular but committed to the essential spirituality of human action, subversive of the main, middle culture of which Modernism is the counter-culture.

Robert Brustein, in his study of that title, describes the drama from Ibsen to Genet as *The Theatre of Revolt.* He invites us in the Foreword, if we so wish, to relate Synge to his thesis of a radical, revolutionary drama; there are several reasons why I think we may do so without strain.

An artist of the very first order, with a fine knowledge of classic English and French drama and perfectly aware of contemporary developments in the theatre elsewhere, Synge nevertheless dedicated himself to a secluded folk culture which he knew was already showing signs of its own demise. His treatment, however, of Irish material is never provincial in a narrow sense; it is the product of a rich mind which brought classical forms to bear upon the native material. The true distinction between Synge and his Modernist contemporaries is not a qualitative one nor even in the choice of subject matter, for Synge's actual themes transcend his local settings, but a distinction of models, of ideal mentors. Synge looks back to sixteenth and seventeenth century drama as his model, to Jonson, Molière and Racine. As an artist he is technically conservative while one of the very purposes of Modernism is in its progressive search for new forms to match the radical programme of the new drama.

Synge's work is a complex composite of the ideas which moved the early Abbey Theatre and the personal quality of mind of the man himself. Without him the actual achievement in dramatic literature of the Movement up to his death would be sparse indeed and would rest largely as an introduction to the development of Yeats. *The Playboy of the Western World* is the major achievement of Synge the dramatist and of the theatrical movement up to that date. Before it the theatre had had its successes, notably in the creation of a style but with this play it realised one of its fundamental aims: the production of a considerable work of literary and dramatic literature native to itself. There is about the writings of all those concerned, up to this date, an air of anticipation, the excitement of people on the verge of discovery, ready to believe that the next play would be it, the play which would give meaning to earlier experiments with Irish speech and to the methods of stage presentation which the Fays had brought to the theatre. *The Playboy of the Western World* was that play and it was this conviction which helped Yeats and Lady Gregory to defend it so vigorously, even if they had their own reservations about its language themselves.

Now *The Playboy* well illustrates that curious mixture of reaction and subversion in Synge. Firstly, it draws its detail, its ethos, from the rhythm of life of a remote corner of the West of Ireland. And, however much we may cherish this way of life for what it represents, it was already an anachronism in 1907, as is exemplified by Synge's problems in translating it to a Dublin stage. Secondly, the form of the play is that of traditional Romantic Comedy but the play ends, not in the conventional marriage, but in the ironic frustration of the lovers. Yet even here Synge has many precedents deep within the European tradition, as Berowne remarks wryly at the end of *Love's Labour Lost,*

> Our wooing doth not end like an
> old play; Jack hath not Jill.

This traditionalism in Synge, however, does not account for the full maturity of his art and it is the other elements, less easily identified, that make him the complex artist who resists categorization. When we begin to assemble those other elements which shape his imagination we find that they act upon the traditional forms, often in a radical fashion, rather than being simply of the forms and in service to them.

The Playboy opens with Pegeen Mike laboriously writing out a colourful order for her trousseau 'to be sent with three barrels of porter' in time for her wedding to Shawneen Keogh. It ends with a pathetic cry of anguish a day later with Pegeen driven back into that loveless marriage having enjoyed briefly 'the love-light of the star of knowledge' through all the eloquence of a poet who has suddenly discovered the capacity of language. The whole force of the play is derived from that swift blossoming of the delicate, fragile, shared vision of Christy and Pegeen in Act Three, its precious, timeless innocence and its mortality before the way of the world. There are those in the play who abide by the rhythm of life about them and there are those who try to defy it. Synge reserves his sympathy for the love of Christy and Pegeen which tries to defy it but it is the rhythm from which they try to escape which is finally triumphant.

It is in this way that Synge uses the form of traditional Romantic Comedy. Shawn Keogh is a satiric representation of respectable marriage, marriage sanctioned by the Church and, more importantly perhaps, by the kind of barter system which operates as a marriage contract within the community. Both religion and the community are ridiculed in his person because as a man, as a sexual candidate he enjoys the respect of no-one. 'It's true all girls are fond of courage,' the Widow Quin taunts him, 'and do hate the like of you.' Rather as he dismisses the young priest as irrelevant to Maurya's suffering in *Riders to the Sea,* Synge at the very beginning of this play puts aside the whole conventional, established idea of marriage. His true subject is exceptional love. In the scheme of the play respectable marriage is at the lowest end of the scale and there is a progressive ascension from that to the ecstasy of Christy and Pegeen. Between the extremes lies the wild, spirited world of Michael James and the Widow Quin, only partly touched by social respectability and only partly in touch with the kind of vision briefly enjoyed by Christy and Pegeen.

The figure of Michael James in the play rises up out of the raw earth itself, a great male voice bellowing with drink, the very voice which, significantly, interrupts the lovers' duet in Act Three. If this is a comic play about the ancient ritual of patricide it is also a play about the survival of the patriarch because while Old Mahon may have been subdued by Christy, Michael James and all he stands for continue to flourish at the end. He is indeed the true father-figure of the play and he, and not Old Mahon, is Christy's real antagonist in dramatic time in the struggle of the assertion of manhood. The lyrical style of Christy as lover could never prosper in the world of Michael James and nowhere is this more evident than in the blessing which the old man pronounces over the two, that extraordinary pagan hymn to the flesh, mixed with the shrewdness of a stock-breeder and with that ludicrous Christian apothegm tagged on at the end. Synge understood, and the play is a dramatisation of it, what such a world excluded, the tenderness of passion, the poetry of love. The greatest obstacle to romance and sexual fulfillment in the play comes from the nature of the culture itself and this is one of the distinctions of the play as a Romantic Comedy.

Within this wider tradition of European Romantic Comedy Christy is but one of a whole gallery of heroes representing assertive masculine vigour, passion and romance who pit themselves against the conventions of a community. Christy, of course, fails but there are certain qualities to his make-up, peculiar to Synge, which make his final exit, even without his lover, triumphant. For, after all, the final question which the play poses, and one which continues to trouble audiences, is why Pegeen does not go along with him. She doesn't go and she realizes the horror of her choice almost at once because, ultimately, the world about her is stronger than the appeal of Christy.

Christy is one of those Synge characters (The Tramp in *In The Shadow of the Glen* being another) who comes in out of the open air, out of Nature you might say, and goes back out to it, to the open road, with a free heart at the end 'romancing through a romping lifetime from this hour to the darkening of the judgment day.' Again and again there is this evocation in Synge, particularly in his occasional writings, of a life beyond the burdens of society, a freedom and a purity of will which Synge associates with Nature, with a kind of animism of which Man is but a part. His models of this daemonic sense of life are the tramps, tinkers, wanderers and it is clear that this rôle is more than just an unconscious projection of the dramatist's own personality.

Yeats, who deeply understood the nature of Synge's genius, speaks of this facet of his personality in words which place Synge within the mainstream of Modernism : the artist in a creative solitude engaged in an uneasy dialogue with the world outside, the artist questioning the very possibility of art to communicate at all. The predicament, the abrasive relationship between the artist and his culture, has become almost a commonplace in our century. This passage, from the Yeats open letter of 1919 to Lady Gregory, actually anticipates Beckett's defence of Joyce ten years later against an identical obscurantism.[6] The issue in each case is the same : the unwillingness or inability of the public to grant the work of art its distinct and total self-containment or, to put it another way, the confusing of art with journalism, sociology or history. What Yeats is talking about, what Beckett writes about in his defence of *Work in Progress,* is the belief, on which the most of Modern Art rests, that art is a unique and superior medium of knowledge about human existence and that it can only be understood and judged according to laws of its own creating:

> The outcry against *The Playboy* was an outcry against its style, against its way of seeing; and when an audience called Synge 'decadent'—a favourite reproach from the objective everywhere—it was but troubled by the stench of its own burnt cakes. How could they that dreaded solitude love that which solitude made ?[7]

The position of Synge, then, is a special one both within the particular idea of a theatre which moved the early Irish Dramatic Movement and the wider tradition of modern European drama. The purpose of this paper is to suggest that we do him something of an injustice when we confine him to our own tradition; what we take from outside it is the man's sense of innovation, his creation of a personal dramaturgy where no native tradition existed before. Even when at pains to distinguish what he was doing from the current Modernist drama, Synge is substantiating a wider claim for his art than what was simply offered by the local material. '*The Playboy of the Western World*,' he wrote, as one of his public defences of the play, 'is not a play with a "purpose" in the modern sense of the word, but although parts of it are, or are meant to be, extravagant comedy, still a great deal that is in it, and a great deal more that is behind it, is perfectly serious when looked at in a certain light . . . There are, it may be hinted, several sides to *The Playboy* . . .'[8]

One of the crises in Modernist drama in this period was in the virtual exhaustion of pure tragic and pure comic forms. When Chekhov described his work as comic he was using that term in a highly revolutionary way; the truth is that after *The Seagull, Uncle Vanya, The Three Sisters* and *The Cherry Orchard* the terms tragic and comic no longer carry their stable, traditional connotations in the main development of European drama. Chekhov marks the final disintegration of these categories, although we may qualify this fact backwards or forward in time. One of the features of provincial literatures, on the other hand, in the modern period, such as the modern Irish or that of the Southern American States later in the century, is the access to the integrated Classical tradition which the writers of these movements continued to enjoy without anomaly. In the great writers, like Synge, Yeats and Faulkner, this is never deployed as an escape out of the modern condition, it becomes rather another version of Modernism but one which begins with a particular place, at a particular point in time.

Much has been made of Synge's education as a playwright in his practical involvement with the players of the Abbey Theatre. But, as his editor, Professor Saddlemyer, points out, his plays were formed at the typewriter and not in workshop theatre and in a very real sense it was Synge who was educating his theatre in stage-craft, not the other way around.[9] Synge turned to a pre-modern aesthetic as a groundwork of his plays, quite unself-consciously seeing the wholeness, the coherence of Irish peasant culture, its seclusion from the upheavals of the nineteenth century which created Modernism, its retention of certain ethical absolutes by which a given dramatic action might be measured. But it required an individual talent of exceptional tact and perspicuity to mate specific theatrical forms of the past with subject-matter of a tradition which had never possessed a theatre at any stage of its history. This is the context within which we look at the neo-Classical formalism of *Riders to the Sea* or the sophisticated use of Romance in *The Playboy* or the Mediaeval-style baiting farce of *The Tinker's Wedding.*

Modernism, however, is not just a preference for one form above another, it is, in its fullest meaning, a mode of perception, of knowledge with a very definite idea of how art should express such knowledge. In Zola's remarkable theatre notes of the 1870's there is this conviction and much else that has a bearing on Synge. Here, as so often in Modernist proclamations, a theatre like the early Abbey would seem to be eccentric, even irrelevant. But when Zola is characterizing the poetics of Modernism, the modern artist's conception of his own rôle as artificer and his unblinking gaze into the variety of life about him, the description applies to Synge:

> . . . To-day the naturalistic thinkers are telling us that the truth does not need clothing; it can walk naked . . . Writers with any sense understand perfectly that tragedy and romantic drama are dead. The majority, though, are badly troubled when they turn their minds to the as-yet-unclear formula of to-morrow . . . For them poetry resides in the past and in abstraction, in the idealizing of facts and characters. As soon as one confronts them with daily life, with the people who fill our streets, they blink, they stammer, they are afraid; they no longer see clearly; they find everything ugly and not good enough for art. According to them a subject must enter the lies of legend, men must harden and turn to stone like statues before the artist can accept them and make them fit the disguises he has prepared . . . The future is with Naturalism . . . it will be proved that there is more poetry in the little apartment of a bourgeois than in all the empty, worm-eaten palaces of history; in the end we will see that everything meets in the real . . .[10]

II

'I do not think biography—even auto-biography—can reveal the person,' Synge wrote, with characteristic irony in a fragment of autobiography which was unpublished in his lifetime, 'but art may.'[11] When he presented such material of his past as he wished to use he did so in a kind of series of musical movements. It is remarkable how much of his personality emerges in this way, the personality which is vitally present in the plays. Introspective, withdrawn even to those nearest to him, prone to illness, his sensibility in both tragedy and comedy is a dark one. The kind of colours which Synge uses (and he is a superb colourist) take their essential tones from an abiding sense of life's conflicts, not its repose. The two elements which he himself sees as central to his early years, a fascination with Darwin and Nature on the one hand and with music on the other, are as important artistically to the plays as the purely local sources of his work in Irish folklore and character, although this is rarely acknowledged. Finally, he gives us in this unfinished autobiography the origins of his life-long suspicion of organized Christianity which gives several of the plays an underlay of satire.

The question of Synge is very much a question of biography, however one may describe it. I believe that much of the portrait of Synge the artist, the roots of his alienation, is explicable within the exceptional attitude which he had to his own class. He was of that minority, Protestant middle-class, with its ramifications in the Church of Ireland, the Crown Civil Service and landlordism, with its particular system of ethics, rhetoric and education and which then dominated the Catholic majority. As an artist Synge was driven to exclude himself from his own background, driven into himself, rather as Beckett was later and from an identical background.

It is the class which produced Farquhar, Sheridan, Wilde, Shaw and some of the most important literary contemporaries of Synge himself. Yeats, who was of the same stock, contrived to give it an aristocratic veneer but it becomes so only within the special terms of his poetry. In fact, and despite its immense contribution to Irish culture, as a class it had its own bourgeois antagonism to art as Synge knew very well in his family life.

Synge, however, chose to write about a race removed from his own people and politically subservient to them. There is about his work, as there is about the painting of Gauguin or some scenes in Melville, the freshness of discovery, as if his characters had been newly minted so free are they of the debasements of conventional society. As with all sophisticated primitivist art, Synge's plays constantly recall the 'normal' society beyond the perimeter of the dramatic action, only that its institutions, pretensions and morality might be mocked and restored to a proper proportion. This is the oblique and very serious level of social commentary in Synge. He is an Outsider, both in the sense of his alienation from all that his own background had to offer him and in that he remains outside his own elected material, however passionately he was involved.

The death of Synge moved Yeats to write one of the most haunting passages in the literature of the period. He was the only contemporary before whom Yeats was in awe, he was the only man who seemed to have the same deep, personal significance that so many women had for the poet in his lifetime.

After his death Yeats realised that the original dramatic movement had come to an end. The peasant theatre of Yeats, Gregory and Synge had been founded upon the distance which separated the playwrights from their source material. At its greatest this distance, as in Synge, had been filled by a complex personal style, a highly artistic sense of the potentiality of the material. When playwrights of a peasant background appeared, a different kind of peasant play appeared with them, tending more and more to a kind of sociological realism. As such the peasant plays of the Abbey repertoire moved further and further away from the kind of poetic truth of *The Playboy of the Western World*.

It is his frustration with this state of affairs which pervades Yeats's open letter of 1919 to Lady Gregory moving him to opt for 'an unpopular theatre and an audience like a secret society where admission is by favour and never to many.' The success of the early Abbey Theatre had led to the infiltration of those very modernist qualities which the original idea had sought to keep at bay. But the new Irish realists lacked the dialectical finesse (and are at times painfully naive in the treatment of ideas) which is the foundation of Ibsenite realism, so that to speak of them as Modernist is to abuse the word.

> You and I and Synge, not understanding the clock, set out to bring again the Theatre of Shakespeare or rather perhaps of Sophocles . . . We thought we could bring the old folk-life to Dublin, patriotic feeling to help us, and with the folk-

life all the life of the heart, understanding heart, according to Dante's definition, as the most interior being; but the modern world is more powerful than any Propaganda or even than any special circumstance, and our success has been that we have made a theatre of the head, and persuaded Dublin playgoers to think about their own trade or profession or class and their life within it, so long as the stage curtain is up, in relation to Ireland as a whole. For certain hours of an evening they have objective modern eyes.[12]

NOTES

1 By Modernism I mean that revolution in European culture of the latter half of the nineteenth century which has precise philosophical, sociological and aesthetic boundaries. See Lionel Trilling 'On the Teaching of Modern Literature', in *Beyond Culture* (Harmondsworth, 1963) for some of the literary implications of Modernism.

2 See Lennox Robinson, ed., *The Irish Theatre* (Macmillan, 1939), p. 92. The statement by Ibsen is from a letter of 1883 as quoted by Robert Brustein, *The Theatre Of Revolt* (London, 1965) p. 61.

3 See Ann Saddlemyer, ed., *J. M. Synge: Plays,* Oxford Paperbacks.

4 As quoted by Ann Saddlemyer, *In Defence of Lady Gregory, Playwright* (Dublin, 1966), p. 9.
p. 213, n.I.

5 T. S. Elliot, *Selected Prose,* ed. John Hayward, (Harmondsworth, 1953), p. 74.

6 See Samuel Beckett and others, *Our Exagmination Round his Factification for Incamination of Work in Progress* (London, 1961). This is a reprint of the 1929 edition.

7 W. B. Yeats, *Explorations* (London, 1962), p. 253.

8 See David H. Greene and Edward M. Stephens, *J. M. Synge 1871-1909* (New York, 1961), p. 246.

9 See Professor Saddlemyer's Introduction to the *Plays,* (Oxford Paperbacks, 1969), p. XI.

10 See Eric Bentley, ed., *The Theory of the Modern Stage* (Harmondsworth, 1968), p. 362 ff., an excellent anthology of Modernist dramatic theory.

11 Alan Price, ed., *The Autobiography of J. M. Synge* (Dublin, 1965), p. 13.

12 *Explorations,* p. 252.

XI: J. M. SYNGE—A CENTENARY APPRAISAL

DAVID H. GREENE

J. M. Synge was a strange man whose personality has always struck me as being unchangingly enigmatic. This is perhaps an unusual admission for a biographer to make. But on the basis of the information we have about him and the assumption that we are not likely to have any startling revelations in the future I have to believe that the only fully understandable Synge we are likely to get in the future will be a product of the imagination. My admission will come as no revelation to anyone who has read the Greene and Stephens biography. In the introduction to that book I quoted Synge's own conviction—'the deeds of a man's lifetime are impersonal and concrete, might have been done by anyone, while art is the expression of the abstract beauty of the person' —and then advised my reader to go to Synge's art, and not his biography, for the 'abstract beauty of the person' himself.[1]

I suspect that if I had actually known Synge I would still have found him an enigma. John Masefield, one of the only two men who knew Synge well, the other being Stephen MacKenna, observed that Synge 'gave one from the first the *impression* of a strange personality.'[2] 'I do not know what Synge thought,' Masefield wrote. 'I don't believe anybody knew, or thinks he knows.'[3]

Very few people in Synge's life came even reasonably close to knowing him well. His mother quite clearly did not understand him, although she seems to have thought she did. Other members of his family saw only one side of this complex man. As a creative artist he was completely outside their world. None of them ever saw a play of his performed during his lifetime. Of course this fact alone is not so unusual—one thinks of the remark James Joyce made that only two people in his life, his wife and his aunt Josephine, both women of extremely modest intellectual equipment, had any understanding of what he was trying to do.

Synge was a silent man, and silence is not one of the normal forms of communication. Masefield and others confirm the fact of his reticence. To Yeats he was 'meditative.' Masefield, to be sure, asserted that Synge's talk to women had a lightness and charm. But Masefield believed that all men talked their best to women, an assertion which might be challenged especially as far as Irishmen are concerned. The letters to women which Synge wrote do something less than overwhelm us with their lightness and charm. In fact they reveal him as very much an ordinary human being but not a particularly eloquent one. As a letter writer he is quite clearly more in Joyce's class than Yeats's.

Admittedly not many of Synge's letters to women have survived. Excluding his letters to Lady Gregory, which were not personal, the only substantial collection we have are those to Molly Allgood, whose stage name was 'Maire O'Neill.' These are shortly to be published, I understand, under the editorship of Professor Ann Saddlemyer. I have not read all of them, for I understand that Professor Saddlemyer discovered letters which were not available to me in 1955. The impression of Synge which appears in the letters to Molly which I was able to read is of a man deeply but unhappily in love with a young woman whom he seemed to have nothing in common with except the theatre. The letters do not on the whole make pleasant reading, and they give the impression that Synge believed he was writing to a child.

I talked to Molly Allgood only once, in 1939, thirty years after Synge's death and after she had been married to two other men. Naturally I found it difficult to find in her anything of what I assumed would have been the Molly of 1909. Her recollections of Synge seemed indistinct, although I was aware of the possibility that she preferred to keep them to herself. Of course none of her letters to Synge which were returned to her after his death, appear to have survived. So we have only one side of the correspondence, and it reveals an aspect of Synge which is not only unattractive but also incompatible with the complex personality of the man who wrote the plays.

The real Synge has evaded us, and even the discovery of more letters is not likely to alter this fact. One of the discoveries I made about him was the fact that none of the people to whom I talked who had known him personally—Molly and Sarah Allgood, Jack Yeats, W. G. Fay, R. I. Best—seemed able to give me any very clear impression of what he was really like. Sarah Allgood told me, for example, that she had a vivid recollection of Synge sitting in the empty Abbey Theatre watching the company rehearse and looking exactly the way he does in the pencil sketch which J. B. Yeats did of him called 'Synge at Rehearsal.' As useful as this observation was it was actually an endorsement of somebody else's impression. Impressions which other people gave me seemed to come more from the published record than from personal observation or knowledge. Synge's fame has now, of course, submerged the man in the legend. He has become his admirers, as W. H. Auden wrote of W. B. Yeats—'scattered among a hundred cities, and wholly given over to unfamiliar affection.'

One accepts the fact of Synge's reticence. I find it difficult, however, to accept the assumption by Yeats and others that Synge was an unhealthy man, sick and in pain during much of his writing career.

> And that enquiring man John Synge comes next,
> That dying chose the living world for text.

It was Masefield, however, who was responsible for suggesting that Synge's view of reality was abnormal because of his ill health. 'His relish of the savagery,' Masefield observed after hearing Synge read one of his ballads about a murder, 'made me feel that he was a dying man clutching at life, and clutching most wildly at violent life, as the sick man does.'[4] But the fact is that Synge was a physically powerful man, who spent much of his life outdoors, walked vast distances and was capable of riding a bicycle sixty miles in a day. He did of course suffer from asthma, though not I believe, excessively. It bothered him when he slept under a thatched roof in Kerry or on Inishmaan, but it did not interfere with his life in any other way. He was also, as we know, operated upon in December of 1897 for the removal of swollen glands in his neck, which was the first appearance of the disease which destroyed him eleven years later. Although he occasionally spoke to friends about his glands there is no indication that he did not recover fully from his operation or that he was aware of the fact that he had an incurable malignancy. Of course he was a very sick man for the last year of his life and his writing career was over.

In the summer of 1907 there was a recurrence of the swollen glands. In August of that year Synge met Dr. Oliver St. John

Gogarty on the street in Dublin and later reported in a letter to Molly that Dr. Gogarty had noticed the enlarged glands and suggested to Synge that they be removed. In 1956, forty-nine years later, Gogarty recalled the incident instantly when I spoke of it to him and told me that he had diagnosed Synge's condition on the spot as Hodgkins disease. But he also remembered that he was very careful not to mention this to Synge. Since Dr. Gogarty was a distinguished eye, ear, nose and throat specialist, even such a curbstone diagnosis is probably not so remarkable. When I asked him if he thought it likely that Synge knew what disease he had Gogarty said that he probably would not have known, that it was not a general practice at the time for a physician to tell a patient that he was not going to recover. I found Gogarty's testimony remarkable because in 1956 only Edward Stephens knew the actual cause of Synge's death. The usual explanation given in print about Synge was that he had died as a result of tuberculosis. I find it difficult therefore to believe that Synge was not a reasonably healthy man for most of his career. He was certainly not in any way prevented from living a life which called for a sound constitution, physical robustness and a state of mind which one can only describe as enviable.

If I am right about this—you are thinking—what about Synge's well known morbidity, the preoccupation with death which is characteristic of much of his work? Here I am still inclined, as I was in 1959, to credit the testimony of Edward Stephens who felt that it was a family characteristic. One of Synge's ancestors in the seventeenth century, as Stephens pointed out, was described by Ware in his account of the Irish bishops as being *vir gravis admodum et doctus*[5]—an extremely grave and learned man. There is ample evidence, according to Stephens, that the words describe a type which recurred in the Synge family through two centuries. Masefield, incidentally, used almost the identical phrase in describing Synge—'his face was dark from gravity. Gravity filled the face and haunted it, as though the man behind were forever listening to life's case before passing judgment.'[6] I am also inclined to believe that the fear of death which Synge's mother had planted in him as a child by her religious teaching, which he eventually recoiled from, provides a possible explanation for his morbidity which is more easily accepted in the age of Freud. It would be quite wrong, or at least misleading, to think that Synge's morbidity, in any case, gives us anything more than an oblique, though authentic, view of the man who wrote one of the most ebullient comedies in the modern theatre.

Where in Synge's art can one hope to catch a glimpse of the abstract beauty of his person? Playwrights, as we know, submerge themselves in the characters they create. One naturally likes to think that there is more of Synge in Christy Mahon than in Shawn Keogh but one can never be certain. All we know is that Synge created both of those gentlemen out of something in himself or his own experience. Drama is the art of externalization, and we must accept the characters as characters and not self-portraits.

Poetry, on the other hand, particularly lyric poetry, is a personal utterance. Masefield wrote that Synge's poems gave a direct impression of the man speaking—'They are so like him that to read them is to hear him.'[7] But Masefield, unlike us, was fortunate enough to have heard Synge reading his poems, and naturally they *were* the man speaking directly. As Synge himself once observed when he was comparing the modern experience of reading poetry to the ancient one of hearing it, 'The modern poet composes his poems with often extremely subtle and individual intonations which few of his readers ever interpret adequately.'[8] Writing verse was only an occasional activity for Synge, in any event, and his verse represents only a small portion of his output. His early verse is conventional and derivative. His ballads and poems of Irish rural life are of course personal statements and one is grateful for the revelations they make. Many of them, to be sure, display a preoccupation with death and violence. But what young poet at the turn of the century was not similarly preoccupied with death—'As for living, our servants will do that for us.' And the violence may reflect not so much a natural appetite as a conviction Synge had about contemporary poetry. In the preface to his poems he argued that 'before verse can be human again it must learn to be brutal.'

Synge's prose writings tell us a great deal about him, and sometimes quite directly. The narratives published under the title of 'In the Congested Districts' were written on commission from *The Manchester Guardian* and are little more than mere reporting. For that reason Yeats wanted to exclude them from the canon of Synge's works and when he was not allowed to exclude them withdrew as editor of the works and published his introduction elsewhere. They are interesting and accurate observations about life in a poverty-stricken part of Ireland because Synge did his job like a good journalist. Almost all of the Wicklow pieces similarly appeared in various magazines and newspapers and like the *Guardian* articles attempt objectively to describe the people of the Wicklow mountains and glens. In 'The Vagrants of Wicklow,' however, he romanticizes the life of the tramp as he was to do in 'In the Shadow of the Glen,' and thus justifies an important side of his own personality. He thought of himself as a kind of vagrant and he usually signed his letters to Molly 'Your Old Tramp.' Synge's vagrants were a colourful feature of the Irish countryside, but whether many of them were gifted, younger sons, driven by their frustrations and creative urges to a life on the road, as Synge imagined, is a theory which obviously would not stand up under real scrutiny.

'A Landlord's Garden in County Wicklow' is almost a counter-piece to 'The Vagrants of Wicklow' because it expresses sympathy for the tragedy of the landlord class. In fact Synge casts himself in the rôle of a combatant in the class war by expelling from the garden an invader who turns out to be a relative of the 'small boy who came to the house every morning to run messages and clean the boots.'[9]

The narrative entitled 'In West Kerry'[10] is based upon four visits Synge made to the north and south peninsulas and to the Great Blasket. One can see how relaxed Synge was among the country people, beginning with the crowded train ride from Tralee through Kilgobbin and Anascaul to Dingle. The train is jammed with a confused mass of country people, the floor littered with sacks of flour, cases of porter, chairs rolled in straw and other household goods while a drunken young man sings songs and begs Synge is happy to be part of it as he watches and listens to everything. Eventually he strikes up a conversation with a young woman—'one of the peculiarly refined women of Kerry, with supreme charm, whose every movement is an expression,' who seems 'to unite the healthiness of the country people with the greatest sensitiveness,' and whose 'face and neck flush with pleasure and amusement.' When the train arrives in the evening at Dingle, he makes the long journey by side car over the hills to the house in Ballyferriter where he is to stay. He is delighted with the mountain scenery, and Smerwick Harbour is 'a wild bay with magnificent headlands beyond it.' But his landscape descriptions take on their vitality when there are people in them. Thus, the next day when he lies on the grass looking out to the Blaskets, enjoying the grayness of the atmosphere and the silence over land and sea, his enjoyment reaches its peak when he notices in the distance a procession of people crossing the olive-coloured bogs. 'The sight seemed to ring me with an emotion that is partly local and patriotic, and partly a share of the desolation that is mixed everywhere with the supreme beauty of the world.'

Several days later, after a walk to the top of Sybil Head, where the air is 'like wine in one's teeth,' he falls in with two men and sits with them under a hedge to take shelter from a sudden shower and all three of them have a wonderful conversation about 'fevers and sicknesses and doctors' and traditional cures and especially about a miraculous local plant which in the old days 'the women used to be giving . . . to their children till they'd be growing up seven feet maybe in height.'

But his trip out to the Great Blasket is of course the high point in the narrative. The ride in the *curagh* gives him 'indescribable enjoyment' and reminds him of Aran. On the Great Blasket he stays with the 'king' of the island, but it is the king's daughter, his hostess, who interests him and becomes the model for Pegeen Mike. His account of the accommodations in the house of the king and the joy with which he gives it make one wonder how a morbid and unhealthy man could have volunteered for such an experience. The room in which he sleeps has two beds. The hostess balances the lit candle on the end of the bedpost, takes off her apron and hangs it over the window as a curtain, lays another apron on the earthen floor for him to stand on when he takes his shoes off. After he has retired for the night the 'king,' who apologises for neglecting the guest, joins him and gets into the other bed, lights up his pipe and, writes Synge, 'we had a long talk about this place and America and the younger generations.' The next morning he wakes up at six o'clock. He and the 'king' —like bardic poets of old—salute the new day with a glass of whiskey and a pipe and a long conversation in bed before breakfast. Perhaps one can be excused at least for preferring to believe that this, and not the author of the poems, was the man who wrote *The Playboy.* The Kerry narrative is not nearly as important a work as *The Aran Islands,* but it is less self-conscious, less controlled. The author of it is no longer a lost apprentice searching for a medium. He is not only enjoying himself but willing to acknowledge it to his readers.

Although I find 'In West Kerry' important because it reveals Synge in a way no other work of his does I would hasten to add that *The Aran Islands* is the essential book for anyone who attempts to understand him as a dramatist. The Aran experience was crucial. *The Aran Islands* is a less personal work than 'In Kerry,' even though it records the experience which transformed Synge into a writer of genius. Like the notebooks of Dostoievski or the letters of Keats it is therefore an important document.

In the introduction to *The Aran Islands*[11] Synge offers his reader a disclaimer. 'I have given a direct account of my life on the islands, and of what I met with among them, inventing nothing, changing nothing that is essential.' This would give the impression that he had written a travel book, to acquaint us with life in a distant and unfamiliar clime. But to take Synge's statement too literally is to oversimplify. Despite what he says, he was selective in what he chose to record or to publish. A study of the notebooks and diaries upon which the Aran book is based shows how he excluded anything which tended to make revelations about himself. Most significant in this respect are the passages in the notebooks which reveal how he felt drawn to, and was disturbed by, some of the young women. 'I saw suddenly the beautiful girl I had noticed on the pier, and her face came with me all day among the rocks.'[12]

The islanders were friendly to Synge, as they were and still are to everyone. They must have looked upon him as a rather harmless visitor, a Protestant gentleman from Dublin come to the islands to study Irish. Masefield supposed, from something Synge said to him, that the islanders had the impression 'that he was a linguist who had committed a crime somewhere and had come to hide.'[13] The islanders knew all about linguists, folklorists and antiquarians. The islands had once been visited *en masse* by members of the Royal Society of Antiquaries. Martin Coneely told Synge that he had known George Petrie and Sir William Wilde and had taught Irish to two European philologists named Finck and Pedersen—Finck published a study of the dialect of

Aran in Marburg in 1899. Synge himself tells us that during one of his visits to Aran a French priest-philologist was also on the islands studying Irish. In fact the frequent visits of philological students to Aran, Synge noted, had led the islanders to conclude that linguistic studies were 'the chief occupation of the outside world.'

The islanders observed that in addition to learning Irish Synge also was interested in copying down the stories of the *shanachie*. He was therefore a folklorist like Jeremiah Curtin who had also visited Aran. But they did not suspect that Synge's real purpose was neither to learn Irish nor to record folktales or that they would provide the inspiration and the medium for his plays. They certainly never became aware of the fact that he was more interested in their English than their Irish.

Although *The Aran Islands* is organized simply into four parts, each part corresponding to one of the four visits Synge made to the islands between 1898 and 1901 and the narrative follows a straightforward chronological plan, it is nevertheless managed so as to achieve a dramatic effect in places. Consider for example the ending of Part III. The boat leaves Kilronan after 4 p.m., having discharged a very large cargo. It is dark when she docks in Galway. The only man Synge can find to carry his baggage is drunk and complains goodnaturedly about the weight of the bag—'It's real heavy she is your honour. I am thinking it's gold there will be in it.' At midnight the train leaves for Dublin. It is the evening of the celebration honouring the eighth anniversary of the death of Parnell and the train is crowded with intoxicated people, all going to Dublin to participate in the commemoration. A young girl who sits beside Synge finally loses her shyness and they strike up a conversation while he points out the sights to her through the grey of early dawn. 'This presence at my side contrasted curiously with the brutality that shook the barrier behind us. The whole spirit of the west of Ireland, with its strange wildness and reserve, seemed moving in this single train to pay a last homage to the dead statesman of the east.'

Synge's train moves between two worlds—the west with its wildness and reserve and the east, paralyzed by the downfall of its leader, the vital past and the prostrated present. One is reminded of Frank O'Connor's story 'In the Train.' O'Connor's trainload of country people returning to their village from a murder trial in Cork City are also passing between two worlds, one urban and one rural, each with its values, each incomprehensible to the other. One is also reminded of James Joyce's masterpiece 'The Dead,' in which the west, epitomized in the image of the 'dark mutinous Shannon waves,' is expected to revitalize and inspire the living dead of a paralyzed Dublin.

One observation which should be made about *The Aran Islands* is that it tells us where Synge got the dialect which became his hallmark. The first audiences to hear it believed it to be entirely synthetic, a language which no one in Ireland spoke, and that impression has to a certain extent persisted until today. William G. Fay, the first stagemanager of the Abbey Theatre, who directed and acted in Synge's plays, wrote of Synge's language, 'The dialect used was entirely strange to us, which was hardly surprising seeing that Synge had invented it himself . . . I was quite at home with the traditional "stage Irish" of the "Arrah" and "begob" and "bedad" school as well as the stage Irish of O'Keeffe, Boucicault and Whitbread . . . it was all the more disconcerting for me to encounter an Irish dialect that I could not speak "trippingly on the tongue." '[14] It need hardly be observed that the stage dialect Fay *was* familiar with was as phoney as anything Synge might have invented.

The actual fact, I prefer to believe, is that the dialect of Synge's plays was a real language, actually spoken by people whose primary language was Irish and whose exposure to normal English was extremely limited. It was in fact the English spoken until the end of the nineteenth century by the people of Inishmaan, who had learned it in the Cromwellian period. Evidence of Cromwellian influence on Aran still exists in the remains of Arkin Castle on Inishmore and in the presence of Cromwellian names on the islands. In fact my friend, James Goulden, tells me that there is no evidence that the Cromwellian garrison on Inishmore was ever recalled. It would probably be as impossible now to determine how English was spoken on Irishmaan seventy years ago as it would be to determine how English was spoken in Shakespeare's day. But a theory which enjoys some acceptance among Shakespearean scholars today is that Elizabethan usage and pronunciation survived in the west of Ireland until comparatively modern times.[15]

It is obvious, I think, that as the flood of English-speaking visitors to Aran increased in the twentieth century and as island life changed after 1922, spoken English yielded rapidly to modern influences. My own impression is that Inishmaan people today, to the extent that they speak English at all, use an idiom which is common to the west of Ireland. But in 1898 this was not the case. As Synge observed within a few hours of his landing at Kilronan, the people spoke English 'with a slight foreign intonation that differed a great deal from the brogue of Galway.' Synge was if anything a sensitive observer, especially of language. He was surprised, he tells us, at discovering how many people in Kilronan spoke English with 'abundance and fluency' and that Irish 'seemed to be falling out of use among the younger people of the village.' In the neighbouring village of Killeany, however, the linguistic picture was drastically different—'English was imperfectly understood.' Some men he talked to were uncertain about what the word *tree* meant. After a hurried consultation in Irish they asked if it meant the same as *bush.* Considering the treeless landscape of Inishmore one would have to concede that this example is something less than conclusive.

On Inishmaan Synge discovered that considerably less English was spoken. His hostess, old Mrs. McDonough, had no English at all. Young Martin McDonough—the Michael of the published narrative—was the only member of the family who could read or write English. The women, Synge suspected, had learned some English in school but since they had had no occasion to speak with anyone who was not a native of the islands they used English only when speaking 'to the pigs or to the dogs.' The children, Synge observed, were taught some English in school but outside the schoolroom spoke only Irish. The men of Inishmaan, however, were all bilingual and most of them were surprisingly fluent. They used Gaelic idioms continually, however, and when their English vocabulary failed them they used 'ingenious devices to express their meaning.' Furthermore he noticed that foreign languages were a favourite topic of conversation and that the men had 'a fair notion of what it means to speak and think in many different idioms.' In fact it was their ability to handle two languages so well which led him to admire their self-sufficiency and the variety of their skills. 'Each man can speak two languages. He is a skilled fisherman, and can manage a *curagh* with extraordinary nerve and dexterity. He can farm simply, burn kelp, cut out pampooties, mend nets, build and thatch a house, and make a cradle or a coffin.'

Twenty-five letters which islanders wrote to Synge survive among his papers. Some of them are in Irish. Five of them, with changes and deletions by Synge, were used in the book. Fifteen are from Martin McDonough, ten from other correspondents including two young girls. But the differences between oral English and the written language of a people unaccustomed to writing a great deal would be substantial. Synge's correspondents, for example, greeted him with such salutations as 'John Loyal Friend,' or 'Old Loyal Friend,' or 'Old Friend John,' or 'Friend of My Heart,' or 'Dear Loyal Sir'—which are Irish vernacular forms of address. Despite the fact that the letters are stilted and self-conscious Synge nevertheless found nuggets to mine. Thus the closing words of Pegeen Mike's letter to 'Mister Sheamus Mulroy, Wine and Spirit Dealer, Castlebar,' echo a phrase in a letter from Inishere—'Hoping you are quite well and enjoying your music, wishing you the best compliments of this season, from your little friend, Barbara Coneely.'[16] Maurya's great speech in 'Riders to the Sea' similarly echoes a passage from a letter in which Martin McDonough meditates on the tragic death of his brother's young wife. 'Ann was visiting the last Sunday in December, and now isn't it a sad story to tell? But at the same time we have to be satisfied because a person cannot live always.'[17]

The reality that Synge's language was neither exotic nor synthetic but based literally and directly upon English as he had heard it spoken on Inishmaan is, fortunately, substantiated by Synge himself in a letter he wrote to a correspondent named Spencer Brodney in 1907. *'I look upon The Aran Islands as my first serious piece of work—it was written before any of my plays. In writing out the talk of the people and their stories in this book, and in a certain number of articles on the Wicklow peasantry which I have not collected, I learned to write the peasant dialect which I use in my plays.'*[18] Of course the language of literature is always to a certain extent synthetic. Imagine what the real Molly Bloom would have sounded like without that avalanche of poetry in her famous monologue. The chief reason why Synge's dialect mystified W. G. Fay and Synge's audiences of the time was the fact that obviously very few of them had ever heard English spoken the way it was in Aran. Because of the isolation of the islands—Synge comments on the fact that steamer service to Aran was only a recent innovation—there is reason to believe that the English spoken by the islanders would indeed have sounded strange to urban Irishmen. In 1898 Synge was witnessing, before it disappeared for good, a linguistic survival from the seventeenth century.

Nobody with the linguistic training necessary has yet to my knowledge made a definitive study of the language of Synge's plays. A. G. Van Hamel, a philologist of reputation, in 1912 published the results of a modest study he had made of Anglo-Irish syntax in *Englische Studien*.[19] He categorized Synge's language as 'a very realistic and vigorous western Anglo-Irish.' Dr. P. L. Henry, presently professor of Old and Middle English in University College Galway is uniquely equipped to make the study we need. He has published full-length studies of the Anglo-Irish of County Roscommon and County Down. One hopes—now that he has exchanged Belfast for Galway—that he will do the definitive study of Synge's language which is needed. We will want to know first what relationship Synge's idiom bears to Irish. We will want to know something about the English spoken around the turn of the century on Aran or in other parts of the *Gaeltacht* where there is a clear record of Cromwellian influence as there is on Aran. Possibly enough letters written at the time to relatives in my native city of Boston, Massachusetts, where so many Aran people live, could be assembled so as to provide more of the kind of evidence which exists in the letters of Synge's friends on Inishmaan.

For the present at least I would like to contend that Synge's landing on Inishmaan in 1898 was the making of him. If it had been only a question of his immersing himself in Irish rural life before he discovered his latent talent, it would have happened without his going to Aran at all. He knew the countrypeople of Wicklow long before he discovered the west of Ireland. His family had its roots in Wicklow. He had spent his summers in Wicklow, and as a young man had walked over every foot of it. But the Wicklow man was a monoglot English speaker, and the Wicklow experience, though it made its contribution as Synge acknowledged in his letter to Brodney, was not crucial.

One of the persistent questions which the facts of Synge's life impel is how could the man who wrote those pedestrian book reviews, those early poems derived from all that is conventional in the poetry of Wordsworth and the English romantics, that very bad play 'The Moon Has Set' and those morbid—the word is Synge's—fragmentary abortions 'Etude Morbide' and 'Vita Vecchia' be the man who wrote the best one-act play in the English language and the incomparable *Playboy?* The fact that most of these effusions were unfinished indicates how clearly Synge saw that he was on the wrong track altogether. Except for one short speech of the mad woman in 'The Moon Has Set,' where is there any foretaste of the torrent of language which bubbled below the surface until it surfaced on Inishmaan?

There is no record of what the islanders thought of Synge's book about them when it was published in 1907. One can assume, I think, that they were not pleased by it. Significantly Synge did not return to Aran after it was published. Despite his attempts to avoid giving offence and his tactful editing of the letters which he published it is not likely that they enjoyed seeing even a sympathetic account of their daily lives given to the world as though they were a subject of curiosity. Synge however published a portion of his narrative, under the heading 'The Last Fortress of the Celt,' in the New York *Gael* in 1901, and the consequences of this we learn about from a letter Synge's mother wrote to her son Samuel. It seems that the long arm of Aran intelligence reaches far. Some expatriate Aran man in New York saw Synge's article in the *Gael,* recognized Martin McDonough's letter which Synge had reproduced, and sent it to Martin who was deeply offended. Whether he communicated his anger in a letter to Synge or not we do not know—this is one letter Synge might have been careful not to preserve—but Synge received the message loud and clear and told his mother he would not return to the islands. 'I am very thankful,' Mrs. Synge writes, 'John heard of it before he went to the islands, as it might have been very unpleasant to have found himself among an angry set of islanders quite at their mercy.'[20] Whatever Synge's apprehensions were, he went back to Inishmaan nevertheless and patched up his friendship with Martin McDonough.

Since Synge's time many other people who have written about Aran have learned that the islanders have their agents in all the principal cities of the English-speaking world. If they were angry about Synge in 1907 they are now at least willing to accept him as an attractive legend. Visitors to Inishmaan are shown 'Synge's chair,' a pile of rocks on a cliff overlooking the ocean, and when this isn't enough to satisfy one's interest other fictions can be produced. Island life has changed so much since 1898, with calor gas, automobiles on Inishmore and most recently regular airplane service during the winter as well as the summer months, that the Aran islander of today would be the last person to know if Synge's account of life there seventy years ago was accurate or not. Obviously what has to be said, at least by me, is that Synge's account of what he saw so clearly and described so factually has the ring of truth about it.

Synge's interest was in people, the way they lived and talked and looked at life. There are many things he saw but did not bother to describe because they were not significant in his view. He has almost nothing to say about the spectacular stone ring-forts on Aran or even the remarkable collection of early Christian remains. He probably noticed that the people themselves took them for granted and paid little attention to them. He seems also to have been unaware of the fact that the islanders were all Roman Catholics and that their religion must have had an influence upon their attitudes. I find it hard to believe that this can be attributed to his obtuseness. How could anyone, much less a member of the Ascendency, be unaware of a fundamental fact of class in Ireland? Quite clearly it was his judgement that religion, which the people probably wore like a glove since it was so much a matter of habit, was not really as significant a fact in understanding them as most people would have believed. And Synge was not like most people. He was a great dramatist, which means that he understood human beings.

In discussing Synge's achievement I have talked not at all about his plays, which are his real achievement, but about the man himself and how he suddenly and miraculously discovered his capabilities when he went to Aran. One reason why I have not had anything to say about his plays is that some of my colleagues on the program will probably have a good deal to say about them. But I would like to conclude what I hope has been a tribute to a great dramatist by making one observation about his influence as a dramatist. The usual theory among historians of the Irish dramatic movement is that Synge was viewed by his contemporaries as a realist and that his influence impelled the dramatic movement away from the direction Yeats had charted for it towards realism. Thus it was Synge and not Yeats who was responsible for Lennox Robinson, Brinsley MacNamara, Sean O'Casey, Paul Vincent Carroll and Brendan Behan. Yeats and Lady Gregory talked about the folk, and yet the Abbey Theatre produced only one folk dramatist—George Fitzmaurice—whom it then proceeded to ignore. Earlier critics claimed that Fitzmaurice was a disciple of Synge, but it would have been more accurate to have described him as a casualty of Synge's influence. After Synge, it seemed, realism counted.

Synge, of course, wrote one play—'In the Shadow of the Glen' —which romanticized an authentic folktale. But the audience were unable to recognise the fact that the play *was* based on a folktale and insisted upon seeing it as a realistic treatment of loveless marriage among the country people. No wonder Synge was puzzled by the violent reaction his work received. His unfortunate statement in the preface to *The Playboy* about lying with his ear to a crack in the floor listening to the servant girls talking in the kitchen of a County Wicklow house and his defense of the authenticity of the language of that play not only made things worse but diverted attention from his real purpose. Synge, as we know now, was not a realist. His vision was unique, personal, poetic, romantic. His view of Irish rural life was, in its own way, just as romantic as Yeats's. Yeats wrote nonsense about the peasant being the key to the collective unconscious of the race. Synge indulged in no such fantasies, but he nevertheless tended to idealize Irish rural life. He could, for example, convince himself that tramps were all artists or that when he listened to Pat Dirane reciting an ancient Gaelic poem he could hear the intonation of the original voice of the ancient poet. These are of course more acceptable myths, but myths nevertheless. And one is reminded of Yeats's reply to a questioner in New Haven, Connecticut, who asked him at his lecture why he read his verses in a sing-song manner. 'Because that is the way Homer read his verses,' the poet is reported to have replied. 'But how do you know, Mr. Yeats, in what way Homer read his verses?' Yeats replied, 'Because the merit of the man justifies the assumption.'

Synge's influence encouraged Irish dramatists who followed him to look closely at the realities of Irish life, urban as well as rural, and to use the poetic resources of the language to the full. It is this particular characteristic which has made—and continues to make—the work of Irish dramatists unique in the modern theatre. And that fact above all others is what impels us to honour Synge's memory on this, the one-hundreth anniversary of his birth.

NOTES

1 David H. Greene and Edward M. Stephens, *J. M. Synge, 1871-1909,* New York, The Macmillan Company, 1959, p. X.
2 John Masefield, *John M. Synge: A Few Personal Recollections With Biographical Notes,* Letchworth, Garden City Press Ltd., 1916, p. 6.
3 *Ibid.,* p. 14.
4 *Ibid.,* p. 22.
5 Greene and Stephens, p. 70.
6 Masefield, p. 6.
7 *Ibid.,* p. 24.
8 Unpublished manuscript in the possession of the Synge estate, See Greene and Stephens, p. 84.
9 J. M. Synge, *Collected Works, II, Prose,* ed. Alan Price, London, Oxford University Press, 1966, p. 233.
10 *Ibid.,* p. 237ff.
11 *Ibid.,* p. 47ff.
12 *Ibid.,* p. 54, fn. 1.
13 Masefield, p. 29.
14 W. G. Fay and Catherine Carswell, *The Fays of the Abbey Theatre,* New York, p. 137.
15 In his review of Lady Gregory's *Cuchulainn* of *Muirthemne* in *The Speaker,* June 7, 1902 Synge observed that 'The peasants of the west of Ireland speak an almost Elizabethan dialect...' *Collected Works,* II, 367.
16 Greene and Stephens, p. 103.
17 *Ibid.,* p. 105.
18 *Collected Works,* II, 47, fn 1.
19 XLV, 274.
20 Greene and Stephens, p. 118.

CONTRIBUTORS

MAURICE HARMON, who has edited this volume, teaches at University College, Dublin. His publications include several studies of Anglo-Irish literature.

ROGER McHUGH is Professor of Anglo-Irish literature and drama at University College, Dublin and a well-known authority in the field.

SEAN O TUAMA poet, playwright and critic, is Associate Professor of Modern Irish Literature at University College, Cork. He has published extensively in Irish.

SEAN O SUILLEABHAIN is Archivist to the Irish Folklore Commission and has written several books on Irish Folklore.

ALAN J. BLISS is Associate Professor of English at University College, Dublin, Joint Editor of Methuens Old English Library and Secretary to the Royal Irish Academy's Committee for Anglo-Irish Literature and language. He has written several books on Old and Middle English studies.

HUGH HUNT Professor of Drama at Manchester University, is artistic director of the Abbey Theatre.

HILARY BERROW teaches at University College, Dublin. She has edited James Stephen's *The Charwoman's Daughter* and J. M. Synge's *The Playboy of the Western World.*

ANN SADDLEMYER, Professor of English at Victoria College, has published several books on Synge. She edited the Collected Plays in two volumes of the Oxford edition of his works.

T. R. HENN has been Reader in Anglo-Irish literature at the University of Cambridge. He has written several well-known books and edited Synge's poems and plays.

SEAMUS DEANE teaches at University College, Dublin. His publications include several eighteenth century studies and he is preparing a work on the influence of the eighteenth century on the Romantics.

JON STALLWORTHY is the author of two critical works on Yeats and four volumes of poetry. He works for Oxford University Press.

THOMAS KILROY, author and playwright, teaches at University College, Dublin. His plays, *The Death and Resurrection of Mr. Roche* and *The O'Neill* received considerable attention when produced in Dublin. His novel *The Big Chapel* has been well received.

DAVID H. GREENE is Head of all University Department of English at New York University. Together with Edward M. Stephens, Synge's nephew, he wrote a definitive biography of Synge.

INDEX

Abbey Theatre, 69-70, 72, 75-87, 175, 178.
actor, role of, in Synge's plays, 63-74.
Allgood, Molly, 88, 92-3, 100, 158-60, 162, 181.
Allgood, Sarah, 181-2.
Anglo-Irish dialect, *see* Hiberno-English.
Anglo-Irish literature, idea of, 1-2.
Antoine, André, 67.
Aran Islands, 3, 131, 189-94.
Aran Islands, The, 89, 104, 114, 120, 132, 157, 187-9.
Aucassin and Nicolette, 90.
Autobiography, 132, 154.

Ballad of a Pauper, 148-9.
Baudelaire, Charles, 153-4.
Berrow, Hilary, 75-87.
Blasket Islands, 186.
Bliss, Alan J., 35-62.
Blunt, Wilfrid Scawen, 90.
Bourgeois, Maurice, 43, 45, 50, 51, 52.
Boyd, Ernest A., 51-2, 55.
Brahm, Otto, 68.
Brodney, Spencer, 191.
Brustein, Robert, 170.
Burbage, Richard, 71.

Carleton, William, 36.
Chekhov, Anton, 86, 175.
Coleridge, Samuel Taylor, 116, 117.
Colum, Mary, 75.
Colum, Padraic, 43, 76.
Conneely, Martin, 187.
Coquelin, Constant, 67, 70-71.
Corkery, Daniel, 15-16.
Cú Chulainn, 22-3.
Cusack, Cyril, 68.

Deane, Seamus, 127-44.
Deirdre and the Sons of Usnach, tale of, 88-105.
Deirdre of the Sorrows, 12-13, 20, 22, 68, 88-105.
Delaney, Maureen, 63.
Donoghue, Denis, 162.

Dream, A, 151.
Dublin Metropolitan Police, 78, 80, 81.
Duncan, Ellen, 78.

Eliot, Thomas Stearns, 170.
English language in Ireland, *see* Hiberno-English.
Etude Morbide, 115-16.
Ervine, St. John, 43.
Evening Mail, 84.

Fallon, Gabriel, 67, 68, 69, 70.
Fay, Frank, 66-7.
Fay, William G., 66-7, 69, 72, 76-8, 85.
Fianna Cycle, 23.
Fitzgerald, Barry, 63.
Fitzmaurice, George, 195.
Flecknoe, Richard, 71.
Forbes-Robertson, Jean, 68.
Freeman's Journal, The, 77.

Glencullen, 146.
Gogarty, Oliver St. John, 182-3.
Gorelik, Mordecai, 130.
Greene, David H., 180.
Gregory, Lady Augusta, 67, 75-6, 78-80, 82, 85, 90, 100, 113, 168-9, 178-9.

Henn, Thomas Rice, 108-26.
Henry Patrick L. 52, 192.
Heslinga, M. W., 16.
Hiberno-English, 12-13, 17, 35-62.
Holloway, Joseph, 75, 76, 77.
Hunt, Hugh, 63-74.
Huscher, Herbert, 51, 52.
Hyde, Douglas, 36-9, 51, 53.

Ibsen, Henrik, ix-x, 86, 167-8.
In Spring, 156-7.
In the Congested Districts, 184-5.
In the Shadow of the Glen, 19, 31n.3, 112-13, 140-41, 195.
In West Kerry, 185-7.
In Wicklow, West Kerry and Connemara, 113.
Irish Culture, elements in, 2-4.
Irish National Theatre Society, 66, 72.

Jakobson, Roman, 128.
Johnston, Denis, 50.
Joyce, James, 14-15.

Kenny, Pat, 80.
Kilroy, Thomas, 167-79.

Lawrence, W. J., 75.
Leahy, A. H., 90.
Lynd, Robert, 43.

McCormick, F.J., 63-4.
McDonough, Martin, 191, 193.
McGarvey, Cathal, 83-4.
McHugh, Roger, ix-xiii.
Mac Leod, Fiona, 122.
McLuhan, Marshall, 131.
MacNamara, Brinsley, 77.
MacSuibhne, Mícheál, 24.
Mallarmé, Stéphane, 128, 130, 156.
Martyn, Edward, 75, 77.
Masefield, John, 145, 180-84, 87.
Modernism, 167-79.
Moore, George, 109, 168.
Moscow Theatre, 70.
Mountain Creed, A, 147.
Muset, Colin, 51.

Nic Shiubhlaigh, Máire, 44, 69, 76.

O'Casey, Seán, 70.
O'Connor, Frank, 45, 47, 52, 68, 134, 188-9.
O Criomhthain, Tomás, 6-7.
O'Donoghue, D. J., 77.
O'Neill, Maire, *see* Allgood, Molly.
O Suilleabhain, Seán, 18-34.
O Tuama, Seán, 1-17.

Petrarch, 161.
Playboy of the Western World, The, xi-xii, 21-2, 42-3, 45, 52, 68, 73, 75, 135-40, 171-5.
Playboy . . ., preface to, 122, 128, 130.
Playboy riots, 75-89.
Price, Alan, 50.
Poems, preface to, 122.

Quin, John, 44.

Rabinowitz, Isaac, 128.
Riders to the Sea, 5, 7, 47, 91-2.
Russell, George W. (Æ), 90, 94.

Saddlemyer, Ann, 88-107, 175.
Sapir, Edward, 16.
Saul, George Brandon, 50.

Saussure, Ferdinand de, 132.
Scott, Clement, 86.
Skelton, Robin, 133, 162-3.
Stallworthy, Jon, 145-66.
Stanislavsky, Konstantin, 64, 70, 71.
Starkie, Walter, 78.
Stephens, Edward, 183.
Swift, Jonathan, 36.
Symons, Arthur, 156.
Synge, John Millington, death in, 9-11, 25-6; folklore, use of, 18-34, 131; Irish language, views on, 123; language, use of, 12-13, 35-62, 127-44; Modernism and J. M. S., 167-79; music and J. M. S., 116-17; nature, description of, 117-19; poetry of, 145-66; prose style of, 108-26; religion in, 9-11, 133-5; supernatural in, 26-8; violence, treatment of, 73-4.

Tinker's Wedding, The, 89.
To the Oaks of Glencree, 159.
Trinity College students at Playboy riots, 79-81.

Ulster Cycle, 22.

Van Hamel, A. G., 192.
Verlaine, Paul, 153-4.
Villon, François, 51.
Vita Vecchia, 115, 149, 151, 155.
Vygotsky, L. S., 128-9.

Wall, Mr. (magistrate), 83.
Well of the Saints, The, 21, 141.
When the Moon has Set, 89, 158, 168-9.
Wilde, Oscar, 109.

Yeats, Jack Butler, 85, 182.
Yeats, John Butler, xii.
Yeats, William Butler, 1, 14, 40, 44, 67, 68, 71, 79, 81-2, 85, 86, 90, 94, 109, 120, 122, 146, 149-50, 155-6, 160-64, 167-8, 174, 178-9, 195.